AF413555

# PRIVATE I

## LYNN HERSHMAN LEESON

### A MEMOIR

PUBLISHED BY
Ze Books of Houston, TX
(in partnership with Unnamed Press of Los Angeles, CA)

3262 Westheimer Road, #467 Houston, TX 77098
www.zebooks.com



BOOK AND SERIES DESIGN
With Projects, Inc.

ISBN
9798988670087
Library of Congress control number available upon request.
Manufactured in  China.

Printed in China
October 2025

246897531
First Edition

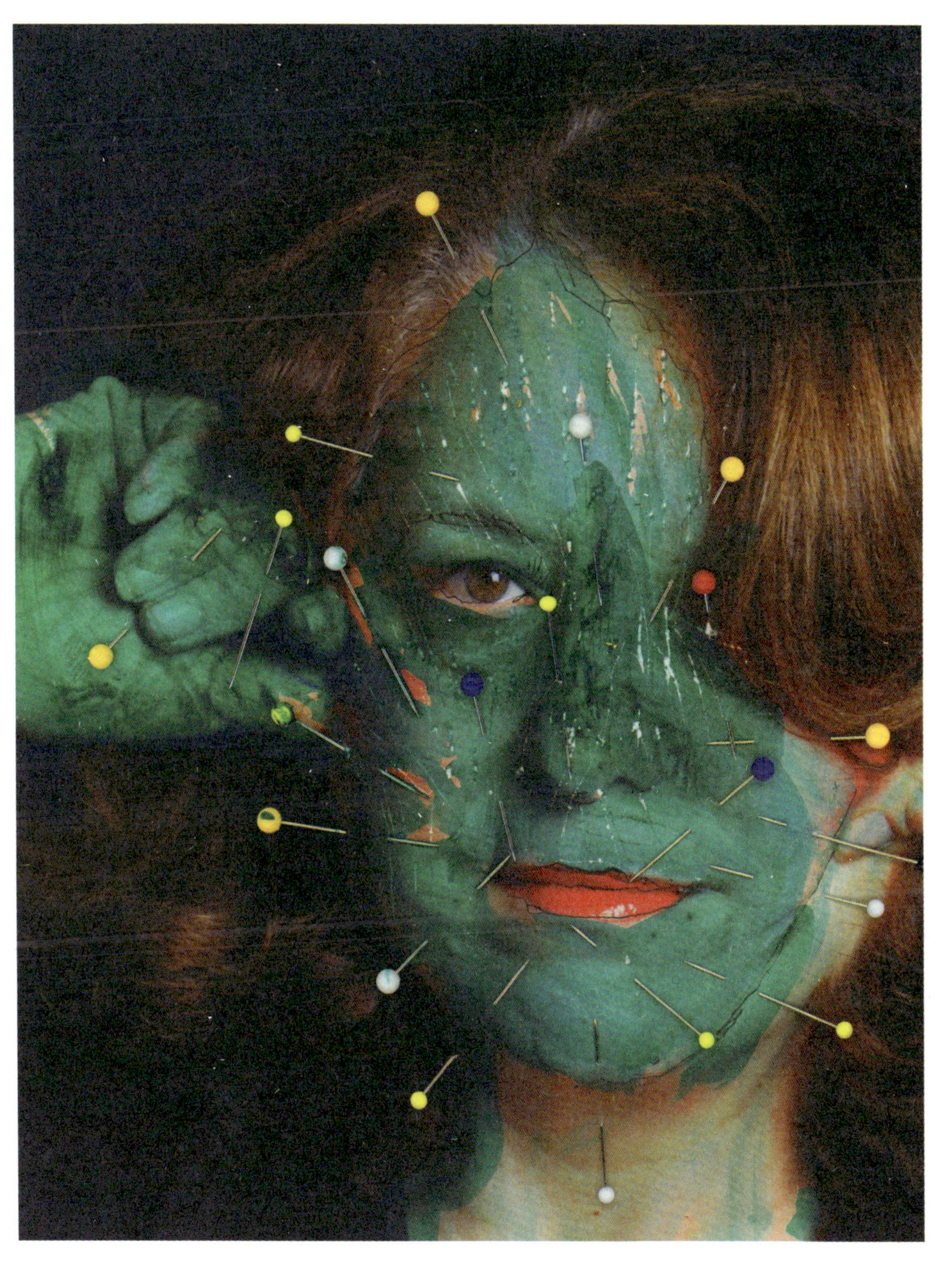

PIN CUSHION, 2010

Dedicated to my grandmother,
Rose

Life can only be understood backwards but must be
lived forwards.
—Søren Kierkegaard

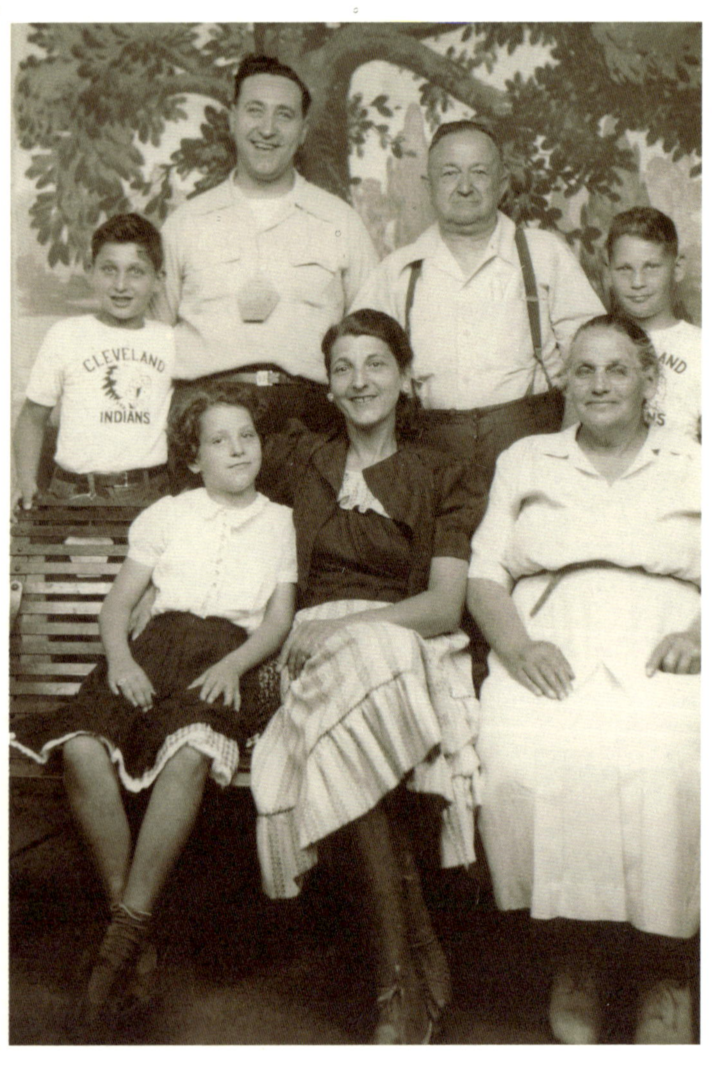


FAMILY PORTRAIT.
FIRST ROW: LYNN, MOTHER, GRANDMOTHER. SECOND ROW: BROTHER GERALD, FATHER, GRANDFATHER, BROTHER ARTHUR. 1946.

# 1
# ORIGIN

> I've been absolutely terrified every moment of my life—and I've never let it keep me from doing a single thing I wanted to do.
> —Georgia O'Keeffe

While reading an old issue of the art journal *Frieze*, I came across the American poet Kevin Killian's 2019 stunning and intimate obituary of the artist Lutz Bacher. His appreciation of this artist's persona prompted me to message Kevin. I conveyed my gratitude for his deeply moving memorial. Then I asked if he might write my obituary, too.

"Oh Lynn," he wrote. "I will email you and it will be obvious that something of the beautiful has been mixed up with the bad, like a Vincente Minelli melodrama."

"Kevin," I replied, "I really do want to commission you to write my obit. I am afraid no one will know who I was or anything about my work." I asked if we could meet when I returned from New York.

Silence.

A few days later his email arrived. "About your offer," it began. "Wow, thanks! But my dear, you are going to out-live me by miles. The last four weeks have proved a trying time. I have been confronted with intimations of cancer.

"I know you are away," Kevin continued, "but I have an idea of how we might collaborate. In the meantime, thank you for showing me how to dream, how to make work, how to perform activism, and how to stick with things even when everything looks scary and awful. You are our hero in many ways."

Kevin's hero? How could that be? I never even met him. He asked to meet in June. Swamped with deadlines, we pushed the date to mid-August.

That same week the artist Carolee Schneemann invited me to her home to pick out one of her sculptures. For three decades, we had been attempting to trade artworks.

As usual, I had a deadline to meet. "Could it wait?" I joked.

"Sure." She laughed, as if that delay were part of a performance we never wanted to end. But before we could meet, she unexpectedly passed.

Shortly after Carolee, other friends left planet Earth in quick succession, including my colleagues Jack Burnham, Okwui Enwezor, and Moira Roth. Most recently, my best friend, collaborator, and co-conspirator, Ellie Coppola, passed away.

Take your time or time takes you. Before I could return to San Francisco, Kevin also was claimed. Everything perishes, even time. So, during the Covid pandemic, I began this chronicle of many episodes, assumptions, presumptions, and challenges, some known, many unknown, in the hope that this history will survive. In doing so, I have honored my family's expressed wish that I not feature them in this narrative (although they inevitably make some appearances).

Jean-Luc Godard noted that his films have a beginning, middle, and end, but not necessarily in that order. That is also the case with this autobiography.

In the early 1970s, the mystery writers Richard Stark and Joe Gores conspired to create two characters whose proscribed destiny would be to meet in each other's books. Their characters appear on either side of a doorway and talk for a moment, thereby creating overlapping fictive spaces that trigger the plot in each separate story.

Alfred Hitchcock called this the "MacGuffin." The MacGuffin is a plot device that sets the characters into motion and drives the story. It can be an object, idea, person, or characters who are either pursuing the MacGuffin, or the MacGuffin can serve as motivation for their actions (like the Maltese Falcon, for example). Usually, the MacGuffin is revealed in the first act.

What is the MacGuffin of my life? I am writing this memoir to find out.

On June 17, 1941, I became the third child in the Lester family. Stella, my mother, worked as a lab technician and high school teacher of biology, while my father, Samuel, a pharmacist, struggled to manage his drugstore. Two boys had arrived before me: Gerald Arnold, born in 1936, and Arthur Herbert, born 1939. We lived in the bottom unit of my maternal grandparents' modest home at 11507 Temblett Avenue in East Cleveland, Ohio, a downwardly mobile lower-middle-class Jewish neighborhood bordering one of Cleveland's poorest black ghettos.

My maternal grandparents, Rose and Martin (we called him Pa) were born in Hungary and were fortunate to have come to this country many decades before the Holocaust. They never spoke of their family members who had remained and were very likely murdered there.

In Hungary, Pa was said to have been a colonel in the army. My grandmother earned her living as a professional cook. They mostly spoke Hungarian to my parents, but when they didn't want us kids to understand, reverted to Yiddish.

Pa, born in 1883, in Rzsapatak, now Romania, arrived at Ellis Island and met Rose, whom he married in 1910. Rose, or as I called her, "Gram," was from Kövárkölcse, Hungary, also now in Romania. After my mother was born in Philadelphia in 1911, they moved to the Upper East Side of Manhattan for a short time, living at 304 East 92nd Street, before moving to Cleveland, where Rose had a cousin, Libby, a survivor of Auschwitz.

My paternal grandparents, Louis and Lena (Rubenstein) Lester, immigrated to the United States in 1918. Louis came from Sokal, which is now in Ukraine; Lena was from Neustadt- Schirwindt, Russia, and arrived in Canada in 1917. They married in Toronto when he was twenty-two and she was twenty and then entered the United States through Buffalo.

I can't say for sure why my relatives came to America, although I assume it was in search of a better life, or more accurately, a life. Even then, it was difficult for Jews in Europe, with state-sanctioned antisemitism limiting where they could live, study or work. There was always an imminent threat of violence. The United States promised a safe haven and the possibility of a better life.

My father owned a pharmacy, Lester Drugs. As was common in those days, the pharmacy had a counter that served ice cream and sodas. In time, both my brothers and I worked there as soda jerks.

I didn't speak until I was almost seven. But just because I was not speaking, did not mean I was not listening. I often heard my parents wondering if I was retarded. Although I didn't understand that word, I assumed that I was considered defective in some way.

My family were masters of repurposing, which may have been their art form. Like constructing collages, a glass pickle jar with a twist-on lid became our soup tureen. The doorway to the kitchen became a stage where my brothers and I performed magic tricks that entertained my family.

For instance, we would take a glass of liquid brimming with diluted yellow watered-down paint and another glass prefilled with blue water and pour them both into a third empty glass. With a triumphant "Ta da!" we announced the magical transformation that turned the two liquids green.

In our small two-bedroom apartment, my brothers shared one room, while my parents occupied the other one. As for me, I slept in the hallway next to the bathroom. It never occurred to me that it wasn't a real bedroom, except that it didn't have a door, and everyone walked through my space to get to the kitchen. Privacy was nonexistent. I never visited other children's homes, nor did any visit mine,

On weekdays, my mother walked Arthur and Jerry to their classes at Chesterfield Elementary School, before heading to her job at a biology lab. Together, Gram and I often embarked on secret adventures. Mostly, we took the bus to Thistledown Racetrack. When the bus stopped in front of the entrance we squeezed through the crowds and then headed to the paddock. Gram insisted on inspecting the ponies. I leaned over the wooden railing and watched as she spoke to the horses. They appeared to understand Hungarian. As she jotted down notes, she could instantly spot wavering eyes, a limp, or a jittery leg.

At the very last minute, we raced to place bets at the $2 window and then caught a ride on the rickety wooden elevator to the bleachers where, stubs in hand, we watched our ponies win. I don't remember my grandmother ever losing. I was given the treat of collecting our winnings. Standing on my tiptoes I gathered the cash for an instant before my grandmother, with one swift movement, opened the golden hinges of her black leather purse and dropped the winnings inside, snapping the closure securely shut. Her profits were parlayed into shrewd real estate acquisitions such as a farm and our home and also covered my mother's college education.

We traveled by bus to many adventures. I sensed passengers viewed Gram as just another elderly woman running errands with her grandchild. But I knew, even then, that she understood how to conjure multiple secret identities. The disguise of banality was a perfect strategy.

At the kosher butcher shop, Gram transformed into an expert at sizing up live chickens. The butcher then demonstrated his murderous expertise by swinging a glistening sharp knife into their throats. The poultry was then defeathered and carefully wrapped in brown paper and tied with a white string. We held these packages tightly while we rode the bus home. Poultry blood dripped, leaving a trail that led back to Temblett Avenue.

My future artistic practice investigating persona was informed by Gram's ability to assume these various identities. Perhaps because I was not speaking, my grandmother confided in me. She knew I would keep our adventures secret.

Pa worked as a grocery store clerk. Gram supplemented the family income by cooking for wealthy families. She was an extraordinary baker who kneaded her special dough, covered it with a wet cloth until it had fully risen, then mashed it with her knuckles. When it was smooth, she rolled it across the dining room table until it was paper thin, sliced it into squares, filled it with farmer's cheese, cinnamon, raisins, chopped walnuts, and sometimes lekvar (Hungarian plum jelly), brushed with butter and egg white and cut into exotic shapes. This wide swath of Hungarian-style origami was placed in a 360-degree oven until slightly brown. Our kitchen simmered with the smell of a happy home. To this day, I make it several times a year, following Gram's recipe.

Friday night dinners with these specially baked desserts were the highlight of our week. Traditional Hungarian dishes such as chicken paprikash and schnitzel were served but desserts were the stars, particularly when she made the crepes called palacsintas or delicious somlói galuska. This was done according to tradition, since we kept a kosher home.

After arriving in New York, Gram cooked for the famous entrepreneur Abe Saperstein, the founder, owner, and earliest coach of the Harlem Globetrotters. She became one of the original investors in the team. When Mr. Saperstein came to Cleveland, he gave Gram tickets to see the Trotters train. I tagged along, and loved watching them shoot baskets. But more, I savored each moment I was privy to Gram's many lives. There was magic in her varied identities.

Coincidentally, our house on Temblett Avenue was not far away from 10622 Kimberly Avenue, the home of Jerry Siegel, one of the two creators of Superman. Perhaps being a superhero and having a secret identity was a common trait among East Cleveland Jews. I was brought up to believe we had no other family beyond our small, insular group. When we were young, we were told that all our other family members were lost or had disappeared. There was never any mention of Nazis or the Holocaust.

When a new deli opened in our neighborhood, I noticed that the owner had numbers tattooed on his arm. I told my grandmother, who rushed to meet him. Remarkably, he was my grandmother's nephew, who survived the Holocaust, alone among his family.

My father's parents, Louis and his wife, Lena, were also immigrants. A few times a year, my brothers and I visited Lena in her dark apartment, where we were fed cookies, listened to records, and had to act as if we didn't notice her crying. Louis, an insurance salesman who was always immaculately dressed in a tailored suit and hat, occasionally stopped by Lester Drugs. We never knew when he might appear or how to contact him. At some point, he stopped coming and I never saw him again. It was only many years later I learned that Louis was murdered. We were never told why or how, just that it had happened.

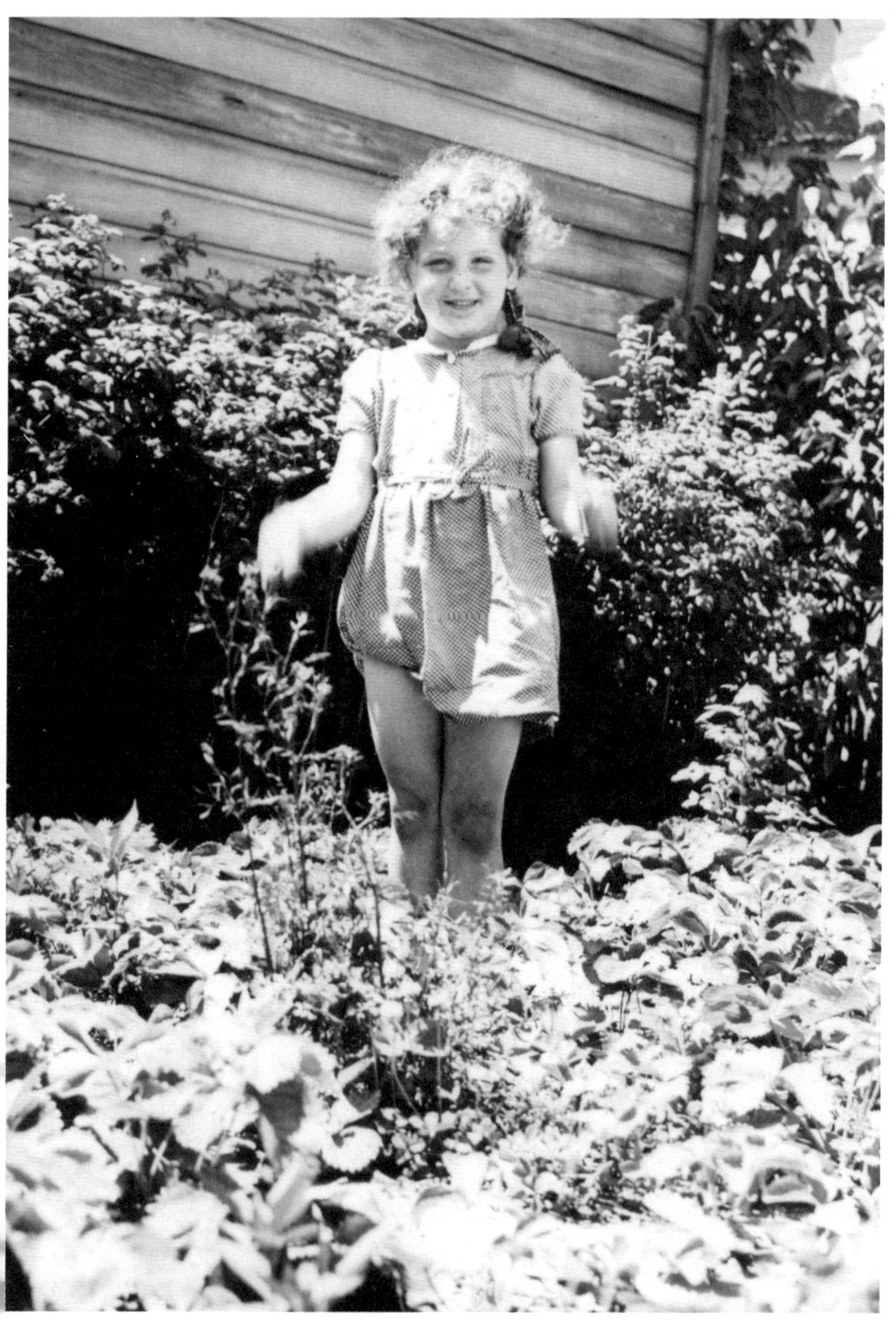

LYNN CAROLE LESTER, 1946

# 2
# AN UNEDUCATION

There are no rules. That is how art is born, how breakthroughs happen. Go against the rules or ignore the rules. That is what invention is about.
—Helen Frankenthaler

On Saturday mornings my brothers and I rode the bus to the Cleveland Museum of Art, navigating the path around a small man-made pond where elegant white swans floated effortlessly. This trail led to Rodin's sculpture, *The Thinker*. I imagined that every museum had *The Thinker* at its entrance.

From there, we climbed thirty steps up to the entrance of what is considered one of the world's most distinguished encyclopedic art museums. We rushed past silent motionless guards in stiff blue uniforms, and took a left into the Armor Court, a cold, open space where voices echoed. Surrounded by enormous tapestries, suits of armor were enclosed in glass cubes. In the center of the room stood an armor-laden horse carrying its armor-suited rider sporting a feathered helmet and holding a long silver lance.

In this room, my brothers met their art teacher and were instructed to copy one of the exhibited artworks. I was not part of this class and never knew why. I assumed it was because of my age and never considered it may have been because of my gender.

While my brothers worked on their assignments, I wandered through nearby massive rooms, entranced by the spectacular artworks of Monet, Degas, Pissarro, Gauguin, Van Gogh, Matisse, Derain, Rouault, and Rembrandt. I never tired of noting how Rembrandt used light in his paintings, or how Gauguin reversed colors or how thick paint oozed from the faces in a Matisse canvas, or Turner's radical abstractions in his watercolors, especially the ones done in secret at night that he hid during his lifetime. Each artwork was a singular triumph, a gift to anyone who took the time to experience it.

Being alone in the museum afforded me a sense of calm that I couldn't enjoy at home. Our house was a place of anger. Paintings became friends with whom I could share my innermost thoughts. The magic of Cézanne's experiments with time and multiple simultaneous perspectives would remain with me. In fact, they still haunt me. I vowed that one day I, too, would paint.

When the bell rang signaling that class was done, I retraced my steps and met my brothers. Ironically, by trying to master the reproduction of drawings their teacher had selected for them, they never had the time to explore the other great artworks in the museum. My older brother, Gerald, continued to paint in his spare time. Arthur's talent was not in art but in science, like my parents.

Back at home, alone one afternoon, I found the food-coloring box my grandmother used for frosting, as well as several empty jelly jars from the kitchen. I set them on the dining room table next to a glass of water, a pencil, paper, rubber bands, and a pair of scissors. Next, I picked up the scissors, and while one of my nine-year-old hands gathered a chunk of my hair, the other wielded the scissors. I took a deep breath and then . . .

Snip, snip, snip.

I collected the fallen strands and affixed them to the pencil with rubber bands, creating a makeshift paintbrush. Dipping my "brush" into food coloring, then water, I tried to make marks on the paper. Much to my disappointment, these innocent attempts failed miserably. The hair on the end of the pencil shriveled pathetically into limp curls, making it impossible to paint like Turner, or anyone else, for that matter. I would need a proper paintbrush and was determined to one day own one. Instead, I reverted to pencils, using their sharpened point to make marks on sheets of paper and envelopes. These became my first drawings.

Later that day, my grandmother was the first to notice that a two-inch-wide chunk of hair had gone missing from the middle of my head. Alarmed, she asked, first in Yiddish then English, "How did this happen?"

I did not respond.

She called my mother, who for the first time left her job at the lab and rushed home.

"When did this happen? Who did this to you?"

They were used to my not talking, but seeing their frustration and realizing my brothers would most likely bear the blame, I confessed: "I did it," I said. "No one else."

"Why?"

"So that I could make a paintbrush," I told them. "I want to paint like Turner."

To say they were surprised is an understatement. They had heard me utter the occasional word but had no idea that I could speak in full sentences, much less express such fully formed ideas. But they were not amused.

As a result, I was forced to wear a brightly colored scarf to hide where I'd cut out a chunk of my hair. To me this was embarrassing, a major punishment that lasted a full month, as my hair slowly grew back. I consider this to be my first brush (literally) with trying to become an artist. But it wasn't just about wanting to make art, it was also about being given the same opportunities as my brothers. Thus began a lifelong struggle for gender parity in art education and art making as well as the start of my lifelong existential need to make art.

For the first day of kindergarten, my mother bought me a reversible skirt, navy on one side, turquoise on the other. The ingenuity of that garment taught me that things were never what they seemed, that anything could be turned inside out; and that simple changes could profoundly revise perceptions. I never forgot the lesson of that reversible skirt.

School was a major adjustment. For one, most important, I could no longer go on adventures with my grandmother. Second, school was about following rules but because of that it also taught me resistance. I presented as a normal, if shy and uncommunicative, child to my teachers, fearing that revealing too much of myself might alienate them. I adopted an external acceptable version of "Lynn." Even at that young age, women were forced to create appropriate personas that hide their true selves.

In third grade, I began fainting in class. Before each collapse, I would feel dizzy, my heart would start pounding, and breathing became difficult. My teachers sent me home, but my parents were convinced I was faking illness. My punishment included severe beatings and being forced to return to school the next day without seeing a doctor. I was fearful of fainting at school and even more afraid of being at home.

My symptoms did not disappear, but they went untreated. At the time, I thought my parents didn't want to spend money on a doctor. But, looking back, I now wonder if the reason was that they didn't want to explain why my nose and my pelvis had both been broken.

It wasn't all bleak. At a garage sale, my mother found an entire set of beautiful golden-edged, crimson leather-bound Harvard Classics, which she bought for five dollars. Disappearing into those volumes launched me on fantastical journeys that made me less lonely. I cherished my many hours spent with the remarkable authors in the Harvard Classics Library.

These books were not meant primarily for children. But I didn't care. I read and reread work that may have been beyond my years, such as by Bacon, Milton, Plato, Wordsworth, and Shakespeare. Like my "friends" in the art museum, these books would become my touchstones and, over time, collaborators in my work. I could not imagine the influence that Thoreau's "Civil Disobedience" would have, when at a much later date I set about fighting entrenched societal norms and prejudices.

My brothers and I were forced to attend an Orthodox temple. At my brothers' bar mitzvahs, my grandmother, mother, and I sat in the balcony seats reserved for women and watched the men below participate in the service. Afterwards, my family went to Corky and Lenny's, a neighborhood Jewish deli, to celebrate. At nine years old, it was my first time in a restaurant.

Before summer recess began, the Cleveland Department of Public Education tested students for a new experimental program for gifted children, to begin in the fall. The program, Major Work, which the Cleveland Metropolitan School District called "the greatest experiment in education" providing "enriching educational experiences for children with high intellectual and/or academic ability."

I remember an interview in a small, dank, nearly empty room with beige walls. A woman sitting at a small desk asked me to count backwards beginning with 20. I accomplished that flawlessly. Then she asked me to identify meanings in images of black splats on white paper. I'm guessing these were part of a Rorschach test. My time looking at art at the Cleveland Museum had given me a visual vocabulary with which to discuss the splats. From these few tests they thought they could determine IQ, and I was selected for the Major Work program. Being selected as a "gifted child" must have surprised my family, as they had told me I was retarded.

The children in the Major Work program gathered into one classroom blending grades 4 through 6 where we participated in Research Talks, Weekly Forums, and a Literature Club. Although we were expected to meet the same grade level content standards as our general education peers, we were never, to my recollection, taught grammar, math, or geography.

The French classes took place in the summer at Case Western Reserve University, and were taught in French, which I did not speak, in a classroom with university students. By August, I was fluent in French and could write bilingual songs and poetry. I was only nine years old. This program did not make me feel special. On the contrary, I was even more isolated from my peers. I felt like a freak.

A saving grace was the university cafeteria, where I was dazzled by the variety of exotic nonkosher lunch options: turkey and cheese, soups or salads with bacon or seafood, and vegetables served in a sauce that would never be allowed in our home. My grandmother kept a kosher household, lit candles on Friday night for the Sabbath, and celebrated Jewish holidays.

At Chesterfield Elementary, fellow students in the Major Works program included Mary Jo LaFontaine, a girl with straight blond hair and blue eyes from the south side of Cleveland, and Myron Levine, who went by Mickey, a handsome and funny Jewish boy from my neighborhood. Mickey and Mary Jo became my best friends. They were also my only friends. Just as my parents and grandmother spoke Yiddish when they didn't want me to understand, Mary Jo, Mickey, and I spoke French to one another, so that our families would not understand our confidences. When we graduated, Mickey, Mary Jo, and I vowed to stay in touch despite moving on to different junior high schools. I had become attached to my friends, and Mickey, although not my first crush, was my first reciprocated crush.

I disliked junior high, and hoped Mickey and Mary Jo were coping better than I was. It was miserable to be placed in a "normal" class after the enlightened and glorious years of Major Work. Like me, Mickey lived in a strict Orthodox home. After some sleuthing at the Hebrew school my brothers attended, I located Mickey's address. It was not far from where I lived. I walked several blocks to his home and knocked on the door. There was no answer. I rang the bell. A voice from an intercom responded.

"Who is it?"

"I'm a friend of Mickey."

No response.

"I'm Lynn. Is he at home? I was in Major Work with him."

No response.

Finally, the voice said, "He's not here."

The next day his parents contacted my parents and asked them to make sure I didn't come to their home again. They said Mickey had hung himself and was dead. No reason was given.

As for Mary Jo, she seemed to have disappeared. Evaporated. As I sit in San Francisco, slogging my way through this global pandemic, I appreciate how much our digital presences today allow us to remain connected to people.

Back then, there were no such options. My grandparents must have suffered deeply from the loss of friends and family murdered in the Holocaust. Yet they survived. I wondered: What do we survive for? I was desperate to make my life meaningful and find a way to contribute to the world.

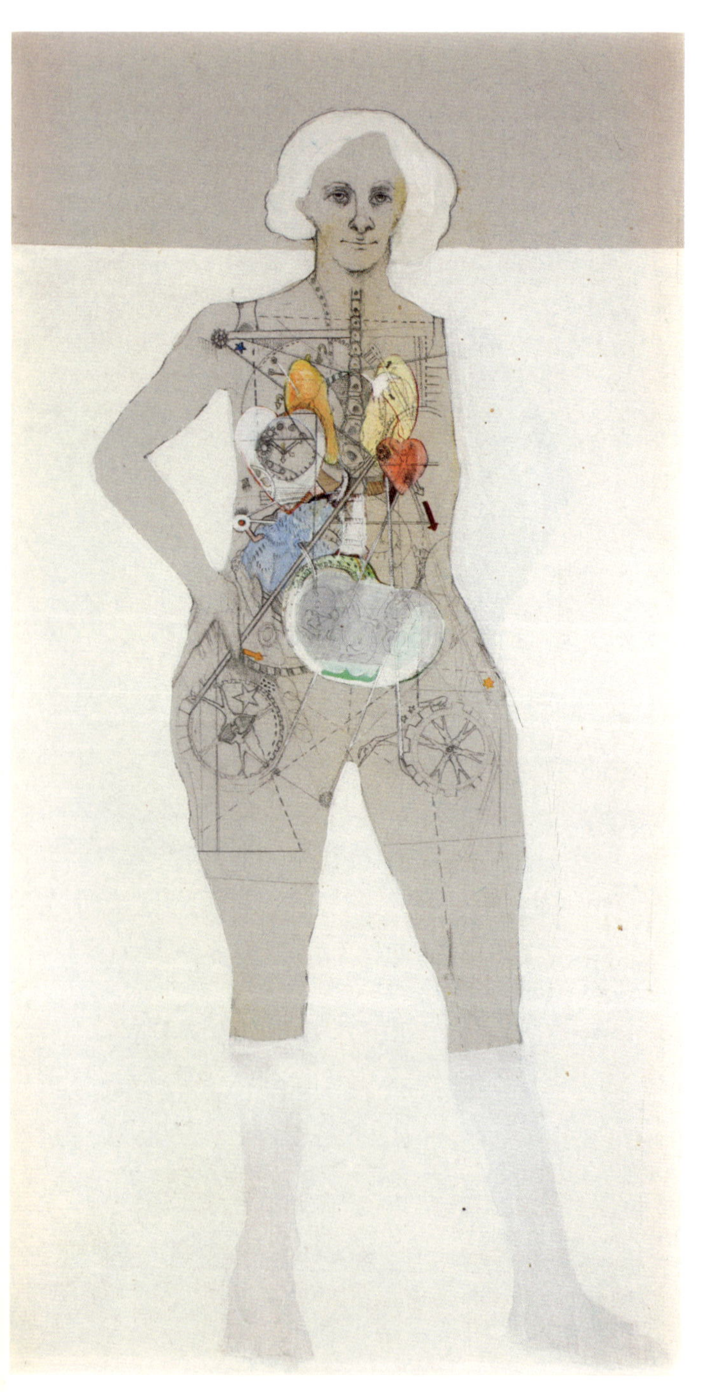

# X-RAY WOMAN, 1966

# 3
# CYBORGS

> The main thing in making art often is letting go
> of your expectations and your ideas.
> —Agnes Martin

The Cleveland Museum was an oasis. Drawings, particularly
the exquisite works of Leonardo da Vinci, launched me
into rapture. I dreamed of being able to draw like him and
sought to imitate his lines. I noted Leonardo's strategy
of alternating deep and subtle lines to define human form.
Our only commonality was that Leonardo used inexpensive materials that, in time, flaked off the canvas. I used
newsprint and thin, nonarchival paper for drawings, which
caused my fragile lines to fade and disappear. After
repeated futile attempts to copy his work, I finally produced
an image of a female nude draped in cloth.

To preserve my drawing, I asked the secretary at
Roxboro Junior High for permission to use the school's
new state-of-the-art Xerox machine. She agreed, so I
also used the office phone to let my grandmother know
I'd be late. She mentioned that my grandfather had come
home from work with a cold and was not feeling well. She
asked if I wanted to say hello to him. Because I was eager
to use the Xerox machine, I told her I didn't have time, but
that I would see him later.

Then, cautiously, I approached the bulky copy machine. It occupied a quarter of the small office. Carefully,
I inserted the drawing into its feeder. I pressed the start

button, then held my breath. My drawing quickly disappeared into the machine. Seconds later, deep churning
sounds gurgled from the machine's innards. I waited
for the copy to emerge, but the drawing stayed inside.
Terrified, I carefully lifted the latch as well as its secret
interior panel and was horrified to realize that my precious
creation was helplessly stuck between two heavy ink
rollers. It was as if the belly of the machine had been
impregnated by this image and refused to release it
as it gestated.

I had to rescue it. My small hand reached inside the
metal enclosure and slowly, carefully, tugged at the paper.
After several sweat-soaked minutes, my mashed and
crinkled former masterpiece was freed from its tight metal
grip. The drawing had been transformed. No longer was
it a perfectly drawn body. The devil machine had mangled,
ripped, and deformed my masterpiece. I could barely
breathe. Pain flooded my body. My eyes squeezed shut
as tears trickled down my face. The original drawing was
gone forever. In its place was a piece of paper in which
deep black ink had soaked into the wrinkles, slashes, slits,
and gashes. Heartbroken, I wondered if I would ever make
as good a drawing.

But when I looked at it again, my perspective
changed. The fragile, hand-rendered human body I had
drawn became vibrantly alive. This process was an
unlikely marriage of human input and technological
output. The resulting hybrid image may have been
inspired by Leonardo, but it was reborn as a work with
no historic precedent or aesthetic preconceptions.
It was the birth of a new species of art that incorporated
technology as part of its creation. The unintended
consequence of this merger was an artwork that represented not just the present but the future.

In this iteration, the machine was neither enemy nor
devil. It was a co-conspirator. Partnering in this symbiotic
human-machine interaction, its unthinking processes had
completed my drawing. Technology could be a partner
in artistic creation. This was 1955. The term *cyborg* would
not be coined for another five years.

When I arrived home that night excited to share my
new creation, my mother and my brothers were already
there. Rose was crying. Pa had died that afternoon.
Between the time when Gram asked if I wanted to say
something to Pa, and on my return home, he had passed

away. I missed my last opportunity to hear Pa's voice, ever. To this day I regret the decision. Making art was important. But speaking with my grandfather was more important. I didn't know that then. I do now. The artwork could have—should have—waited.

Too often, in my life, I delayed making time for friendship, or missed opportunities to connect, because my urge to make art owned my life.

# CLEVELAND HEIGHTS CITY SCHOOL DISTRICT
## CLEVELAND HEIGHTS, OHIO
## HEIGHTS HIGH SCHOOL
### REPORT TO PARENTS

Student's Name: _Lester, Lynn_    Home Room: _127_    Semester _II_  1956 - 1957

| Subject | Teacher | First Report | Second Report | Final | Subject | Teacher | First Report | Second Report | Final |
|---|---|---|---|---|---|---|---|---|---|
| ENGLISH II | RW | C | C+ | C | MUSIC | | | | |
| Industry | | 2 | 1 | 1 | | | | | |
| Attitude | | 2 | 1 | 1 | Attitude | | | | |
| TYPING I | | A- | A | A | PHYS. ED. | | | | C |
| Industry | | | | | 2 G, 1 S | | | | |
| Attitude | Pal | | | | Attitude | | | | |
| B. Scott | | C- | C | C- | SWIMMING | | | | |
| Industry | | 1 | 1 | 1 | | | | | |
| Attitude | | 1 | 1 | 1 | Attitude | | | | |
| W. H. II | | B | C | D | HYGIENE | | | | |
| Industry | S. F. N. | 1 | 1 | 2 | Industry | | | | |
| Attitude | S. | 1 | 1 | 1 | Attitude | | | | |
| French I | | D | D | D | CITIZENSHIP | | | | 2 |
| Industry | | 2 | 2 | | ATTENDANCE | | | | |
| Attitude | | 1 | 1 | | | | First Report | Second Report | FINAL |
| Industry | | | | | Days Absent | | 0 | 1 | 2 |
| Attitude | | | | | Times Tardy | | 0 | 0 | 0 |

Home Room Teacher _MRS. B. C. GOODMAN_

### Signature of Parent or Guardian

First Report _S. Lester_

Second Report _S. Lester_

5600 9-56

# 4
# A BRUSH WITH RACE

There are things that are not sayable. That's why we have art.
—Leonora Carrington

Walking home after school, a group of black girls approached me. Thinking they needed directions, I turned around to greet them but suddenly, with no warning, one of them whacked me across the face with an umbrella. The others joined in hitting me. as they taunted me with "White bitch!" I had never heard those words before and didn't know what they meant. They were laughing. Beaten to the ground, I was hurt and crying, the pavement scraping my skin.

After they left, I wiped the blood from my face and limped home. My leg was bruised, as was my shoulder. I did not understand what I had done to provoke their anger. I have a persistent belief that when things go wrong, it's my fault—a feeling that has haunted my life. When my parents saw me, and heard what happened, things changed. From then on, my brother Arthur, who was very tall, walked me to and from school.

Within a month, our family moved to an upper-middle-class Jewish neighborhood in Cleveland Heights. It was a fifteen-room house on an acre of land that Gram bought with her winnings at the track. I had my own room and hoped that having a door would give me privacy. I didn't realize that closed doors could also hide secrets.

Arriving at Roxboro Junior High School mid-semester, I immediately felt like a misfit. The Roxboro students were a tight-knit group of wealthy kids who had been friends since first grade. Plus, it seemed that every girl at Roxboro owned multiple cashmere sweaters. My one pathetic, ripped beige cashmere was purchased for 75 cents at a Salvation Army sale. At Roxboro I was not assaulted because of race, but I was constantly pummeled by the other students' wealth. I felt lonely, poor, less valued and of less value. Though we lived in a big house, my parents were always broke. I never understood why.

The Major Work program left me academically unprepared for junior high. At Roxboro, I was once again thought to be a dunce. I knew how to produce and present original research and speak French, but Roxboro's French teacher had a southern twang that mangled the language.

My brothers did not suffer from the same social acceptance issues. They made friends easily and sometimes brought them home. My grandmother had opinions about each of them. One she liked was Larry Hershman. He was two years older than me. Why wouldn't she like him? He was Jewish, popular, and class valedictorian. He went on to attend college at Miami University at Oxford, Ohio, where he was president of his fraternity. I didn't like the fact that he was so conventional.

One morning my mother appeared in the living room carrying two suitcases filled with my grandmother's belongings. She scratched her head nervously, which she did when she was upset. Gram followed slowly, saying a sad goodbye, and not looking at me. I didn't know where they were going. I thought maybe she was taking a trip and assumed she would be back. From the front window, I watched Gram slowly climb into the back seat of the car. My mother turned on the ignition and they drove away.

My brothers and I were never told why Gram was put in an old-age home but we were assured we could visit her. I couldn't understand why Gram, having escaped hardship in Hungary to come to America, where she became a professional cook, bought real estate, and raised a family, couldn't live out her life in the home she owned. My parents met my questions with silence. Or worse.

A week later, after I found out where Gram was living. I took a bus to visit her. It was on the way to the racetrack. When I was shown to her single room, she was no longer the Gram with whom I had adventures. She had lost weight, barely spoke, and her spark and vitality were extinguished. The entire time I was there, she looked out her lone window. It was as if she was searching for her past because she could no longer see a future. I continued to visit her but it became increasingly difficult to see her, as I juggled school and work. She died a few years after my first visit. I don't remember going to her funeral. Gram's presence had always made me feel safe. I was on my own now. Perhaps I would be alone forever.

At Roxboro and then at Cleveland Heights High, my grades dipped so much that being accepted to a good university seemed unlikely. Counselors and academic advisors said no college would accept me. That motivated me to prove them wrong.

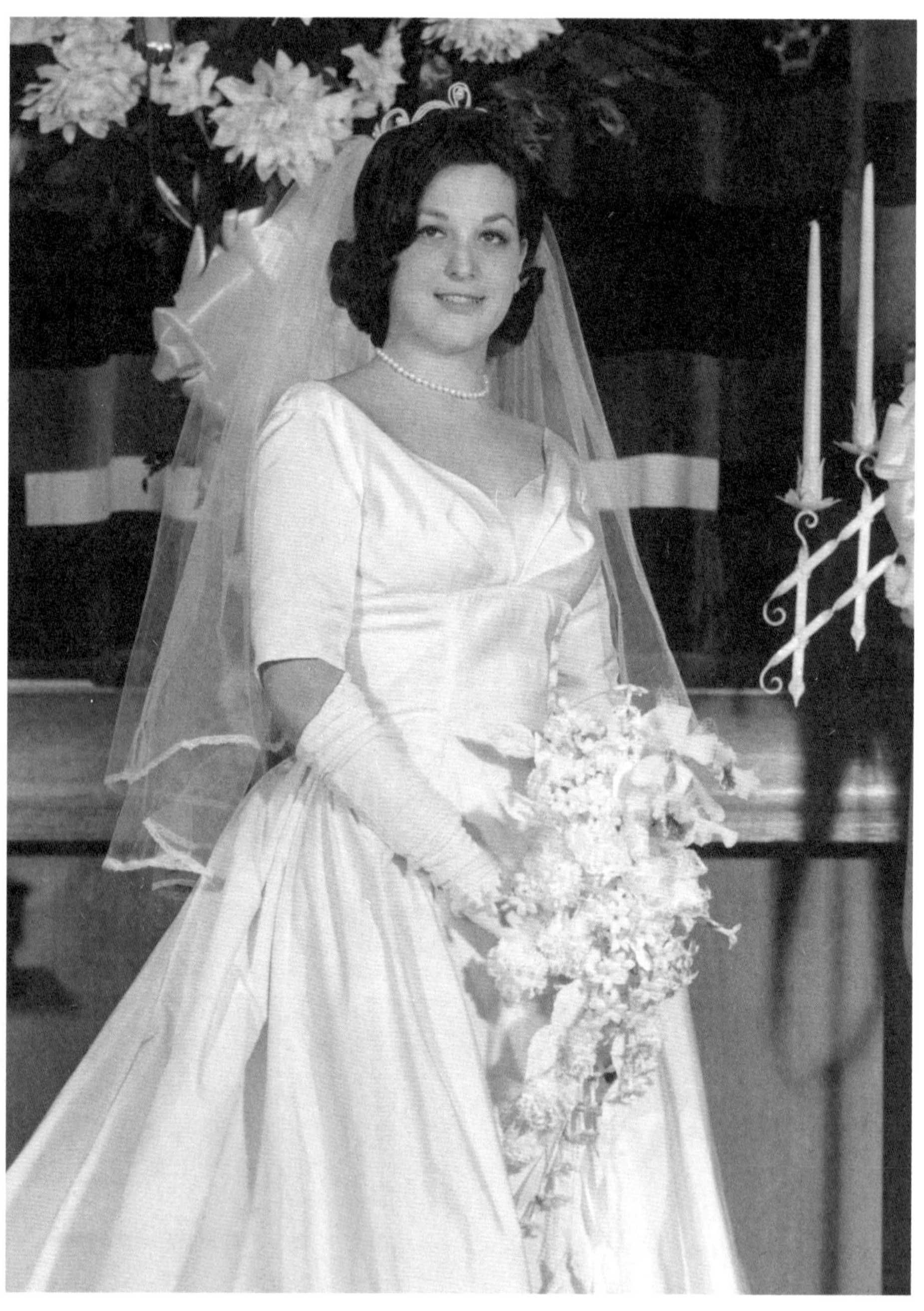

LYNN ON FIRST WEDDING DAY,
1963

# 5
# COLLEGE COLLAGED

I love creation more than life, and I must express myself before disappearing.
—Sonia Delaunay

No money had been put aside for my college education by my grandmother or parents. Aware that attending college would require paying my own tuition, I worked random odd jobs such as delivering newspapers, baby-sitting, and teaching Hebrew classes at our synagogue. Extracurricular activities or after-school clubs or social activities, were not possible. Kelly Girls' Employment Agency found me jobs typing and filing when I was sixteen. One company I worked for was named National Screw. I found the name hilarious.

Still, despite functioning at school and holding down after-school jobs, I felt a growing numbness in my life. There was an ever-present voice inside my head that kept reprimanding me for my failings. At that time, I did not realize the voice was my own. I took it as the voice of Truth.

At home, beatings recurred as random, sudden outbursts provoked for no apparent reason. I had multiple broken bones, including a broken nose from a broom handle striking me across my face and welts from being whipped with a belt. I lived in constant fear of being hit, in a state of imminent danger. I don't remember a single day growing up when there was not some sort of violence in my house. Things happened to me that you weren't supposed to tell others about. I could hear that whispered voice saying, "You're not supposed to talk about it."

My older brother was no longer living at home but his years of abusing me—entering my room to "teach me how to act with my boyfriends or husband"—had traumatized me. Yet I felt that even this must have been my fault.

I had no sense of who I was. My bedroom closet was filled with outfits in several sizes to accommodate my weight fluctuations, as if there were several different people living inside me. There was no stable or one "me." My existence felt intolerable.

Consumed by feelings of worthlessness and that I didn't deserve to take up space on the planet, I saw no purpose to my life. I sliced my arms with razor blades. Episodes of self-harm escalated into a desperate series of failed suicide attempts, including pill overdoses. One time, I got into my mother's car, closed my eyes, and accelerated, driving straight into a brick wall. The car was totaled, and I was trapped inside.

Police arrived and took me into custody. When my parents came to claim me at the police station, they were angry not just at losing the car, but because I was causing them so much trouble. As I was a minor, the police released me to my parents with the understanding that their options were either to hospitalize me in a psychiatric ward or, if I stayed at home, to place me under the care of a private psychiatrist. To my surprise, they opted for the latter. There was never extra money at home, so I don't understand how they were able to pay for these sessions, which were not covered by insurance.

Dr. Rachel MacDougall was a highly respected psychiatrist with a small office located a few blocks from the Cleveland Museum of Art. I began seeing Dr. MacDougall twice a day, four days a week, which in time decreased to three visits a week. Between appointments I often visited the museum. At first, I did not speak in our sessions. I reverted to the muteness of my early childhood. But when I began to trust Dr. MacDougall, our encounters became collaborations. Understanding that I could make my own decisions was a profound revelation.

Dr. MacDougall had lost a daughter who would have been my age. Her daughter had died of rabies after a stray cat scratched her while on a family vacation in

Mexico. I think this made Dr. MacDougall particularly sensitive to me.

Four years into our collaboration, I made an offhand reference to incest. I now suspect Dr. MacDougall already knew. We never spoke directly about the perpetrator's identity. I kept silent out of shame, fear of retaliation, and also to protect family members. After revealing the incest, Dr. MacDougall shifted our work process to one focused on muting the critical voices in my head and developing strategies to negotiate future confrontations. Part of this process included visualizing choices to a given problem and weighing the possible outcomes of each depending on which decision was made.

Our visits together brought forward the realization that I could possess a secret, hidden self, a defiant "secret agent," that would be an affirming voice in my psyche. Accessing it would counter the critical voices that once dominated my thinking. Over time I came to appreciate that, despite the violence that permeated my childhood, I had acquired vital skills such as an ability to read behavioral and physical cues. A certain sideways glance, or a tone of voice, or a specific turn of neck was a sign that rage was imminent. I never fought back. To this day I am terrified of confrontation. Instead, I find ways to avoid or defuse charged situations. My current therapist says I grew up in a war zone and that I am still suffering from posttraumatic stress disorder.

Reading cues also allowed me to spot developing cultural patterns and innovations in technology. I could foresee their potential for transforming society, particularly as regards online identity, privacy, the surveillance state, and artificial intelligence.

Dr. MacDougall also gave me the analytical skills necessary to map outcomes to possible situations. Controlling potential confrontations was achieved by charting forking paths that listed the anticipated pros and cons of each choice. Years later, scientists, mathematicians, and computer programmers would use the same sort of "decision trees" to create algorithms that power voice recognition, predictive software, and artificial intelligence.

Above all, Dr. MacDougall made me realize that creating art was my life force and gave me reason to live. I learned how to live with my parents. But I'm not sure they ever learned to live with me.

After graduating high school, my savings were enough to pay for one full year of tuition, room, and board at Ohio University in Athens, Ohio. I entered college as a biology major and lived in a dorm. I hoped that I might one day work in a research lab, like my mother.

After discovering a joint program between the Cleveland Institute of Art and Case Western Reserve University, I transferred. There were pros and cons to this decision: Attending college in Cleveland meant living at home again with my parents and working nights and weekends to pay for tuition and materials. But I would also be close to my beloved museums and libraries. As I have done my entire life, I chose art over my own personal safety and comfort.

At the art institute's library, I first learned about Jean Tinguely's *Homage to New York*, a 1960 self-destroying mechanical sculpture that enacted a performance about suicide and resurrection in the garden of the Museum of Modern Art in New York. I found it profoundly moving (even though I never saw it). Another discovery was Yves Klein's *Leap into the Void*, a manipulated photograph that celebrated freedom—and that presented fiction as fact. What seems like a photo of a man diving from the second floor of a building is in fact the merger of two photographs—one in which the man dives but there is a group of people holding a tarp to break his fall; and one in which the street is empty. Klein collaged the negatives seamlessly to make that print, which creates the illusion that man can fly. He distributed a mass-produced broadsheet of the image to Paris newsstands. Klein's photographic creation reminded me of Lee Miller's subversive passport photos that challenged how official government forms might skew identity and how an artist could make art that refused to succumb to cultural expectations.

In my watercolor class at the Cleveland Institute, for the first time, I used a real brush to imitate Cézanne, Turner, and other artists I admired. Their techniques taught me to see in a different way. Other students were better draftsmen; and, at that time, I certainly didn't think of myself or the art that I made as exceptional. But one teacher, Paul Travis, who was an artist himself, appreciated my watercolors and encouraged me to do more. At that time, like many in my generation, I was also influenced by the Beat poets: Jack Kerouac, Allen

Ginsberg, Diane di Prima, Lawrence Ferlinghetti, and Gregory Corso. I read all that I could by them and attended their in-person readings in Cleveland.

Another influence was the WJW 850 AM Cleveland radio disc jockey and concert promoter Alan Freed, who coined the term *rock 'n' roll*. Students talked about the Cave, a local club in a basement where there was live music. I was curious to go there. One night around midnight, I slipped out the second-floor window of my bedroom and silently climbed down the ladder to the ground. I still had a key to my mother's car, and drove to 105th and Euclid in East Cleveland to find the club. I was the only white person in the room. Since my earlier assault by a group of black girls, I was often fearful and cautious about my personal safety and sensitized to issues of race. However, I remained seated inside, enthralled by the live music.

When the Cave closed at 2 a.m., I was intoxicated, not from alcohol (I didn't drink), but by this exotic new world. I would return night after night. Although I was underage, no one checked IDs and there was no entrance fee. The club featured now-legendary artists such as Miles Davis, Bob Dylan, and Joan Baez. My family, who would have been horrified, never discovered my midnight romps. They didn't even approve of my going out on dates.

I fell in love for the first time with Glenn, a pre-med student I met by accident in the Case Western Reserve cafeteria. Because he was blond, my parents assumed, wrongly, that he wasn't Jewish. He invited me to dinner at his parents' home. My parents let me know that I was not to meet his family and locked me inside my bedroom. They also installed a lock on my window to prevent me from sneaking out onto the balcony. When he arrived to pick me up, no one answered the door. I never saw Glenn again. I was devastated. I was in college yet still being beaten and locked in my room.

Larry, my brother's friend who was now a college graduate, asked me out on several dates. Like me, he came from an observant Jewish family. My grandmother was still living in the old-age home when I started dating him. She urged me to marry him. He was everything she wanted for me. Perhaps it was because she knew I had to leave my parents' home for my own safety. So I agreed to get married as soon as I graduated college. Frankly, I felt no one else would ever ask me or want to be with me.

At twenty-two, I graduated from both college and Dr. MacDougall's care. I married Larry, the man my grand-mother chose for me. Though he became an accountant with a position at Ernst & Ernst, I convinced him that he should get a graduate degree. He was accepted into a PhD program at the University of California at Berkeley, where I hoped to take art classes. Berkeley was a long way from Cleveland. I had never been out of Ohio but was excited to start a new life in California.

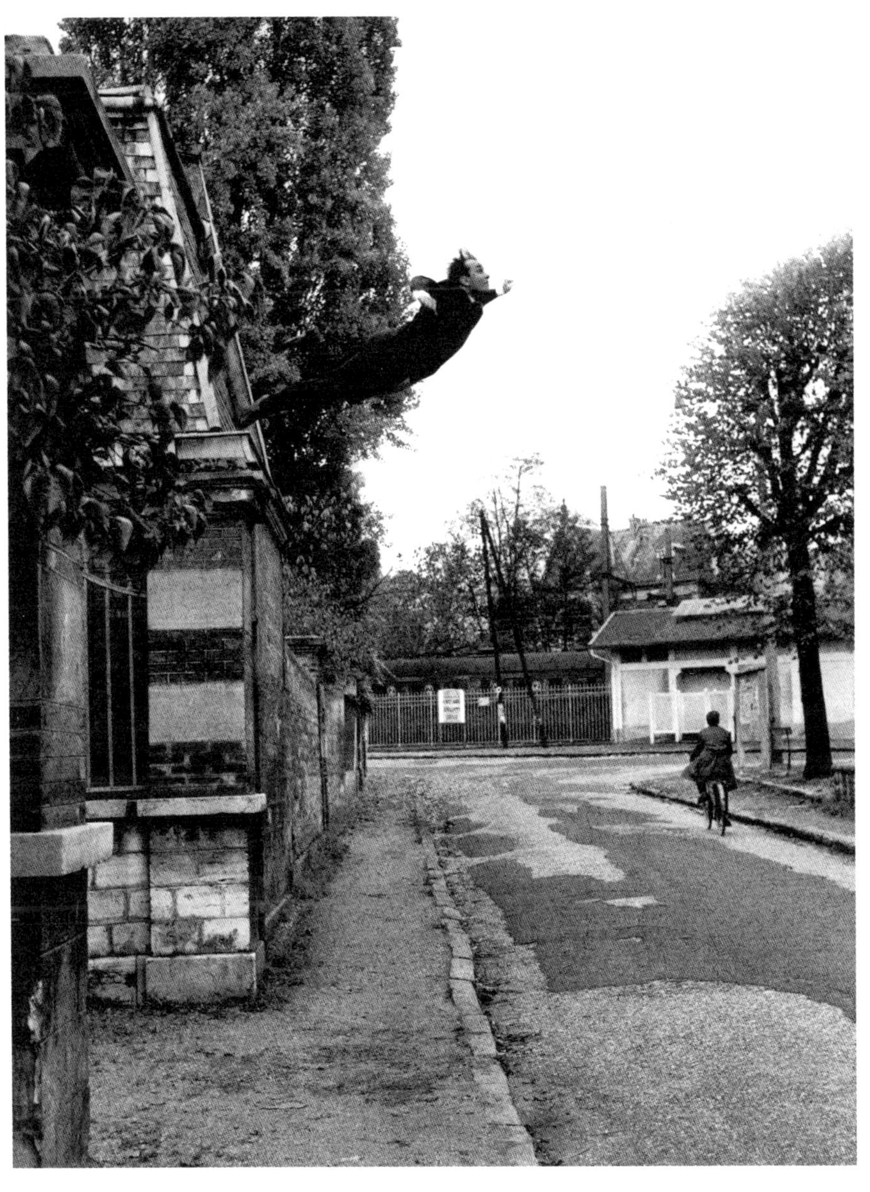

# YVES KLEIN, *LEAP INTO THE VOID*, 1960. COURTESY OF GETTY RESEARCH INSTITUTE, LOS ANGELES.

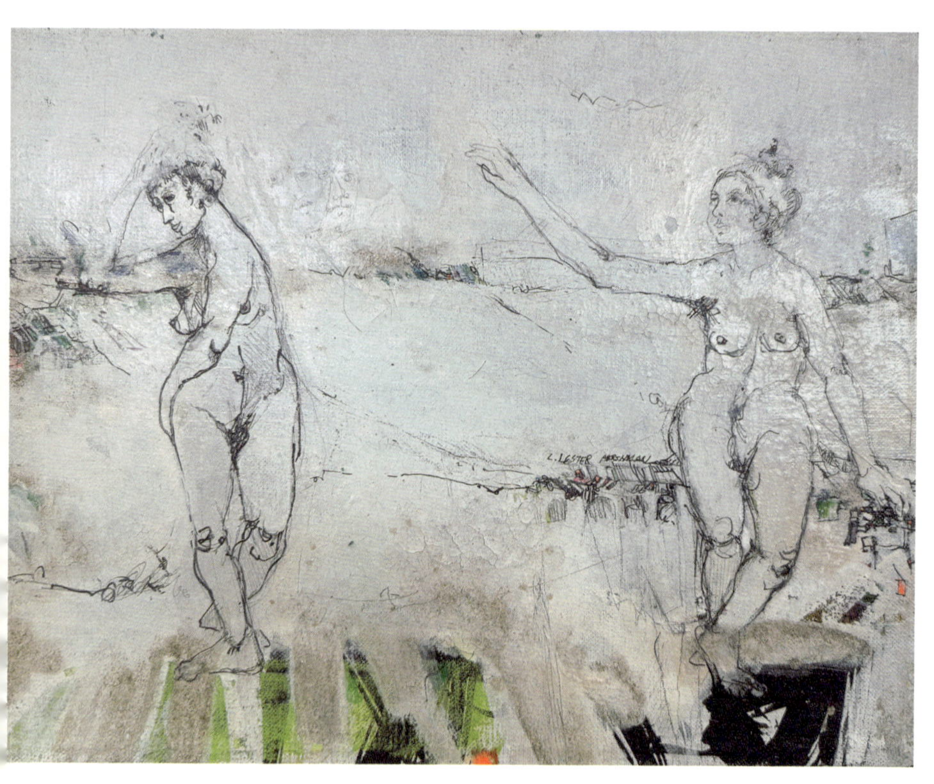

GOODBYE TO THE PAST, 1966

# 6
# REVOLUTION

> I wanted to start a revolution using art to build the sort of society I envisioned.
> —Yayoi Kusuma

In 1963, Berkeley was undergoing a seismic change. College students were agitating, creating a supercharged atmosphere with the Free Speech Movement and the protests at People's Park. While Larry was taking his graduate courses at Berkeley, I became absorbed by the revolutionary spirit of the sixties.

Our apartment was a few blocks from Sproul Plaza, allowing me to hear harbingers of the coming revolution such as Malcolm X and Medgar Evers; while over in Oakland, Bobby Seale and Huey Newton formed the Black Panther Party for Self-Defense, writing a ten-point manifesto demanding change for their community and founding a visionary organization that emphasized racial pride and economic empowerment.

Inspired, I quit my graduate program at Berkeley where I had been making paintings and drawings, mostly of women. I still have a few of these early works. Looking at them today, I can see the seeds of ideas my work would eventually explore.

One of my earliest works is a portrait of a woman dressed entirely in black. It is done in a style that calls to mind Manet's *Portrait of Berthe Morisot in Mourning*.

There is also a painting of a couple: a man is in the

foreground, the woman in the background, almost in his shadow. Looking at it today I wonder if this was a subconscious depiction of my marriage.

I also painted two women, both in profile, with a portion of each face carved out as if to suggest they were not complete.

This was the era of underground comics. M. C. Escher was creating his mazelike works, Ralph Steadman was illustrating children's books and would soon tackle *Alice's Adventures in Wonderland*, as Grace Slick and the Jefferson Airplane were singing "go ask Alice." R. Crumb was drawing *Zap Comix*. I see all these as early influences. My work sought to marry my present with hopes for the future in a style purely my own.

After completing his MBA, Larry was offered an executive position at Hughes Aircraft in Los Angeles. My husband was the only one earning an income, so we moved there.

I was twenty-three years old and three months pregnant. Two months after our arrival in LA, I began experiencing severe night sweats, breathing became difficult, and my legs were swollen. Doctors diagnosed me as suffering from cardiomyopathy, a condition that makes it difficult for the heart to pump blood. My mitral valve had collapsed, and I was in danger of heart failure. I was rushed to intensive care at the hospital and placed in an oxygen tent but still struggled to breathe.

I was so weak I could barely hold a fork or a pencil, and the sound of my struggling to breathe resonated loudly in the hospital room. A few months later, still under the oxygen tent, labor was induced, and my daughter, Dawn, was born. Doctors warned that it would be too dangerous for me to ever have another child. They were also not optimistic about my recovery and cautioned that I might not live long.

How would I take care of Dawn?

Determined to survive, I challenged my doctors' prognosis. The Cleveland Clinic had developed an exploratory procedure to diagnose the root cause of cardiomyopathy. By inserting a microscopic camera into a patient's vein, they could film the extent of damage to the affected heart valves. Back in Cleveland, an angiography revealed untreated childhood rheumatic fever as the most likely the reason for my earlier fainting episodes.

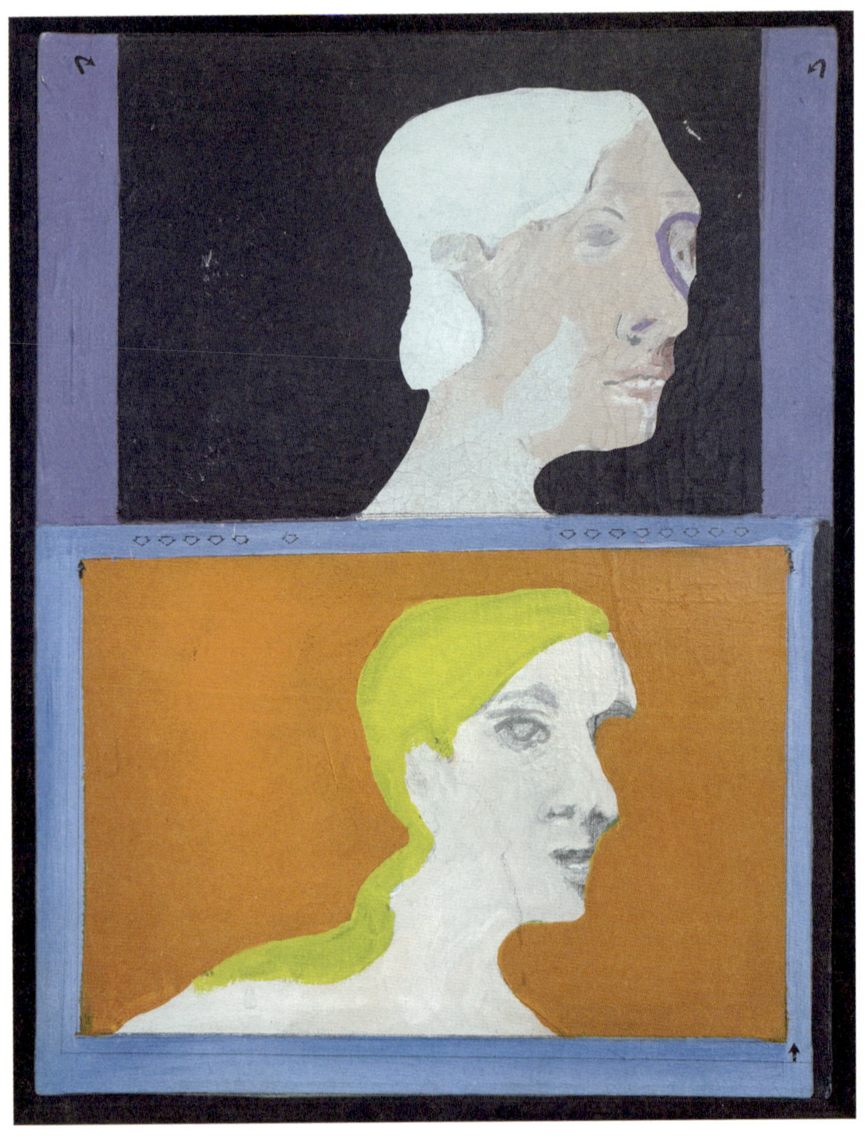

# *DOUBLE HEADER, 1968*

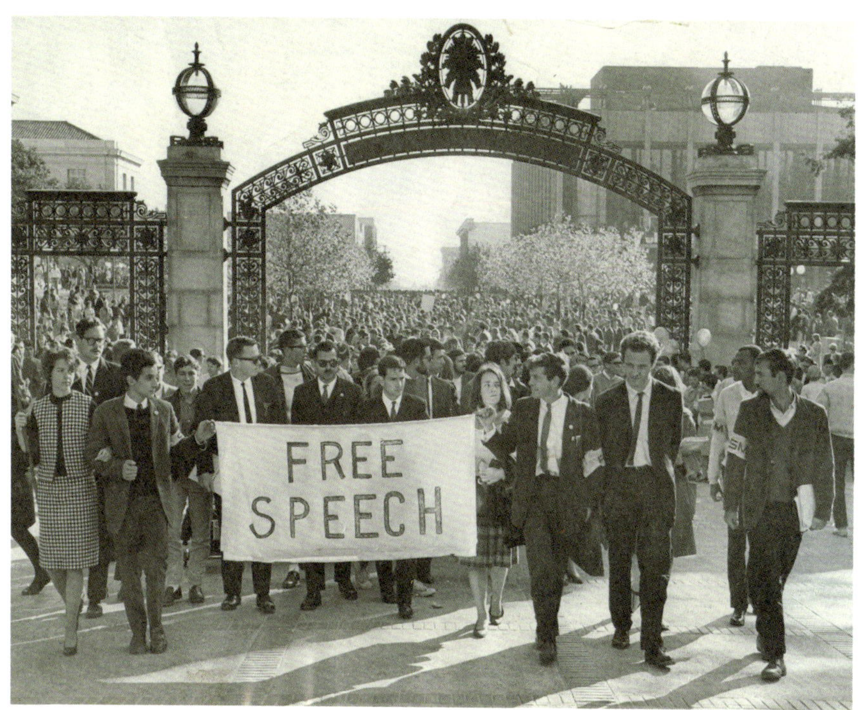

CHRIS KJOBECH, UNTITLED (FREE SPEECH MOVEMENT). © THE OAKLAND MUSEUM OF CALIFORNIA

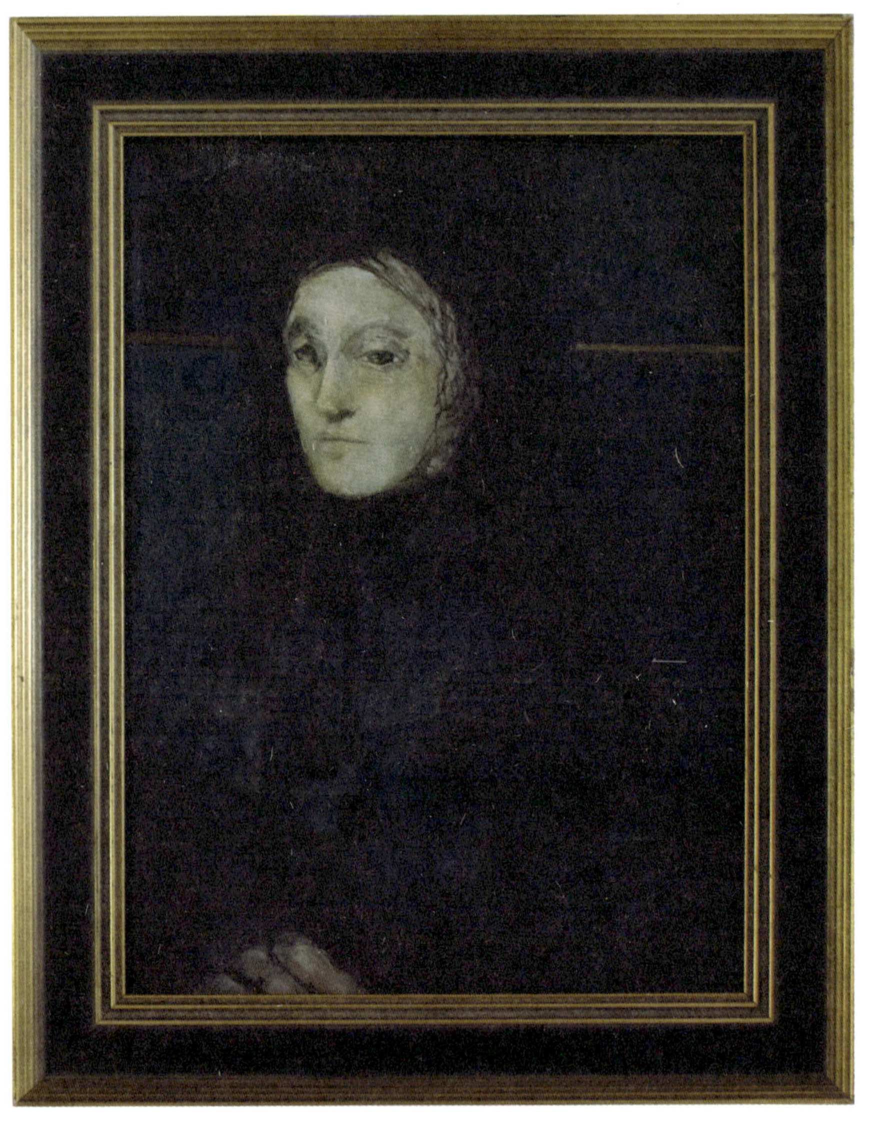

*GLAZE GAZE, 1960*

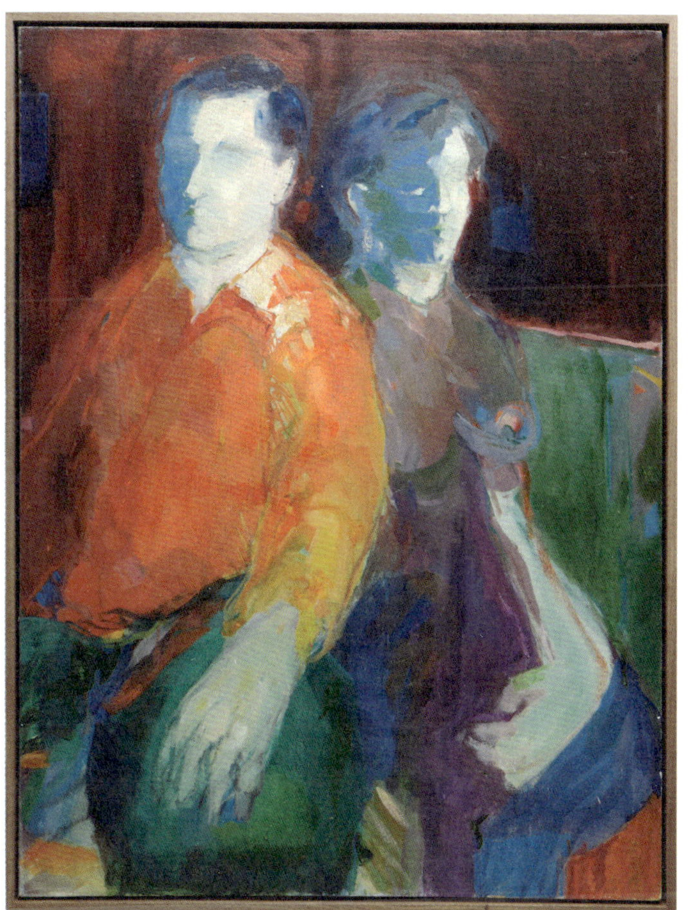

# LYNN AND LAWRENCE HERSHMAN, 1965

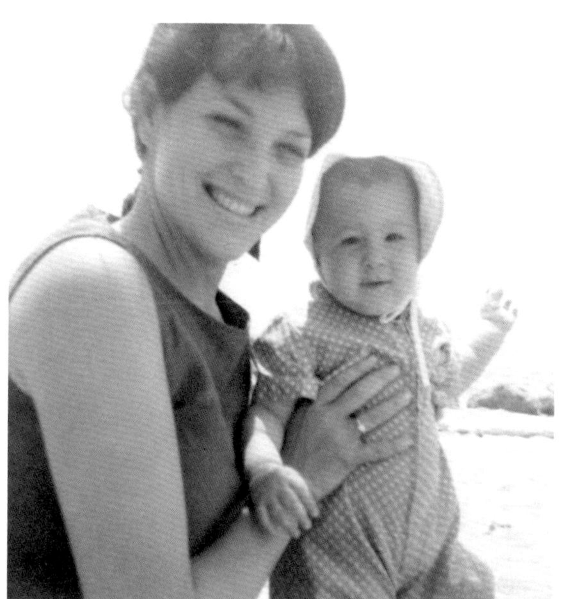

# LYNN, AGE 25, WITH BABY DAWN, 1966

Like the doctors in Los Angeles, those in Cleveland warned that my condition meant a limited lifespan. However, through my own research I learned there were several alternative treatments if I wanted to lessen the strain on my heart, such as breathing exercises, meditation, and strength training. Every day while I cared for my infant daughter, I pushed myself to get stronger.

Dr. MacDougall had pointed out that creating art was something not everyone could do. For me, making art was as necessary as breathing. As I recovered, I forced myself to write single letters on paper. On a good day, I could write one short, completely legible word.

Six months later, I managed to glue a tiny nail to some wood. Over the next two weeks, I shaped a one-inch wax female head with flowing hair, set upright on a nail. Two weeks later, I added another one-inch golden nail with a male face, which sat next to her, regally.

I named this first work *Conversation Piece*. At the time, no one understood it. Today, it seems not only prescient but of the moment—and speaks to our interconnected neural networks and systems of communication. Like me, these tiny humans manifested an autonomous life.

Six months later, when I first stepped outside, my senses were ignited. Sunlight surrounded me, as crackling leaves whistled through tree branches, singing a duet with the wind. This symphony accompanied each victorious step.

As I continued to investigate these new art forms, I incorporated sensors and sound into sculptures called "Breathing Machines." This occurred decades before multimedia artworks included technology. These early works prefigure my explorations of identity, particularly my Roberta project. Making art was my reason to breathe. I was using art to explore the varied personas women embody in contemporary society.

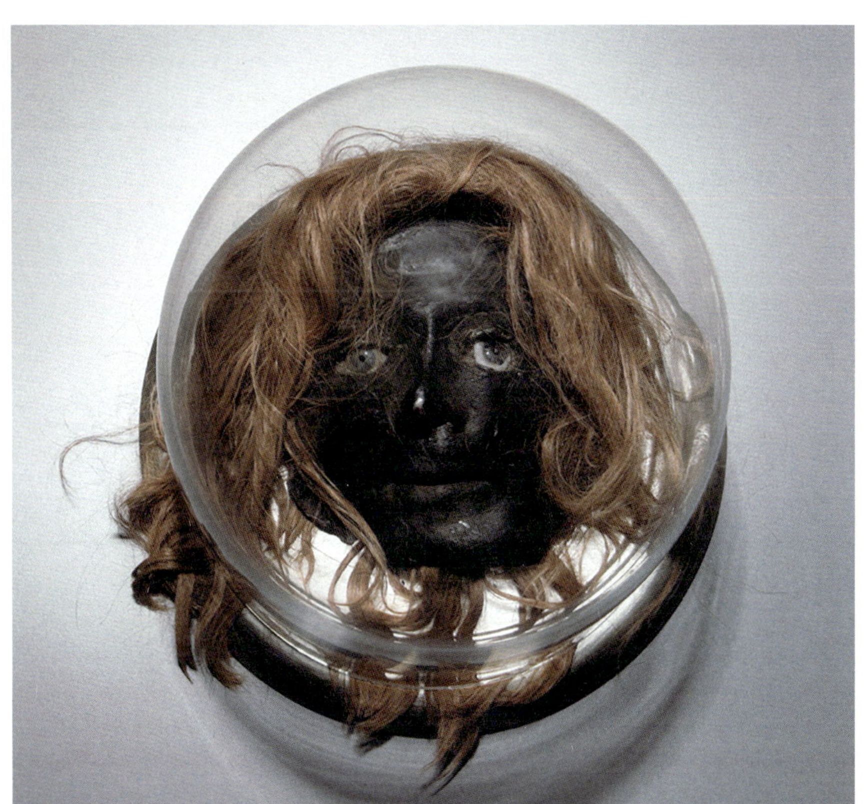

*BREATHING MACHINE*, 1967.
PHOTOGRAPHY BY
KIM HARRINGTON.

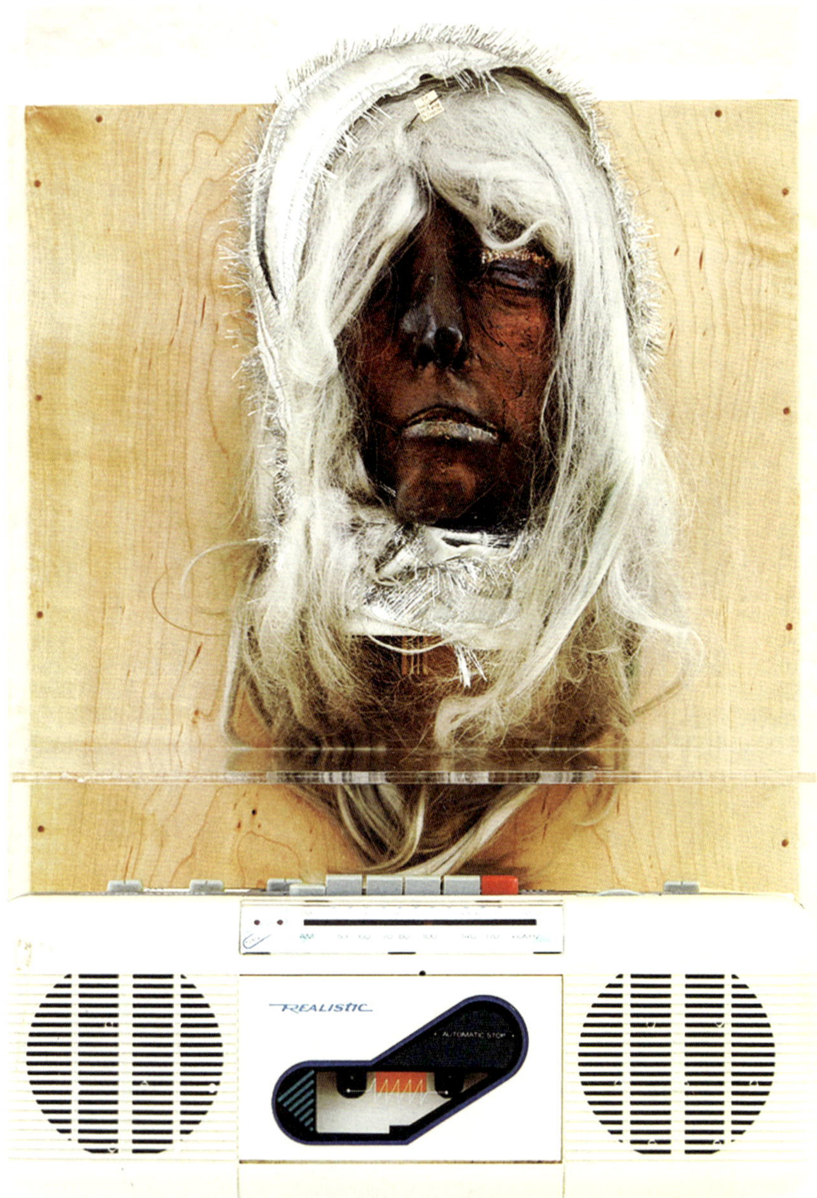


# SELF PORTRAIT AS ALBINO FROM *THE BREATHING MACHINES* SERIES, 1968

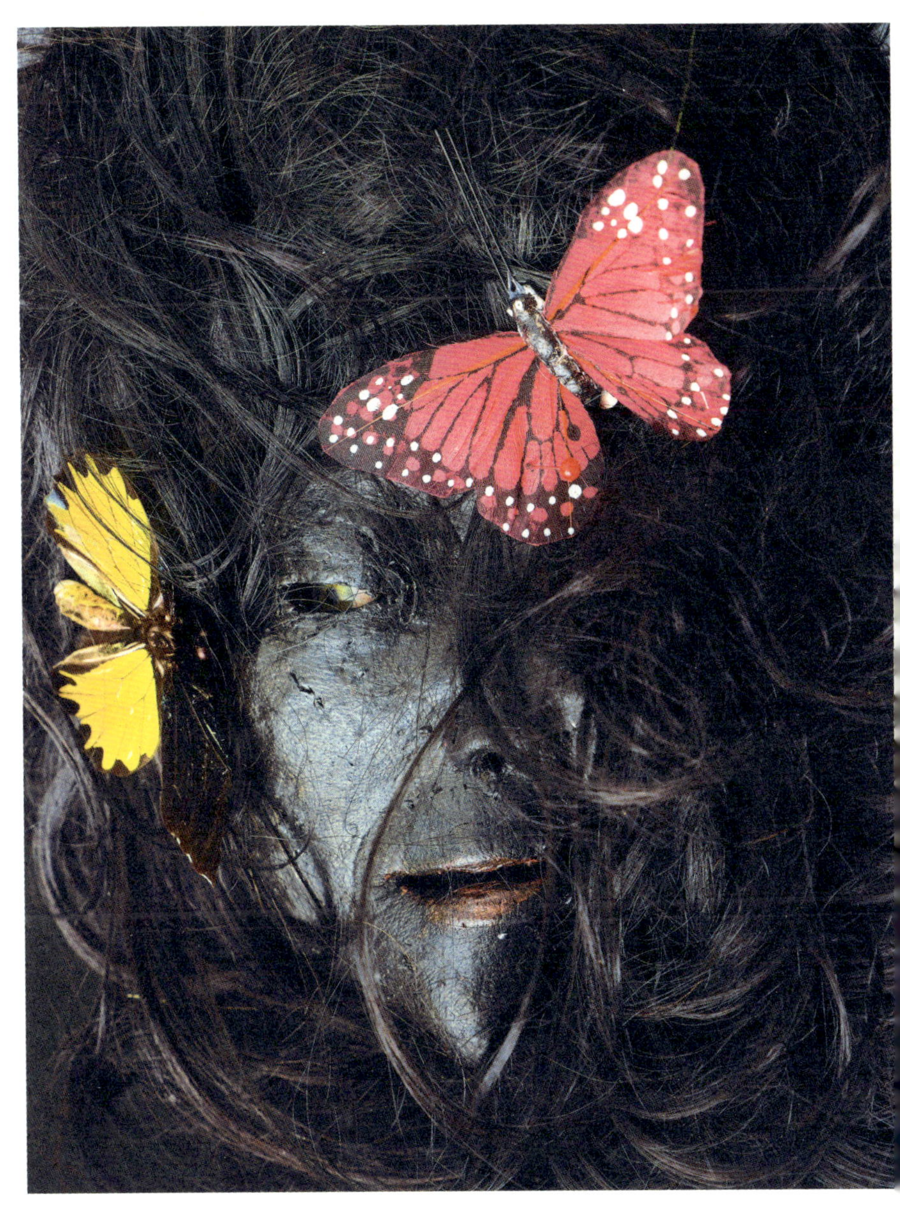

*PARANOID* FROM THE
*BREATHING MACHINES*
SERIES, 1968/2022

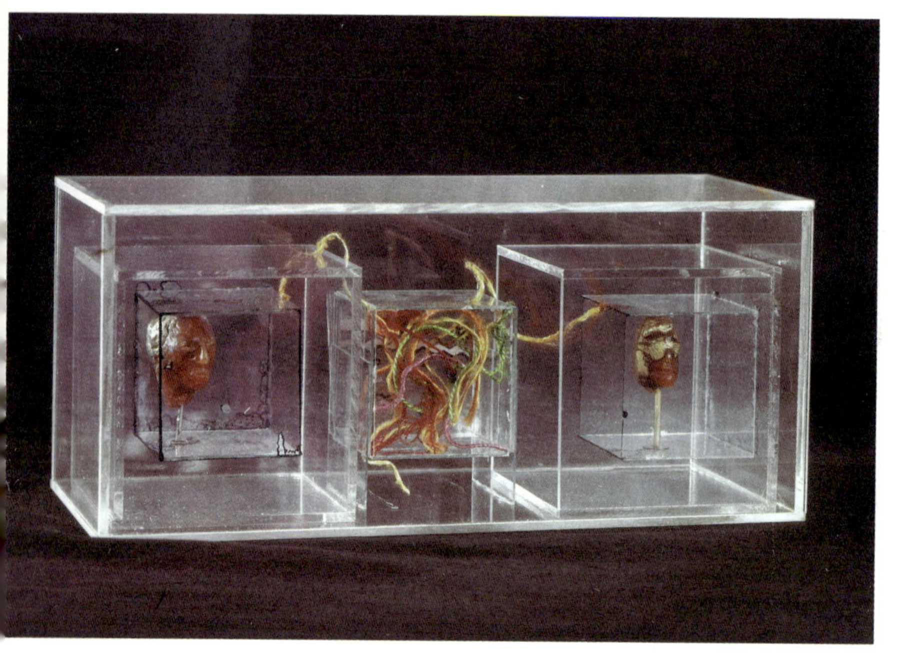

# CONVERSATION, 1966

# 7
# UNREST

I got involved in 1970 in the women's movement
when I finally realized that my exclusion from the art
world was based on the fact that I was a woman, not
just because I was an African American. I realized I
had to incorporate that in my struggle, and so I did.
—Interview with Faith Ringgold, 1991

Breathing the polluted smog of Los Angeles was difficult.
So we returned to the Bay Area, around the time that both
Malcolm X and Medgar Evers were assassinated. The FBI
director, J. Edgar Hoover, declared that the Black Panther
Party "represent[ed] the greatest threat to the internal
security of the country." Under Hoover's leadership, the
FBI waged war on the Panthers, jailing and murdering
organizers and igniting discord among its leadership. As
San Francisco protests became more active, the government ramped up its response. In May 1969, then Governor
Ronald Reagan declared a state of emergency in Berkeley
and sent 2,700 National Guard troops to invade both
Sproul Plaza and People's Park. Protesters were tear-
gassed, and buckshot was fired at them. More than 800
people were arrested. Hundreds were hospitalized. One
was killed, another blinded. One year later, on May 4, 1970,
four Kent State University students were killed and nine
injured when members of the Ohio National Guard opened
fire on a crowd gathered to protest the Vietnam War and
its expansion into Cambodia. Student strikes on campuses
nationwide forced the closure of colleges and universities.
    Simultaneously, the Women's Rights Movement
began agitating in response to the absence of women in

art history. In 1970, Judy Chicago launched the Feminist Art Program at Fresno State University, designed to address sex discrimination in art history and practice. I wanted to document the women involved in this movement at this pivotal moment, so I borrowed a video camera, taught myself how to use it, and interviewed as many women artists as possible when they visited the Bay Area. The interviews would continue over the next forty years.

I was not a filmmaker then, but I knew it was essential to document these female artists in real time to record the existing societal restrictions on their practices. Our conversations chart their struggles, changes, and successes as they aged. My interviewees included Judy Chicago, Miriam Schapiro, Joyce Kozloff, Sheila de Bretteville, Carolee Schneemann, B. Ruby Rich, and about sixty-five others. More than 1,500 hours of footage can be viewed today at the Stanford Special Collections Library. The interviews describe the tortuous obstacles these women faced as well as their brilliant tactics to defy repression.

Very few galleries showed women artists, and when they did, very few critics, almost all of whom were male, reviewed their work. To challenge this, I created three fictional critics named Prudence Juris, Herbert Goode, and Gay Abandon, all of whom wrote articles about women artists. Though the critics may have been fictive, their writing was not. Prudence Juris's writing appeared in prestigious art journals such as *Studio International*. Herbert Goode wrote for *Artweek*. Gay Abandon's reviews were part of a community newspaper that was left on doorsteps. While each fictional critic had a unique style of writing, they were all in agreement about the lack of women artists' visibility.

In those pre-computer days, everything was done by mail. I never met the editors of any of these publications, nor did they know the actual identity of these critics. Mentions of my own work in these critics' articles were instrumental in my being added to the roster of Paule Anglim in San Francisco, which was one of the few woman-owned galleries. Was my strategy of fictional critics ethical? What are the implications of a culture that celebrates gender exclusion? Does existing bias justify these fictive tactics? Yes!

Marcel Duchamp challenged gender stereotypes with his alternate female identity Rrose Sélavy, the very

name a play on *"Eros c'est la vie* – Love/Sex, that's life."
By becoming Rrose Sélavy, Duchamp became an "other."
Duchamp was considered the first conceptual artist. He
argued that, "An ordinary object [can be] elevated to the
dignity of a work of art by the mere choice of an artist."
Thus, a urinal, or a bottle rack, could be transformed into
an artwork by Duchamp's shifting how we perceived it.

Nonetheless, Duchamp himself was not innocent
of sexism. There are some who say his famous *Fountain*
(the urinal "readymade" mentioned above) was in fact
created by his uncredited collaborator Baroness Elsa von
Freytag-Loringhoven. If the readymade celebrated the
artist's intent, then what intent is demonstrated in keeping
Freytag-Loringhoven's contribution invisible?

Back then, Kenneth Baker was the art critic for the
*San Francisco Chronicle*. He often bragged that he would
not write about anything that moved and did not consider
photography art. Baker also authored a biography of Carl
Andre, a well-known New York–based Minimalist sculptor,
who was known to have a violent history with women. After
Andre's much younger third wife, the artist Ana Mendieta,
fell to her death from their thirty-fourth-floor apartment
window, I, along with Carolee Schneemann and Yvonne
Rainer, created *Conspiracy of Silence*, a 16-minute video
about her final moments, implicating Carl Andre in her
death. Baker was furious. From then until his death, he
refused to write about my work. Between 1972 and 2016,
my work was rarely if ever written about, except by
Prudence Juris, Herbert Goode, or Gay Abandon.

These imaginary critics achieved success during
their short lives, but they were designed to be temporary.
In 1974, they all retired simultaneously when I published all
my critical writing as my master's thesis at San Francisco
State University, titled "Aesthetic Morphology and Its
Application to Art Criticism." My graduate committee
understood how these fictional critics were commentary
on the art critical establishment, but I don't believe they
imagined that decades later, my creations and their writing would also be construed as artwork.

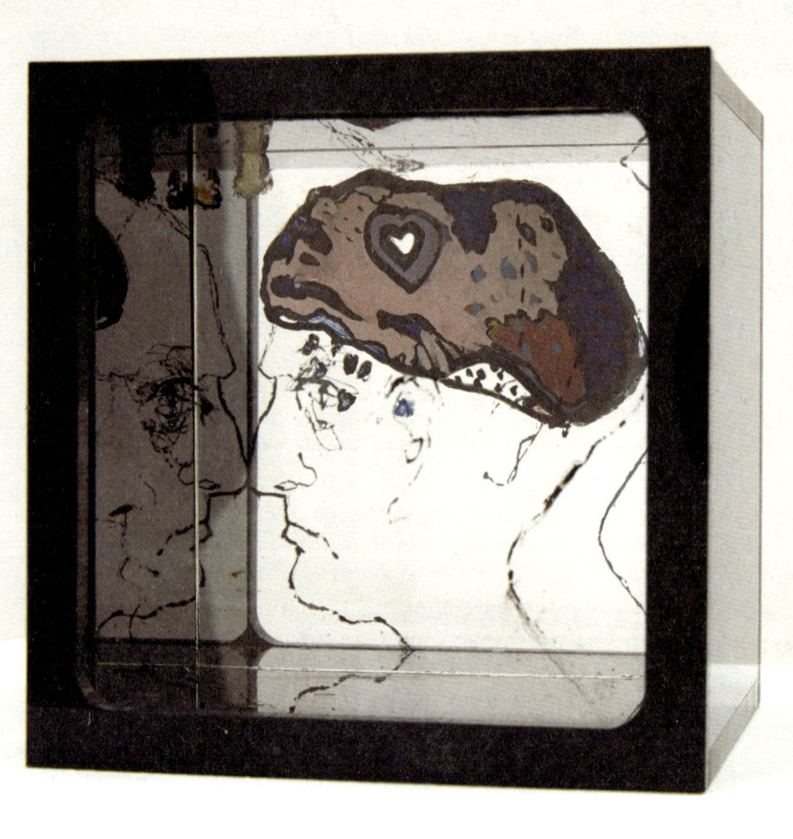

*3D BRAIN (AFTER LEONARDO),*
1964

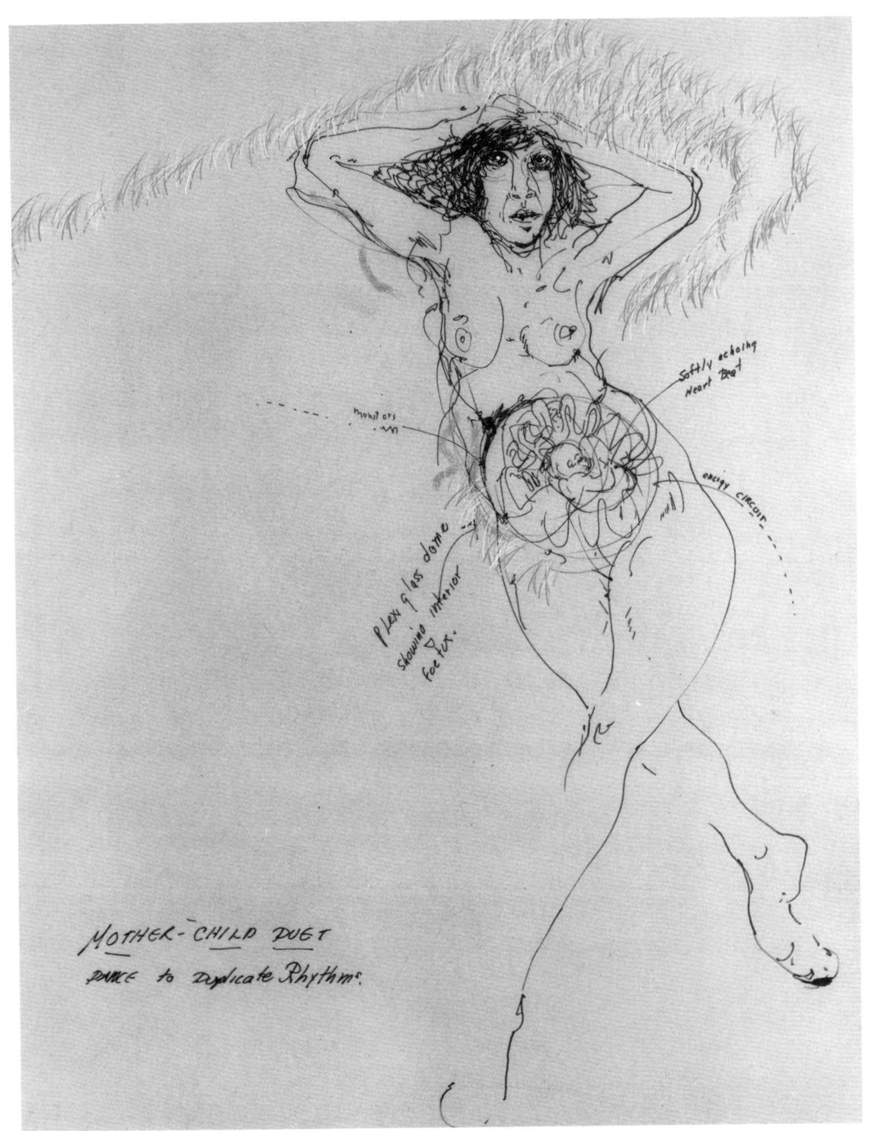


# MOTHER CHILD DUET, 1969

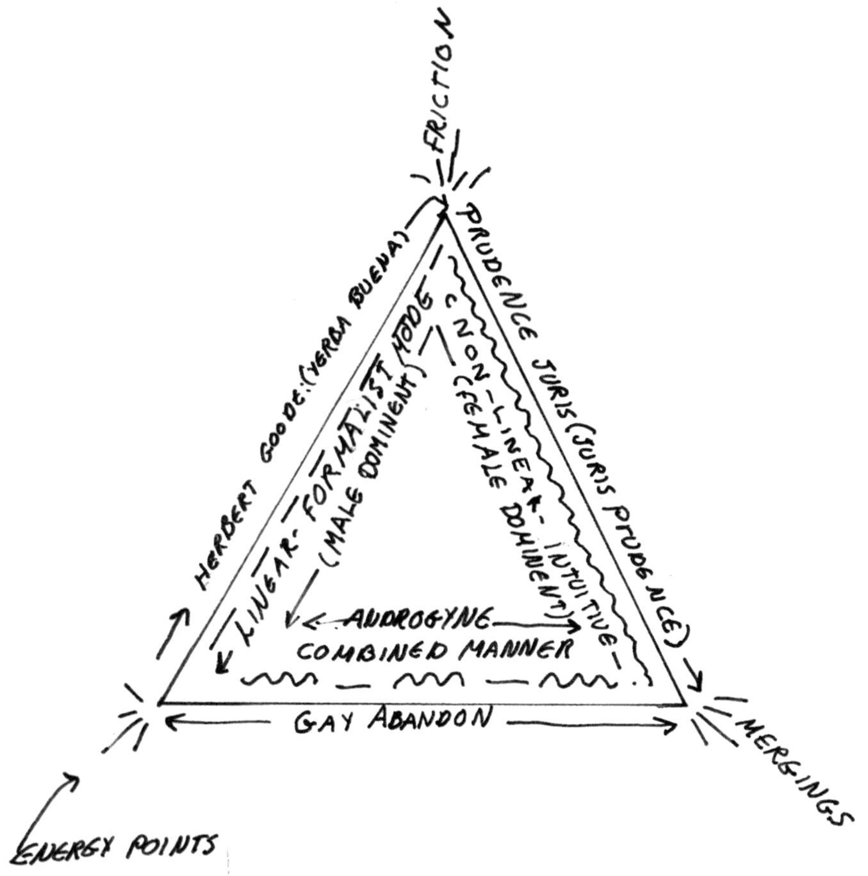


*DRAWING FLOW CHART FOR THE CREATION OF VIRTUAL CRITICS PRUDENCE JURIS, GAY ABANDON, AND HERBERT GOODE, 1968*

# The dadist vision-artists' games at SF Art Institute

**By Prudence Juris**

With genuine pluckiness, the San Francisco Art institute, 800 Chestnut St., opened "The Game Show." Interpretations of the general theme tend to reflect the concerns of the involved participants who, by virtue of their inclusion, become elements in Gallery Director Helene Freed's August gamble.

## Art

Jock Reynolds plays with various boxes set out on a table. When opened, they reveal subtle witticisms with overt dadist formats. This is an interesting enough concept, and Jim Pomeroy offers a variation of the theme through his opening wooden doors. In this contest, through, Marcel Duchamp won hands down.

One of the strongest pieces in the show is Robin Winter's suicide-choice game titled "Chose the Real One."

For 10 cents one has an opportunity to play ring toss at the "Money Lisa" or see John Gilmore Thomas's lovely kaleidoscopic monument titled "Fishe Voyeur," which was devoted (amongst other things) to dancing dolphins and tinny sounds. This piece is worth the admission charge.

Ainsley Pryor's birds twitter at the flick of the wrist. Walter Gabrielson' displays watercolors of war, executive, office and baseball games. Lynn Hershman's wax mask utters cliched social amenities and contact games to those who will listen.

Others in the exhibit are Carol Eckman, Norton Wisdom, Richard Burger, Irv Keper and Susan Subtle, Hilla Fudderman, John White, Peter Jones, Jim Roseberg and Martha Shaw —and, of course, the show would not have been complete without Paul Koss's pool table.

By the way, where is Melchert?

The exhibit is entertaining, but is it art? Marshall McLuhan once remarked that Art is anything you can get away with. Perhaps.

Personally, I tend toward provinciality and threrefore lean more toward the intererpretation of a Bay Area resident philosopher Tom Marioni, whose game consists of a resume along with a letter asking for a job. The post script at the bottom of the letter profoundly states "art is a business, not a game."

## Poetry reading

● Fay Kicknosway will read at Intersection, 756 Union St., next Tuesday at 8:30

# PRUDENCE JURIS IN *ARTWEEK,* JUNE 1973

# 8
# CHANCE

> The only thing I have learned is to find strength in yourself. No one can help you, no one can do anything for you, you have to do the work yourself.
> —Marina Abramović

Two chance encounters changed the trajectory of my life. My daughter was in nursery school and Eleanor Coppola (Ellie), who like me was both an artist and a mother, was in my car pool. We were both trying to maintain our practice while raising young children. When the Paule Anglim Gallery included a small drawing of mine in a group show, Ellie came to the opening. We had our first conversation that night. We soon became co-conspirators and collaborators.

Born in Los Angeles and a graduate of UCLA in applied design, Ellie was an assistant art director on the film *Dementia 13*, directed by her husband, Francis Ford Coppola. Unhappy with life in Los Angeles, Francis moved to San Francisco to open his own independent film studio, American Zoetrope, designed to champion independent filmmakers.

When Ellie invited me to a private film screening held in their home, I sat in the back row, not watching the film, but how everyone in the room reacted to the movies. Afterwards, in their elegant dining room, I stood in line behind a very shy young man who had just graduated film school in Los Angeles. He was in San Francisco because American Zoetrope had agreed to produce a feature-length version of his student film, *THX 1138*, a dystopian science fiction film shot in a tunnel of the Bay Area transit system. As we waited, we engaged in a long conversation about space travel. We both wondered whether, given the physics involved, it was possible that a person who left the planet might return before they left. His name was George Lucas. It was the first of many screenings that I attended at the Coppolas' home. These screenings became my film school.

Other filmmakers showing new work for the first time in Ellie's screening room included Marty Scorsese, Wim Wenders, Philip and Rose Kaufman, and Werner Herzog. Watching as they spoke about making their films made me think that it was not a difficult process. So, in the hope that I, too, might make a film, I enrolled in a one-night-a-week class at San Francisco City College. Eventually, I dropped out, but not before I learned how to edit 8 mm films.

Ellie was incredibly generous to me, and we met often for coffee at the Caffe Trieste, a small cafe in North Beach where Allen Ginsberg had written his poem "Howl."

My second chance meeting occurred in my dentist's waiting room. I was reading a recently published review by Prudence Juris when another patient remarked that he was a fan of hers. He was Peter Selz. He gave me his card and asked me to give him a call.

Before I phoned him, I looked up his background. Peter was born in Munich, Germany, to a prosperous Jewish family. His maternal grandfather was an art dealer who played a major role in Peter's art education. In 1936, as a teenager, he fled Germany to relocate to New York, where he briefly attended Columbia University before eventually enlisting in the OSS, precursor to the CIA. After the war, he received a master's degree in art at the University of Chicago, and then worked as curator at Pomona College, MoMa, and in 1970 was hired to oversee the University Art Museum at Berkeley.

When I called, Peter invited me to a luncheon with other local artists. How exhilarating to hear the percolating ideas of Bruce Conner, Victor Moscoso, Howard Fried, Joseph Raffael, and William Wiley. I was the only woman and sat quietly, not saying a word but enraptured by their ideas. I am certain the men there did not consider me to be an artist. Why would they? I never mentioned my work and it had never been exhibited. The assumption was that I was Peter's "friend."

Later, I showed Peter my drawings, which he seemed to appreciate. I never revealed to him, or anyone else, my secret identity as Prudence Juris.

At Berkeley, women academics were agitating for better representation. Complaints had been filed with the Department of Health, Education, and Welfare because the museum rarely exhibited work by women. As a response, Peter curated a drawing show, inviting me and the local female artists Cheryl Bowers and Cherie Raciti to show our work. I was eager to get reactions to my sound works. I was also excited to meet other women artists. Between raising my daughter and working on art, Ellie was my only friend.

To me, drawings are born of partnerships of pencil, watercolor, acrylics, glue, sparkle lines, razor cuts, ink, even light and sound. Each drawing is a rehearsal for the ones that follow. Erasure, change, and renewal are all part of the life cycle of drawings and of life itself.

In the hospital, I struggled to breathe and make art. The two are intertwined—life and breath. For the U.C. Berkeley exhibition I created an installation called *Breathing Machine*, which featured wax casts of my own face painted in a range of colors from white to blue to black. They were placed inside wooden boxes with their faces partially covered by hair that fell across the wax face's forehead. Glass eyes stared blankly out at whoever looked at them. I also embedded sensors covered by a rug on the floor in front of each piece. When a viewer stepped on the sensor, the wax cast initiated a dialogue through sensor-connected tape recorders. When viewers came close, the face seemed to come to life, making sounds, including laughter and sneezing.

Another work, titled *Self-Portrait of Another Person*, interviewed viewers, leaving silent space for their responses. I knew of no other artist at that time incorporating sound and sensor technology into their artworks. Sound added a new dimension. It permeated the space in a way that interactively engaged the viewer. Robert Irwin, Dan Flavin, and James Turrell used light to define and shape space. Later the Dia Foundation exhibited La Monte Young's sound installations, but no other artist I knew of combined these elements as I did at that time.

Bruce Conner allowed me to cast his face in blue wax. Though Bruce was stoic, his wax cast face appeared to be crying, signaling a hidden despair. I named the work

*Bruce Conner Crying X-Ray*. Thus began my friendship with Bruce.

Another of my works was a sculpture that spoke to feminist political concerns regarding reproductive rights, called *Abortion*, which featured two wax legs that peered out from beneath a sheet stained with human blood. The installation went smoothly.

On the day of the opening, when I went to inspect my room, I was flabbergasted to find that my exhibition gallery was empty. A rope closed off the space. Upset and confused, I barged into Peter's office to ask what was going on.

Sheepishly, Peter admitted that Brenda Richardson, then chief curator, decided not to show my exhibit, *Completed Fragments*.

"Why?" I asked.

Silence.

"WHY?" I repeated.

"Brenda said that it was NOT ART!" Peter told me. "She objects to there being sound . . . and she objects to the abortion piece as political," he replied.

"Is this being done to any of the other women's installations?" I asked. Bowers and Raciti were both considered feminist artists, yet their work remained on exhibit.

"I'm sorry, Lynn," Peter said. "It was supposed to just be drawings like the ones you showed me."

Peter claimed he had not been consulted about the removal of my work. In retrospect, I don't believe such a decision could have been made without his complicity. It is hard to describe what it felt like to be told that my work was considered "Not Art."

Years later I learned that between 1968 and 1971, Robert Rauschenberg made an artwork titled *Mud Muse*, in which a rectangular vat of mud was activated by bubbles. It also made sounds via speakers embedded in the vat, some of which were the recorded sound of bubbles. No one dismissed Rauschenberg's work for being too radical.

The label "Not Art" haunted my work for decades. I was desolate. In despair, I walked down Telegraph Avenue, haunted by the willful erasure of my show. The boarded-up windows at the Bank of America, an artifact of the Free Speech Movement I so admired, were still there. I realized that what challenges the status quo, what is new, is often suppressed at first. I decided that regardless of acceptance by others, I would make my work and wait for the world to catch up.

Perhaps things would have been different if I lived in New York. Perhaps there I would have continued to make traditional drawings and paintings within the context of current art movements. However, given my own personal health situation and living in the center of technological innovation that would become known as Silicon Valley, I stayed in San Francisco and continued to make work I felt was part of both that moment and the future. Making work that addressed current issues was, for me, the reason to be an artist. I did not stop and continued to make sculptures such as *3D Brain (after Leonardo)*, which featured a portrait of a brain encased in plexiglass.

The title of one work from 1965, *Thinking Woman Dreaming of Escape*, reflected my dilemma. The mother of an infant, I was in a marriage I had neither chosen nor knew how to leave.

Brenda Richardson was a fan of Prudence Juris. She occasionally wrote Prudence letters. I was often tempted to blow my cover and respond as me. Instead, Prudence wrote a devastating review of the nonexhibition and, of course, asked why Lynn Hershman's work was removed. Prudence received no response.

Fifty-four years later, in 2014, those same prohibited works were finally exhibited as part of my retrospective at ZKM Center for Art and Media in Germany. They were celebrated as pioneering and prescient. Reviewers acknowledged their historical importance as the first media works to combine sound, sensors, and media and have since been acquired by many important collections, including MoMA and the Cleveland Museum of Art

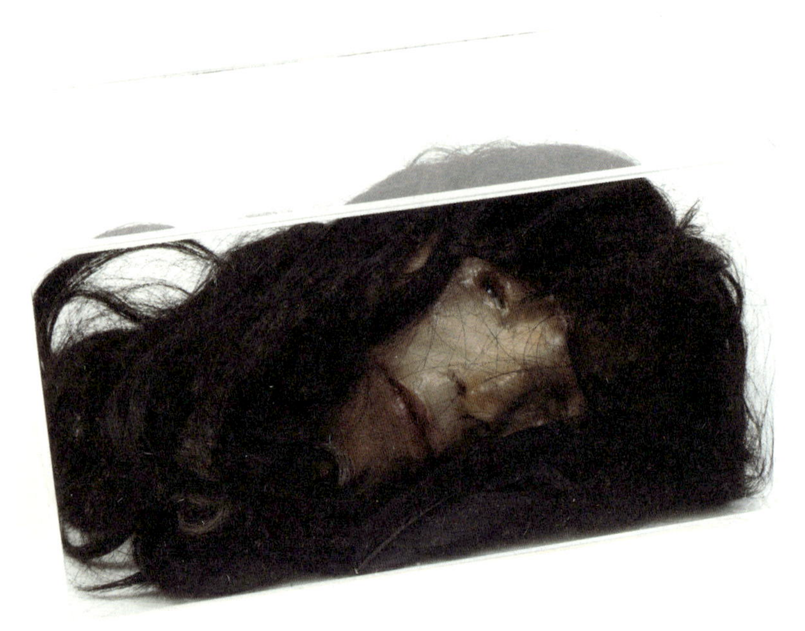

*THINKING WOMAN DREAMING OF ESCAPE, 1965*

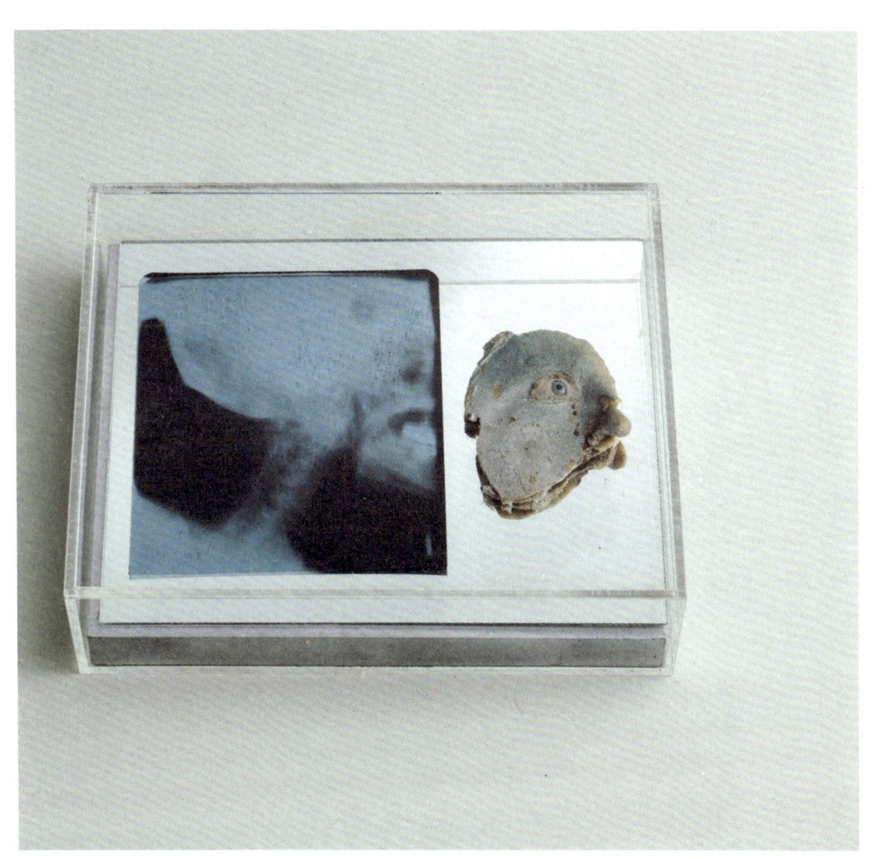

*BRUCE CONNER CRYING X-RAY*, 1965. PHOTOGRAPH BY ROBERT DIVERS HERRICK

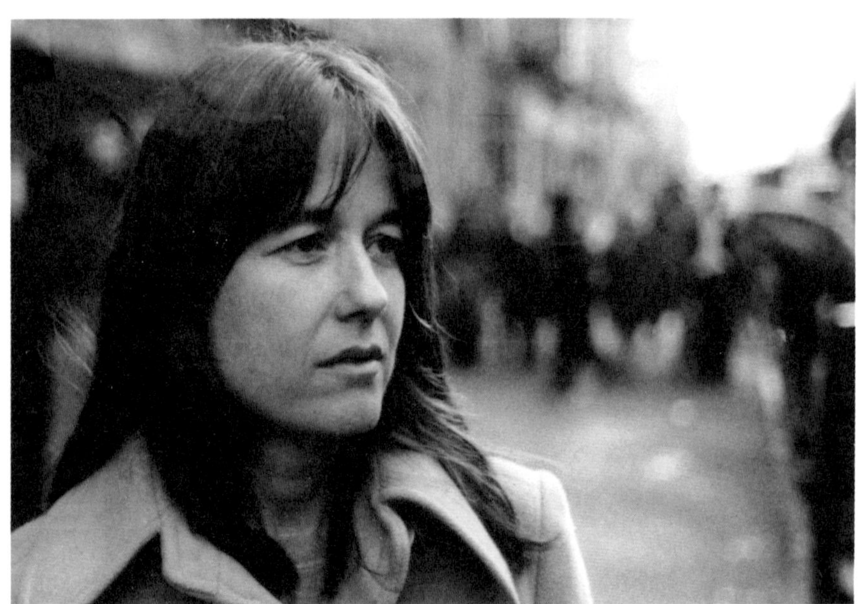

ELEANOR COPPOLA.
COURTESY OF AMERICAN
ZOETROPE.

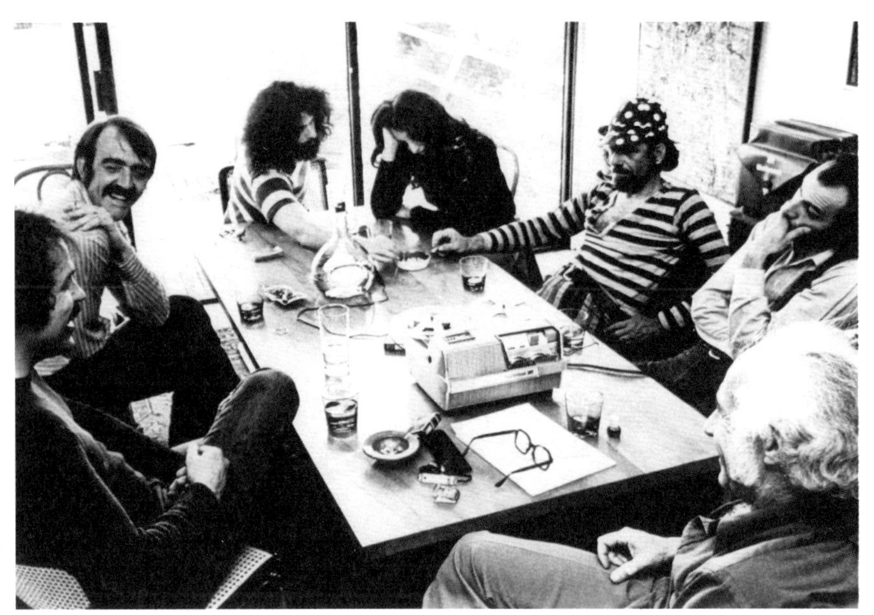

# PETER SELZ, VICTOR MOSCOSO, LYNN HERSHMAN, HARALD PARIS, WILLIAM WILEY, JOSEPH RAFAEL, HOWARD FRIED AND OTHERS, BERKELEY, CALIFORNIA, 1977

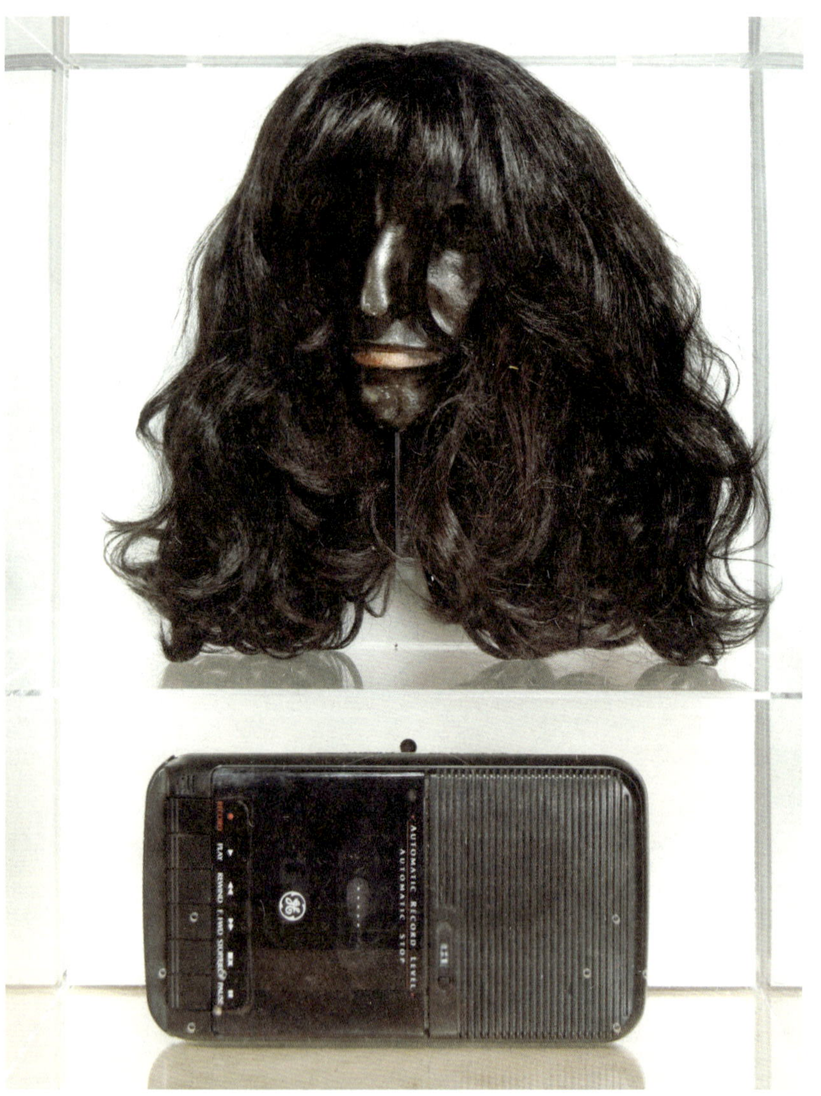

# *SELF PORTRAIT AS ANOTHER PERSON FROM THE BREATHING MACHINES SERIES, 1968*

# 9
# REINVENTION

> Art is the only way to run away without leaving home.
> —Twyla Tharp

After my exhibition was canceled, I called Ellie to convene an emergency meeting at Caffe Trieste, the North Beach spot where we often met while our children were in nursery school. The café was close to City Lights Bookstore, where Beat poets like Allen Ginsberg, Lawrence Ferlinghetti, Gregory Corso, Jack Michelene, and Jack Hirschmann often sat at tables inside.

We discussed how female artists such as Elaine de Kooning, Lee Krasner, Nancy Kienholz, Nancy Spero, Ana Mendieta, Lee Miller, Frida Kahlo, Nancy Holt, and Yoko Ono were only noted as "the partners, girlfriends, or wives of" their more famous male partners. Ellie and I decided we needed a strategy to defy cultural censorship by narrow-minded curators such as Brenda Richardson. The solution we came up with was simple: If museums and galleries would not show our work, we would rent hotel rooms and present it to a broader public. Around the corner from Caffe Trieste was a smallish, inexpensive hotel called the Dante. I liked the name. Rooms were affordable at $30 a week. So, in November 1973, we rented rooms 52 and 47 for our installations. The rent came from my household budget.

At the time, the term *site specific* did not exist, even

though James McNeill Whistler had designed a room for a client in Detroit and Frank Lloyd Wright had made total environments, but those were more architectural and decorative than art installations. In San Francisco, there had been "happenings" and rock performances with light shows, theater and dance performances that were multi-media events, but no one had created an art installation in a hotel room. The hotel rooms were open to the public twenty-four hours a day, seven days a week, allowing visitors to sign in at the front desk to access a key and enter the small, simple environments. The rooms were about 100 square feet with no private bathroom. Each had simple furnishings: a table, bed, chair, and dresser, as well as a small closet.

Ellie's room was open for two weeks during which Tony Dingman, a college friend of Francis, happily lived there rent-free. Ellie trained him to photograph changes in the interior of the room caused by shifts of time, such as a towel being folded or the bed, unmade or made. These images would be posted on the wall, documenting the changing environment.

My room was open indefinitely, allowing dust and other natural shifts to become part of the evolution of the piece. In *Room 47*, artifacts simulated the lives of fictional people who might have lived there.

Rodin created cast body parts that he would constantly recycle. Inspired by his repurposing, my wax cast body parts of faces and hands were designed to be continually recycled in new, temporary installations. Two wax casts in the bed in *Room 47* gave the impression of two women sleeping there. The essence of the characters' identity was articulated through choices of mundane objects gathered from the neighborhood such as menus, matchboxes, and flyers, which were placed on tables, on chairs, or in drawers. An audio tape loop of breathing emanated from the locked closet.

A fictional character authenticated her existence through the accumulation of "real" cultural artifacts. How does one discern reality? When and how does the blurred edge of truth gain veracity?

We advertised our installations by posting xeroxed handouts at nearby stores and cafes. The announcements and word of mouth brought hundreds of people to the Dante Hotel. The *San Francisco Chronicle* even listed the Dante Hotel as one of the ten best art exhibitions

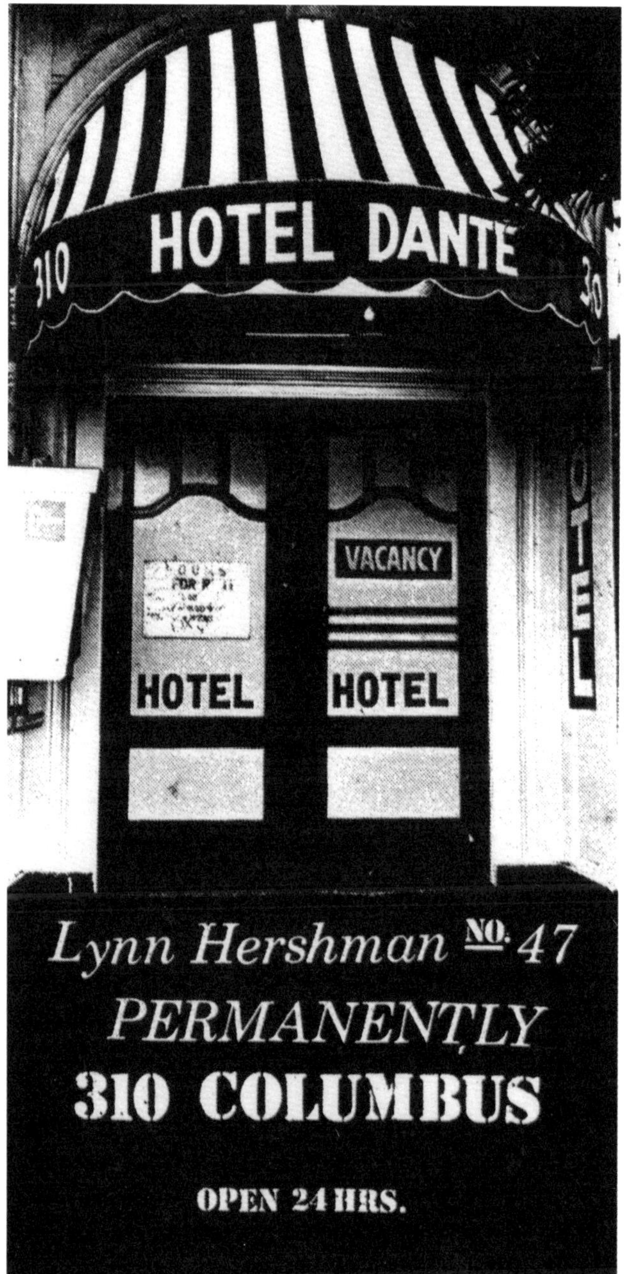


# ADVERTISEMENT FOR THE DANTE HOTEL, 1973

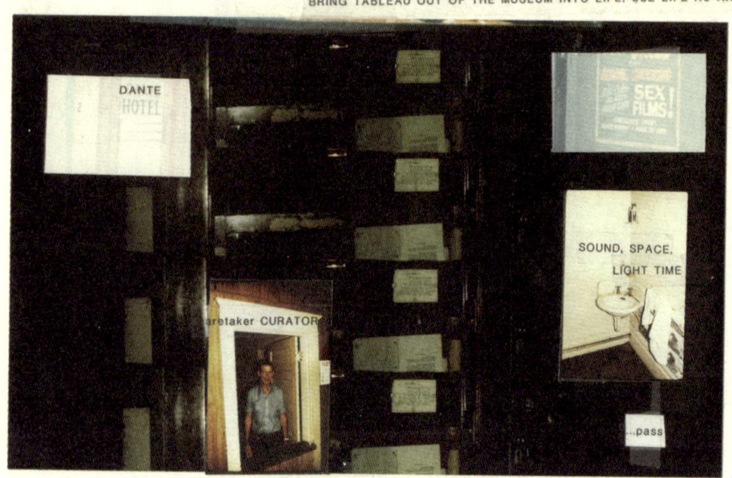


SIGN IN  ENTER NAME BEFORE GETTING KEY  TRESSPASS TRESSPASS INTO SPACE AND TIME

# *DANTE HOTEL STORYBOARD, 1973*

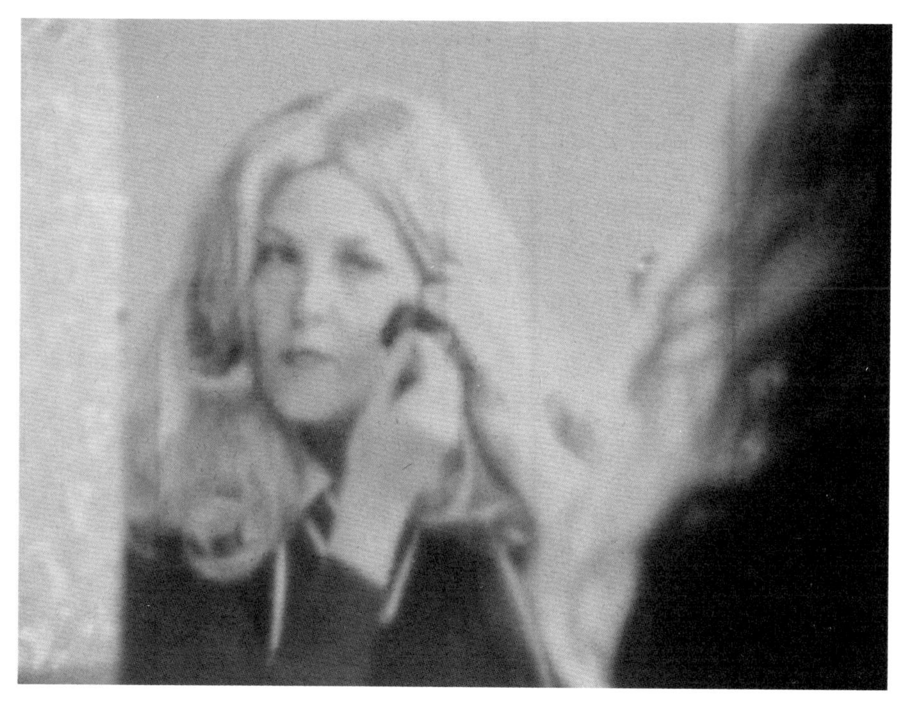

STILL FROM
*CONSTRUCTING ROBERTA,*
A FILM BY ELEANOR
COPPOLA, 1975

of the year, on a par with a San Francisco exhibition of Turner's watercolors.

Ellie's room closed as planned after two weeks. My room was meant to exist indefinitely. However, in the middle of the night, some ten months later, a visitor entered the room and saw my cast bodies lying in the bed, covered and not moving. Imagining they were dead bodies, he called the police. Two patrolmen came to the hotel, opened the door to room 47, collected the wax heads, wax body casts, and artifacts, and took them to the San Francisco Police's Central Headquarters, where they remain to be claimed. This was an apt closure for the narrative of the piece.

Ellie and I were both in traditional marriages where the man was the breadwinner, and the women did not work and instead stayed home and raised the children. Francis had great success as a filmmaker, and Larry had taken a high-level administrative position at U.C. Berkeley. Although the art world was reluctant to fully accept us as artists, our families understood that making art was central to who Ellie and I were.

Many young women today may not understand the contradiction inherent in presenting as a feminist while living off our husband's incomes. As Betty Friedan explained in a 1979 *New York Times* article: "Most of us let ourselves be seduced into giving up our careers in order to embrace motherhood, and it wasn't easy to resume them." Earning a living by making art was beyond our imagination.

A few days before *Room 47* closed, Peter Selz escorted the artists Christo and Jeanne- Claude to the Dante Hotel. Christo noted that a visitor's interaction with space added vulnerability to the work and compared it to the two-week lifespans of his own projects. Christo and Jeanne-Claude were about to embark on their *Running Fence* project. Peter Selz was hired as project director.

# 10
# ROBERTA

> The world is full of fictional characters looking
> for their stories.
> —Diane Arbus

In the process of installing the room at the Dante Hotel, I read a Joyce Carol Oates short story, "Passions and Meditations," about a lonely, starstruck woman named Roberta Bright who stalks a composer by writing unrequited letters. She eventually placed an ad in *The Village Voice* requesting a meeting. Though in this story the composer was the victim, I empathized with Roberta; I wondered what made her so desperate.

Sitting in room 47 at the Dante Hotel, I was inspired by Oates's story and imagined a fictional person who might have lived in the Dante Hotel. The character would move in and out of reality, basing her identity on the evidence, traces, discards, and artifacts that proved her existence.

Working further on the conceptual skeleton of what would become the Roberta project, I constructed her background, starting with her arrival in San Francisco. As I added artifacts, the reality of her existence was validated even though Roberta was a fiction.

I enrolled in a PhD psychology program at Antioch College to understand how to manifest a credible sense of identity for Roberta. After a few classes, having gathered the knowledge I needed, I dropped out.

When the Roberta project began in 1972, there was no finite end in mind. Like the *Breathing Machines*, or *Room 47*, I imagined these projects existing without ending.

Roberta left the Midwest because of a troubled family history. Roberta represented a manufactured image of the ideals fostered in advertising, fashion, and beauty magazines. She was a composite of accumulated stereotypes and psychological data, and like many women, had been traumatized by incestuous sexual abuse at home. *Roberta* was a performative live artwork. I hoped to find someone else to perform as her but when no one was willing to do it, I enacted Roberta's early episodes myself. Roberta and I shared a heartbeat and breath.

Roberta was an ordinary young woman. She was blond, wore heavy makeup, was clumsy, shy, and did not fit in anywhere. Roberta opened a bank account, applied for and received credit cards and a driver's license, had defined handwriting, and assumed a unique posture, walk, and speech pattern. Extensive charts documented Roberta's appearance. Roberta took part-time typing jobs to support herself, though she was always fired within days. Then, as now, rent was expensive in San Francisco, so Roberta moved into a transient hotel until she could find a roommate. She placed ads in local newspapers and then met responders, usually in Union Square. This led to sequential adventures with specific names such as *Meet Mr. America*. People answered her ads and by doing so, became unwitting participants in her fiction, just as Roberta became a part of their reality.

During the near decade that Roberta was live, her existence was documented by Edmund Shea, who photographed Bruce Conner's artwork. Later I hired professional surveillance photographers to track her movements and to protect her if she got into difficult situations.

Roberta was a double mirror. She simultaneously reflected and refracted society's biases. Clothing, checks, credit cards, driver's license, psychiatric reports, diary entries, letters, tape recordings—all became the archived remains of her artificial life. Roberta's detritus allowed viewers to become voyeurs to her history. Archived photographs, objects, documents, and texts proved her existence. Roberta's manipulated reality, decades ahead of the engineered dramas of reality TV, were a model for a private system of interactive performance.

Halfway through the process of constructing Roberta

as a live breathing simulacrum, I enlisted a series of individual dancers, whom I termed multiples, to enact portions of Roberta's life. The first multiple was Kristine Stiles, at that time one of Peter Selz's graduate students. The other multiples were dancers because they could mimic Roberta's posture and body language.

*Roberta* represented the social construction of conditioning and was an investigation of the precarious nature of identity.

After I went out as Roberta, I retreated to my life as wife and mother. I never confused our identities. When I began this project, I thought it would last a few weeks. I never suspected it would be enacted for almost a decade.

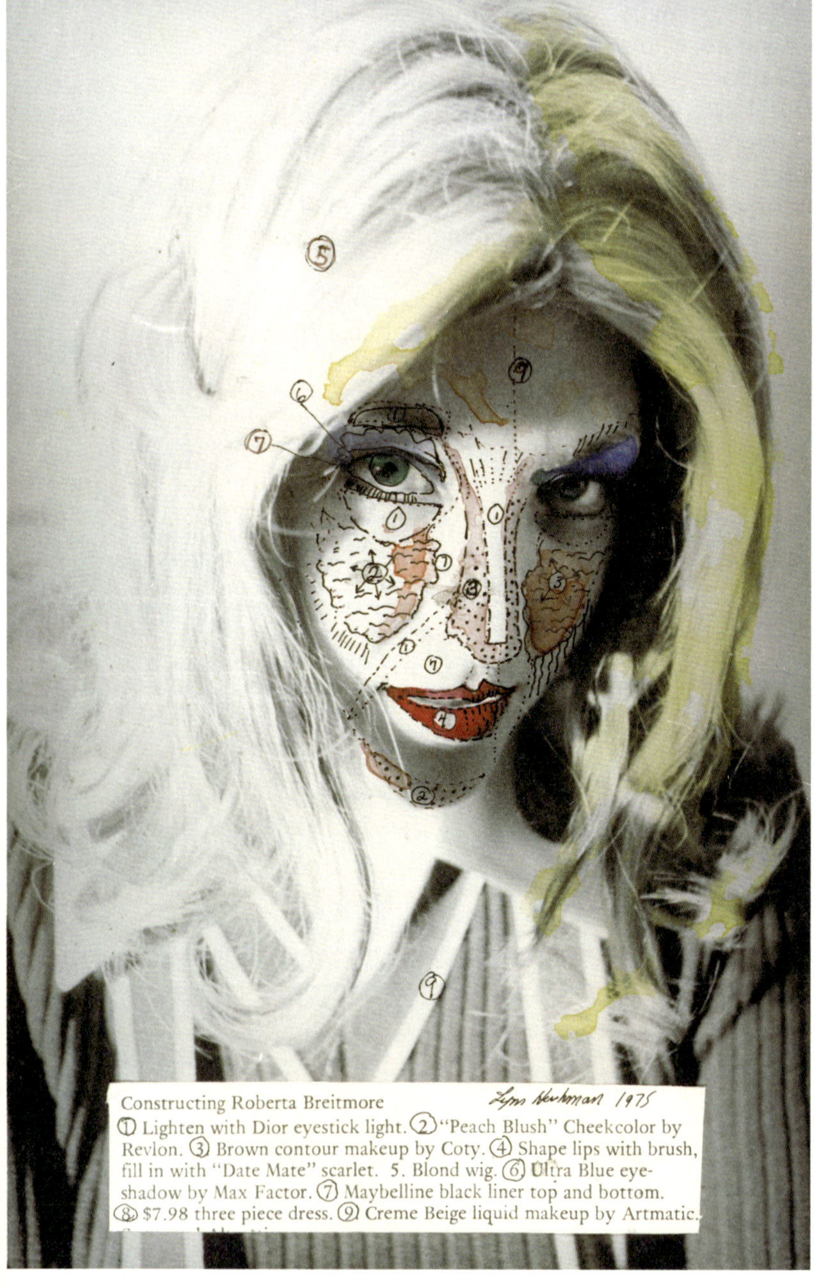


# ROBERTA'S CONSTRUCTION CHART #1, 1975

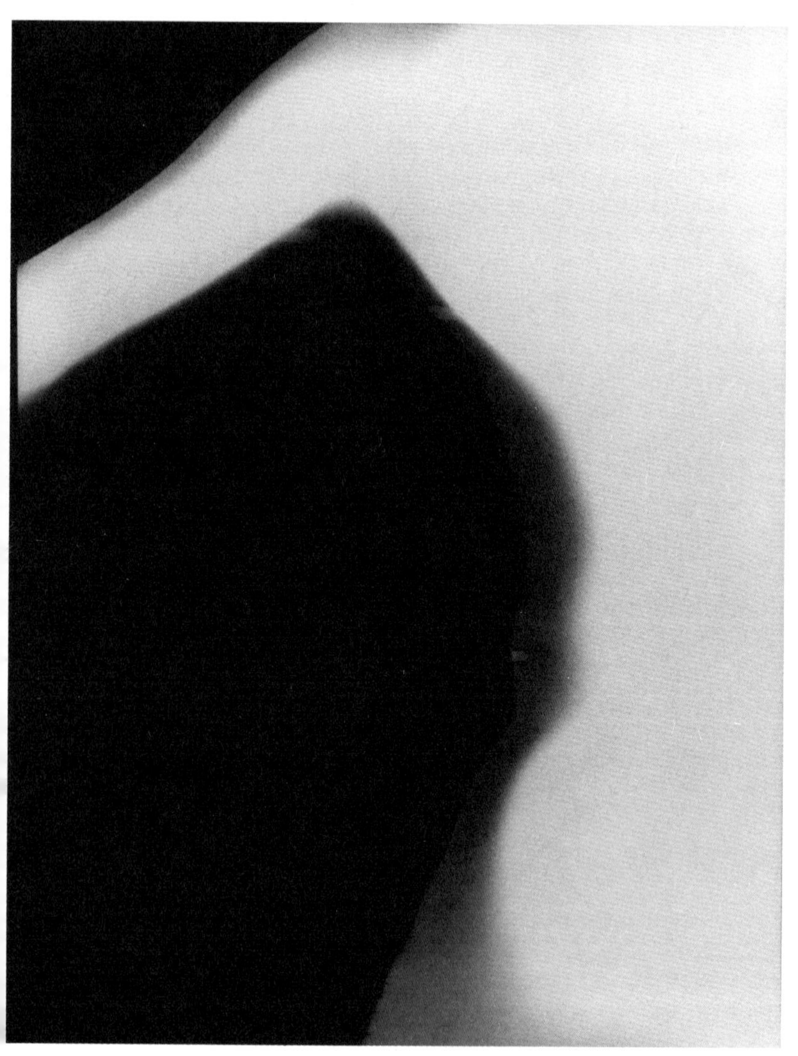

*DEPARTING ANGEL* BY BRUCE CONNER AND EDMUND SHEA, 1973 © 2025 CONNER FAMILY TRUST, SAN FRANCISCO/ ARTISTS RIGHTS SOCIETY (ARS), NEW YORK

# 11 RANDOMNESS

It is important to express oneself ... provided the feelings are real and are taken from your own experience.
—Berthe Morisot

Meeting living artists presented a precious opportunity for inspiration. I was thrilled when Bruce Conner invited me to his studio to watch him edit his current film. In silent fascination I noted his obsession with perfection as he replayed each cut backwards and forwards, changing speed and size, intently studying patterns of movement before making one microscopic change. Then repeating the process again. His fingers flew swiftly, as if they were on a Promethean journey, climbing and falling, holding, then releasing, strips of film, as he decided which frames deserved to live into the future.

When he reached a point where he could take a break, Bruce invited me to accompany him to Mabuhay Gardens, a club in North Beach where Blondie and Devo were performing. With his camera in tow, Bruce showed no inhibitions in capturing them on film. In a frenzy, he climbed onto chairs and tables with unsuppressed glee, shooting footage of them, cackling as he caught a good shot while all of us, including the performers, were enraptured by his obsessive quest to preserve and capture the experience. Later, Bruce collaborated with Devo to make a three-and-a half minute documentary film, *Mongoloid,* for their second music video.

With Ellie's permission, I invited Bruce to a screening at her home. He arrived in a suit of finely woven deep-gray wool with a matching vest, gold pocket chain, and custom-made Italian leather shoes. An elegant, perfectly knotted silk tie complemented his exquisitely hand-tailored cuff-linked silk shirt. Bruce always dressed in the most elegant outfits. So much so that he looked more like a wealthy art patron than an artist. But no amount of fine clothing or good grooming could hide Bruce's true identity as a wild and audacious artist with a fully realized artistic vision.

In 1973, I invented a secret organization named *Nail File (Foundation for Information Not Known)*. This was my heartfelt attempt to empower artists to identify galleries and museums that mistreated them or violated their rights. I believed there was power in artists banding together, exposing the wrongdoers, and warning others against them. Bruce was the first to become a member. Unfortunately, too many artists lived in fear of alienating the gatekeepers who controlled the public's access to their work. Although this organization never got off the ground, my friendship with Bruce became stronger.

When Bruce was looking for a space to create life-sized photograms of his shadow, I approached Judy Newman, also a carpool mother, because she and her husband, Jim, a gallerist and art dealer, owned a large three-story home on Divisadero Street. An interior balcony overlooked a ground-level living room. They collected art and were sympathetic to Bruce.

So Bruce, the photographer Edmund Shea, and I spent a night in the Newmans' luxurious home, staging, lighting, and photographing Bruce at various angles. None of us knew if the photograms could even be processed at the scale Bruce envisioned. Despite that, we worked through the night and into the next morning as Bruce placed his body in various positions on the floor. Edmund managed the process from the balcony above. That night I fully appreciated that risk taking and making art is an act of faith. The collaboration produced spiritual images unlike anything else I had ever seen. Bruce called them Angels.

Despite my long and close friendship and collaboration with Bruce, he never really acknowledged me as an artist. Bruce was entirely focused on Bruce, but he accepted me as part of his support system and occasional entourage.

In 1974, wanting to make new works of conceptual art that expanded and deepened the investigations into manufactured identity I had begun in the Dante Hotel and *Roberta*, I went to New York, where I rented three different hotel rooms, one at the Chelsea, another at the Plaza, and a third at the central YWCA.

In the Chelsea, a live person took up residence with artifacts identifying them as a writer. At the Plaza, the suite was littered with children's toys and coloring books. While the television showed westerns, a phonograph played music from *Alice in Wonderland*, and the bathroom featured a wax cast of a child taking a bubble bath. Plastic sealed off the room at the YWCA, where a male mannequin stood watching a sleeping female mannequin. A hired bus took viewers to all three locations at designated times. To advertise the installation, which ran from October 21 to December 16, 1974, I made a two-minute 16 mm film that featured Peter Selz, and that was broadcast in San Francisco and New York.

Soon after, I staged *Lady Luck: A Double Portrait of Las Vegas*, a twelve-hour art intervention in Las Vegas that featured the circus performer Lisa Charles. In the Circus Circus Casino, Lisa appeared with a wax mannequin double, wearing the same outfit and same hairstyle. A televised commercial invited patrons to gamble next to Lady Luck and her twin. Both Lisa and her double received $1,400 to play at the roulette table. Lady Luck placed her bets based on intuition, and the twin did so based on a recording of random numbers that played from speakers implanted in her chest. The robot-like sculpture won $1,620; the actress lost $1,460.

The *Water Women* series were works in various media from collage to digital prints in which women appeared to be evaporating. To accomplish this, I used images and sometimes actual drops of water to illustrate imperma-nence and that humans are mostly made of water. The themes of erasure, and transformation were inspired by women artists who were invisible to art collectors, galler-ists, museum curators and art critics. Rather than being sidelined, women artists were inspired to invent new forms of art, including performances and site-specific works that used media itself to amplify critical social justice issues such as rape and domestic violence.

I was questioning the notion of what forms a woman's identity and what social cues are used to identify a person.

To explore these ideas, I wanted to use the tools of the present, which were just being invented and which I could integrate into the realm of artmaking.

Looking back, I have no idea how I was financially able to make these artworks. I never received any grants. I had no fellowships or support as an artist. In very rare cases, such as with *Lady Luck*, I was commissioned to make the work. However, making the works often cost me more than the commission. What I do remember is constantly being in debt, putting these expenses on a credit card. The debt weighed upon me for years.

One of the most visible activists for women's rights in San Francisco was Margo St. James, the painter turned prostitute, then prostitute turned attorney. Margo was the founder of COYOTE, which stood for Call Off Your Old Tired Ethics, an organization advocating for the decriminalization of prostitution. Margo and I met at Tosca Cafe, owned by Jeannette Etheredge, originally started by her mother. Jeannette and her mother were devoted to helping Russian dancers emigrate to the United States. Jeanette loved filmmakers and set up a private room for them at Tosca. Margo was friendly, attractive, and funny. I admired the brilliance of her far- reaching activism and was eager to involve her in an event Ellie and I were plotting.

In May 1975, we were invited by the Society of Contemporary Art to give a performance for two groups of wealthy art patrons, one from the S.F. Museum of Art and the other from the Los Angeles County Museum of Art. Although we were suspicious of their motives (we imagined they were just using Ellie to get to Francis), we nonetheless agreed. We named our event *ReForming Familiar Environments* and made certain the date we chose was when Francis was out of town.

Ellie and I designed a game that turned the floor plan of her home into a Monopoly board, with events occurring in each room. With Margo's help, we hired the entire local union of prostitutes to occupy the rooms and engage with patrons in unexpected ways. Some of the young women took baths, some peeled potatoes beneath hand-drawn posters of Joseph Beuys quotes, others slept in beds, and still others interacted with patrons.

Edmund Shea snapped images of money changing hands. These photos were later published in the local newspaper in an ad we titled "Cultural Exchange." The multiple Oscars usually on display in the Coppola dining room were replaced with tiny, one-inch replicas, originally designed to be necklaces. Despite the confusion of patrons who struggled to define what was or was not art/performance, the event was provocative and entertaining. Writing this now, I wonder where we found the audacity.

Eventually, Margo received her college equivalency and enrolled in law school, working as a process server for a criminal defense attorney, and became one of the first women private investigators in California. She fought for the rights of sex workers and founded the St. James Infirmary Clinic, a medical and social service organization run by and serving sex workers in the low-income district of the Tenderloin. Margo died in 2021. COYOTE's and St. James's papers are archived at the Schlesinger Library on the History of Women in America at the Radcliffe Institute for Advanced Study, at Harvard University. I regret that we lost touch.

In 1976, several artists began using the U.S. postal system to distribute their work outside the nexus of galleries and museums. They were dubbed "mail artists." In San Francisco, the artist Anna Banana pioneered what she called "artistamps," postage-stamp-sized artworks, which she would affix to envelopes and mail to acquaintances. In New York, Ray Johnson initiated the New York Correspondence School, which sent notes, letters, and packages to chosen people with no explanation. I created postage stamps that obliterated my identity by covering my face with hair. I pasted these stamps on letters addressed to myself and to friends and mailed them, anticipating that the post office, a governmental agency, would further cancel my image with a date and an official government record detailing when exactly my identity became changed. Ray was the only one who responded.

At first, Ray appeared to be a charming, gentle soul. I was wrong. He was obsessive and flooded my mailbox with his documents. He also often phoned at midnight wanting to chat. After several months of his late-night rants, the calls lost their charm, causing me to turn off my phone after 8 p.m.

I met Sam Francis through Peter Selz after Peter had asked me to collaborate on his overdue book about Sam. I ended up writing major sections of the text. It never occurred to me to ask for a contract or payment for my efforts. I expected to receive credit for my work when the book was published. Instead, not only did I receive no payment, but my collaboration on the text was never acknowledged.

In spring 1969, Sam flew to Berkeley "to paint the sky" with colored puffs of smoke as part of a student demonstration at People's Park. Sam told me that he had been a fighter pilot. His plane was shot down, causing him to suffer such significant injuries that he was not expected to survive. While he was in the hospital, someone brought him a set of watercolors. He started to paint.

"Art saved my life," he once gushed.

Sam recovered and never stopped painting. Much later I learned that the story of his plane going down may have been fiction, and that he was actually hospitalized for spinal tuberculosis. Regardless, he was a formidable painter and generous individual whose career was birthed in a hospital.

At Caffe Trieste, Ellie introduced me to Stephen Schwartz, who was at a nearby table. He had been recently hired to edit a magazine Francis had purchased named *City*. Stephen invited us to a lecture given by Arturo Schwarz, a scholar of alchemy from Milan whose gallery represented many of the Dada and Surrealist artists, such as Marcel Duchamp, Man Ray, André Breton, and Francis Picabia. By 1985, Stephen Schwartz had become editor of *The Journal of Contemporary Studies*, for which I wrote "Politics and Interactive Media Art," an article that pre-dated a publicly accessible internet, web browsers, email, and online avatars.

Ellie and I went together to the San Francisco Art Institute auditorium, where shortly after Arturo began his talk, two men in yellow banana suits took to the stage, waving signs that each read "DA." When they stood together their two signs combined to read "DADA." As Arturo continued his reading, the Dadaists' surrealistic antics turned the event into chaos. Ellie left but Stephen asked me to drive Arturo to the party planned for him.

On the short drive with Arturo, I asked about Christo and Jeanne-Claude, who were spending a lot of time in California designing their next project. Arturo dismissed Christo's work as derivative, comparing it to Man Ray's *Enigma of Isidore Ducasse*, a 1920 sculpture shrouded in fabric and tied with string. Arturo believed Man Ray did it first and better. I told him that Peter Selz had hired me as associate project manager on *Running Fence* and that Christo's vision was different in scale and context. When I asked what Duchamp was like, he said their communications were mostly telepathic, transmitted because of the many hours they spent silently playing chess.

At Arturo's party, I met Daniel Spoerri, an artist who was in residency at the Art Institute and whose work was about to be exhibited at a local gallery. Noting that I had a car, Daniel asked me to drive him to a local flea market to collect material for his upcoming exhibition, and Arturo asked if I might take him to City Lights Bookstore. Somehow, in between Dawn's classes, I managed to do both. I couldn't have imagined saying no or telling them that my time, and my work, was as important as theirs.

The next morning, after dropping off Dawn, I drove Arturo to City Lights, where he whizzed through the book stacks, followed by a clerk with a shopping cart that Arturo filled with books. At the checkout, he gave the directive to send one of each book to Milan and to gift me with a precious second set. Thus began our decades-long friendship.

Daniel Spoerri was born Daniel Isaac Feinstein in Romania in 1930. Daniel began his artistic career as a dancer, then staged several avant-garde plays which brought him into contact with Surrealists such as Duchamp, Man Ray, and Tinguely. Beginning in 1960, Spoerri made "snare-pictures," in which leftovers from his meals were glued to a board and then hung on a wall. Spoerri was also a chef and owner of a famed restaurant in Düsseldorf. For the opening of his exhibition at Eliane Ganz gallery, he prepared a dinner that he named *Transvestite Capsule.*

Lamb chops disguised as chickens were presented as the main course. When dessert was served, without warning Daniel lunged forward, grasped the tin edge of an awaiting meringue pie, and shoved it into the unsuspecting face of the chairwoman of the San Francisco Art Institute, who had the misfortune of being seated next to him. No one knew what she might have said to incite him or, indeed, if she had said anything at all. Daniel proceeded to throw chairs against the wall, followed by crystal, dishes, and finally the table itself. The horrified guests scattered. The owner of the gallery, Eliane Ganz, was in tears. Daniel sat on the floor, chuckling to himself despite the upheaval. He seemed to be enjoying the chaos.

The next morning a truck drove to the gallery's front door and unloaded three hundred blocks of ice, barricading the entrance. It was estimated the ice wouldn't melt until after the exhibition was scheduled to close. A note arrived for Eliane at the gallery from Daniel saying I was the one responsible for the ice. This was Daniel being Daniel.

Women artists would never have been able to get away with those sorts of antics. The reputations of male artists such as Daniel, Bruce, and so many others seemed only to be enhanced by their outrageous behavior.

During this era, I held dinner parties for friends that were performance art. For these events I made special dishes with the ceramicist Diane Flyr and menus describing edible portraits of the person honored. The plates and cups were artworks, featuring elements such as eyes, mouths, and even two little arms grasping a miniature fork and a knife.

Before Arturo returned to Milan, I arranged one of my dinner parties in his honor, designed around the new book he was writing, *The Alchemical Machination*. The guests included Francis and Ellie Coppola, Terry Fox, Lawrence Ferlinghetti, Daniel Spoerri, and a few neighbors. Tables simulated a laboratory with flasks, clamps, and objects that hinted at the supernatural. Beakers held swimming goldfish. Bunsen burners warmed bowls of Black Magic Shrimp soup. Menus were printed in lead-gray ink that transformed to gold as it oxidized in the air. My daughter and her friend Jenny were dressed in white lab coats and served the meal, including rack chicken titled *The Bird Stripped Bare with Herb Bachelors*, and a salad of greens served around a wax impression of my own face that I called *Head Salad*.

Another memorable dinner was given by Peter Selz for an important European curator I'll call Mr. X, who was in town to look for artists to include in the German *Dokumenta* exhibition. Mr. X had recently curated a notable exhibition in Bern that *The New York Times* had named the most celebrated exhibition of new art of the postwar era.

Peter suggested I bring some Roberta photographs for Mr. X to see. I placed a few Roberta painted photographs on the back seat of my car, where they remained while I went inside Peter's home. A throng of well-known local artists were there, Bruce, William Wiley, Joseph Raffael, and Harold Paris—all men, as usual. They secured studio visit dates with Mr. X. By contrast, I had no studio other than my kitchen table and I stored my art under the bed.

As everyone competed for Mr. X's attention, I was overtaken by a feeling of breathlessness, not from lack of air, but from suffocation as I regressed into my earlier self. Unable to speak, I swallowed myself little by little during the evening until I disappeared.

Peter asked me to drive Mr. X back to his hotel. When Mr. X got into my car, he glanced at the Roberta photographs still snuggled in the back seat. He seemed intrigued, but in my social paralysis, I could not bring myself to show them to him. Arriving at his hotel, he leaned closer to me, whispering that I had beautiful eyes and inviting me to his room. I was paralyzed. Stunned. I believe he knew I was married. I didn't know how to respond. I thought to myself, is this what every female artist must put up with? I sat there, frozen. After a few moments of uncomfortable silence, Mr. X went inside his hotel, alone.

Driving home that night, I fretted about the episode, admonishing myself for not describing Roberta or showing my photos to Mr. X. The next morning, I phoned him to offer to bring my work to his hotel, but he said his schedule was completely booked. Who knows if Mr. X would have liked my work and included it in *Dokumenta*, whether that would have changed the trajectory of my artistic career? I continued to believe that creating art in the face of such obstacles was an integral part of my process.

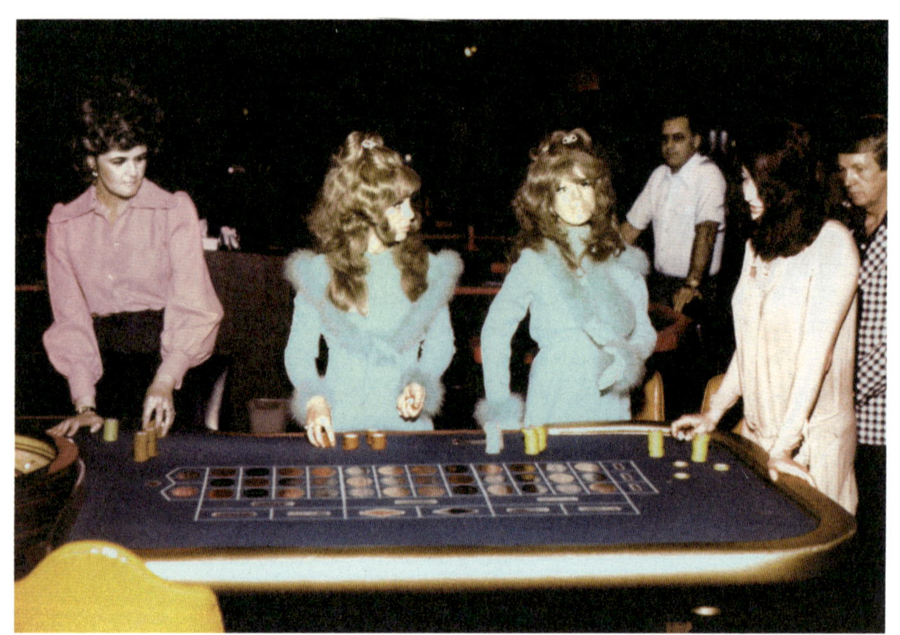

LADY LUCK DOUBLES AND
LYNN HERSHMAN AT
ROULETTE TABLE,
CIRCUS CIRCUS, LAS VEGAS,
NEVADA, 1975

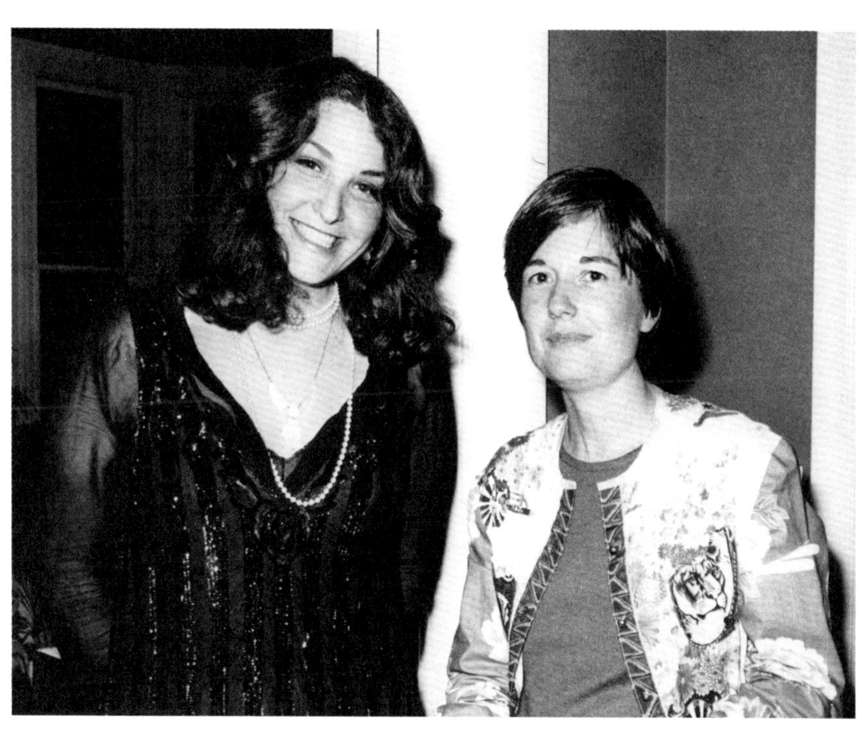

# LYNN HERSHMAN AND ELEANOR COPPOLA DURING THE EVENT FOR RE:FORMING FAMILIAR ENVIRONMENTS, 1975

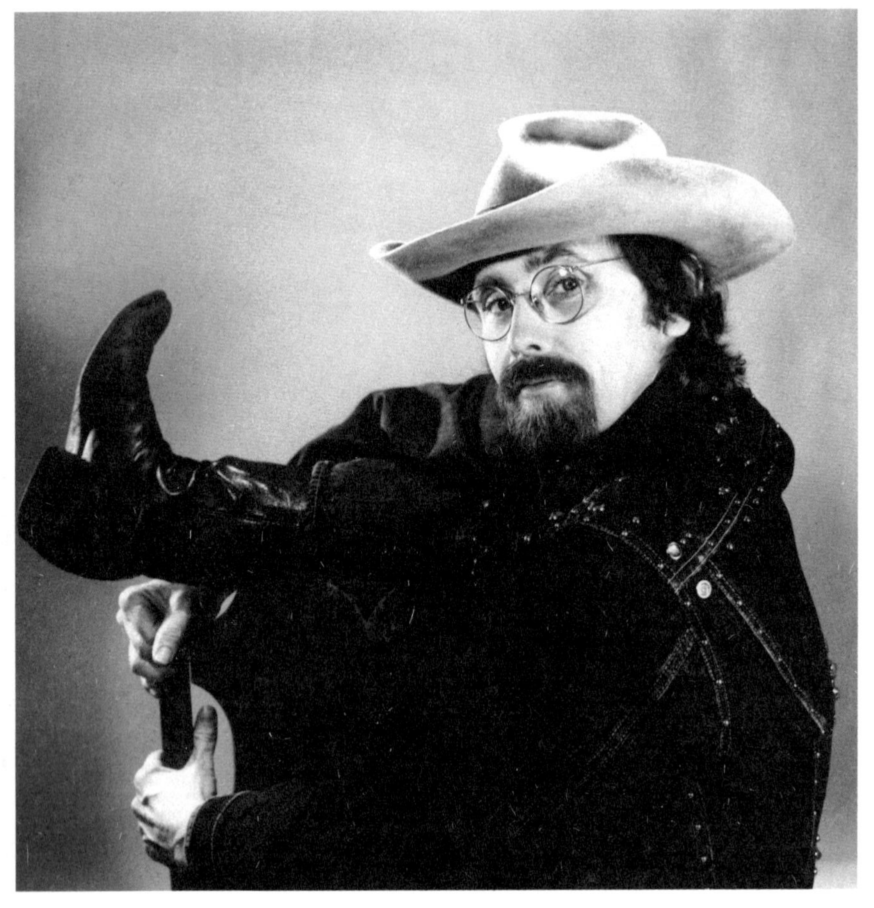

BRUCE CONNER BY
EDMUND SHEA, 1971 © 2025
CONNER FAMILY TRUST,
SAN FRANCISCO/ARTISTS
RIGHTS SOCIETY (ARS),
NEW YORK

**western union**   **Telegram**

| NO. WDS.–CL. OF SVC. | PD. OR COLL. | CASH NO. | CHARGE TO THE ACCOUNT OF | OVER NIGHT TELEGRAM |
|---|---|---|---|---|
|  |  |  |  | UNLESS BOX ABOVE IS CHECKED THIS MESSAGE WILL BE SENT AS A TELEGRAM |

Send the following message, subject to the terms on back hereof, which are hereby agreed to                19

TO                                                                CARE OF OR APT. NO.

STREET & NO.                                                     TELEPHONE

CITY & STATE                                                     ZIP CODE

THIS IS TO CONFIRM YOUR RESERVATION TO SEE LYNNHERSHMAN'S ROOMS

STOP HOTEL CHELSEA W. 23rd AT 7th AVE. OCT. 30 - JAN 1 ROOM 111

STOP CENTRAL YWCA LEXINGTON AVE. AND 53RD ST. OCT. 30 - NOV. 4

STOP PLAZA HOTEL 5TH AVENUE AT 59TH ST. 2:00 Nov. 2 - 12:00 Nov. 3

ROOM 837 STOP BUS WILL DEPART HOURLY SATURDAY NOVEMBER 2 BEGINNING

12:00 FROM STEFANOTTY GALEERY   50 W. 57TH STREET STOP

SENDER'S TEL. NO.            NAME & ADDRESS
                PARTY NOVEMBER   2 6:00 - 8:00 HOTEL CHELSEA

WU 1207 (R 5-69)

# ANNOUNCEMENT OF NY HOTEL ROOMS, 1974

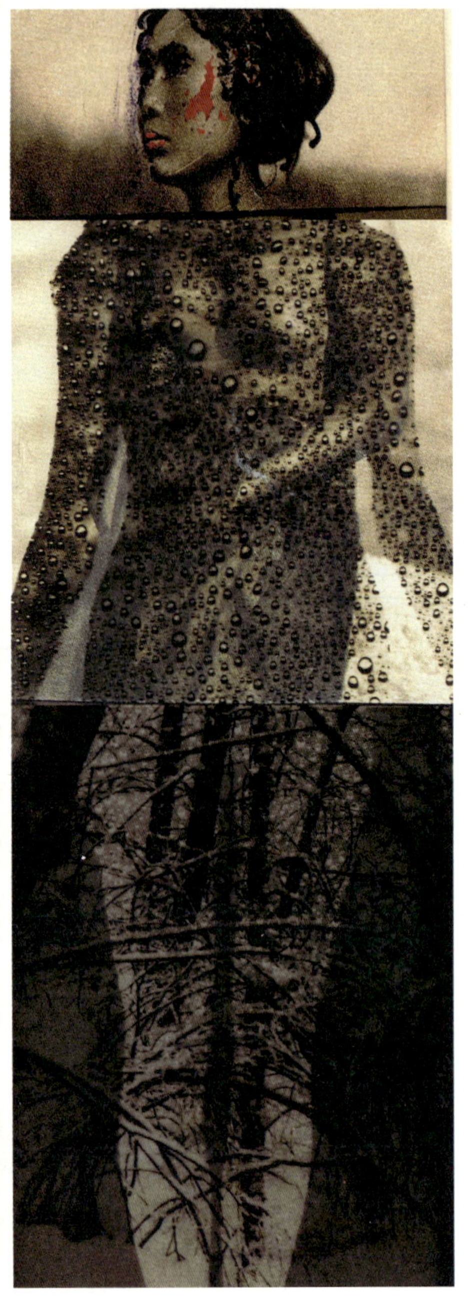

# WATER WOMAN COLLAGE, 1976

          

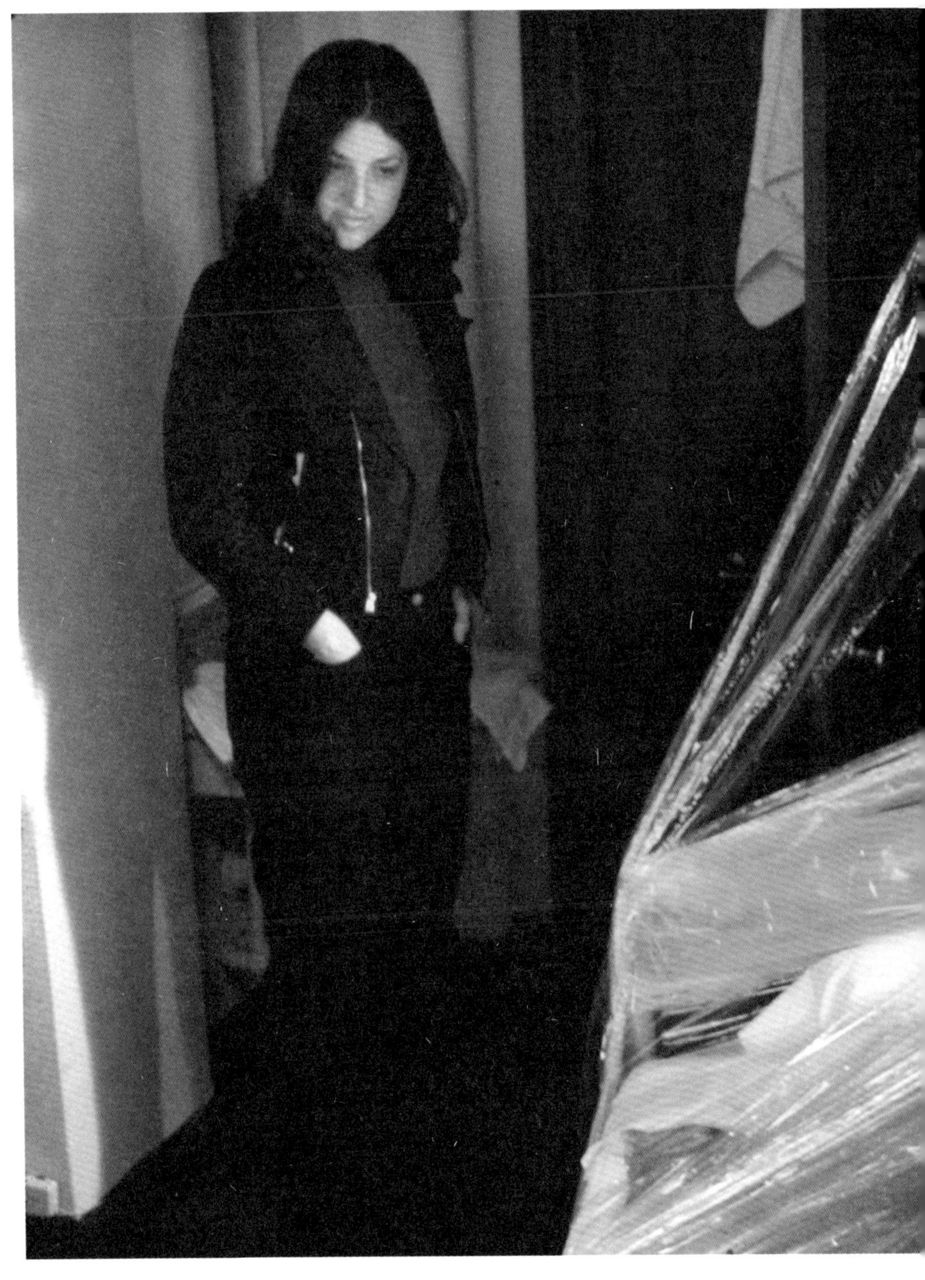

# INSTALLATION VIEW, YWCA, NEW YORK, 1974

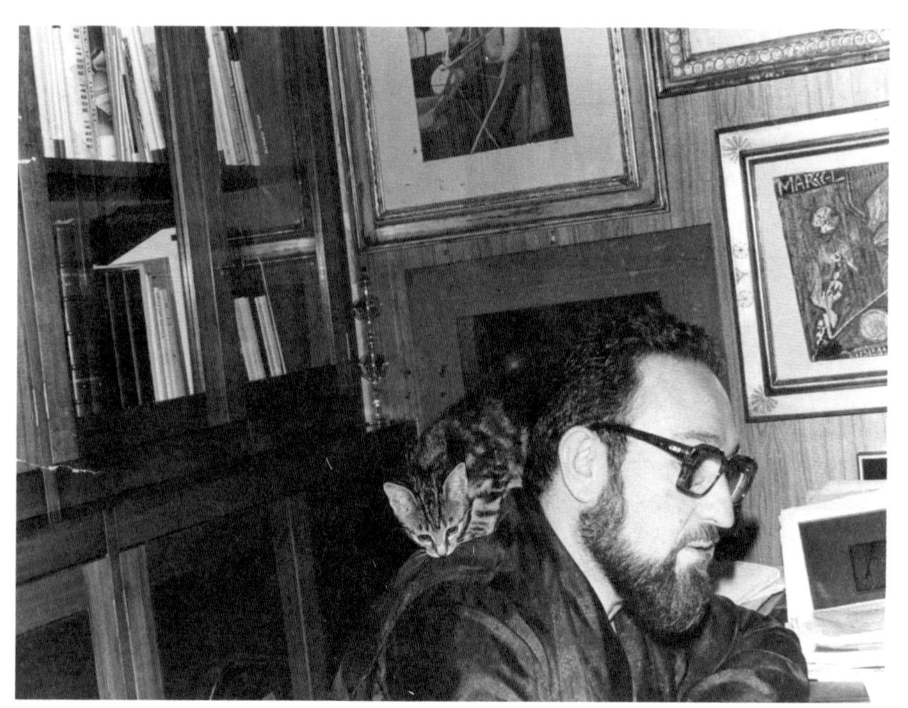

# ARTURO SCHWARZ WITH CAT,
# C. 1976

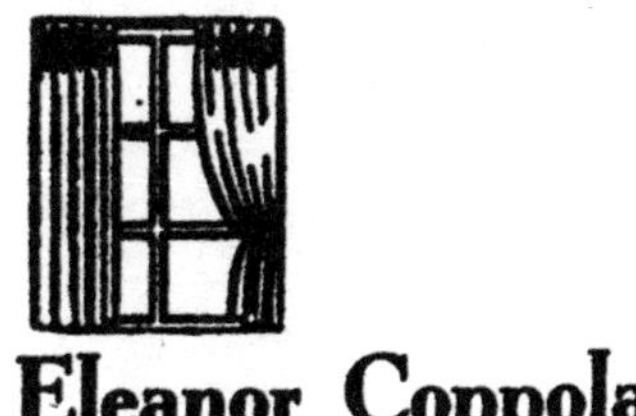


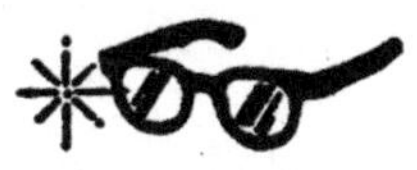


# BUSINESS CARD, 1975

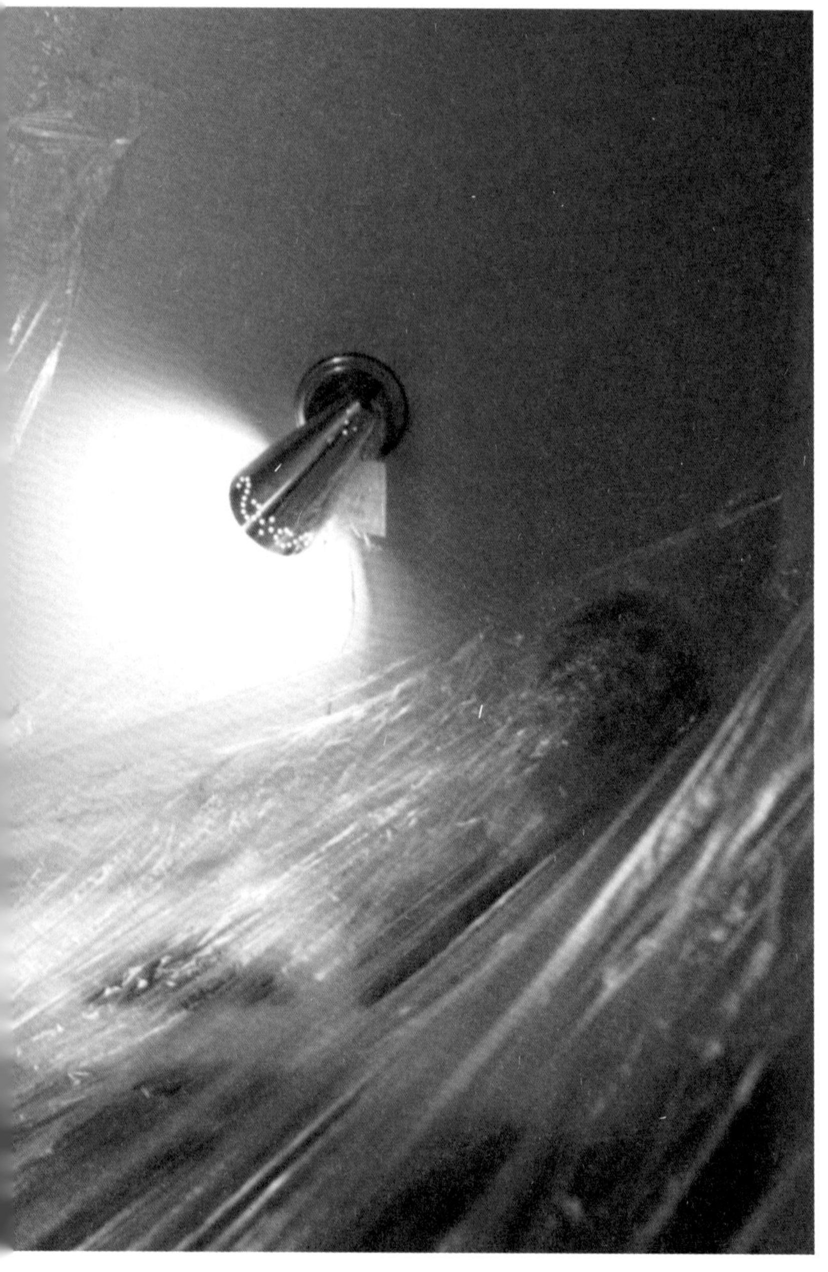

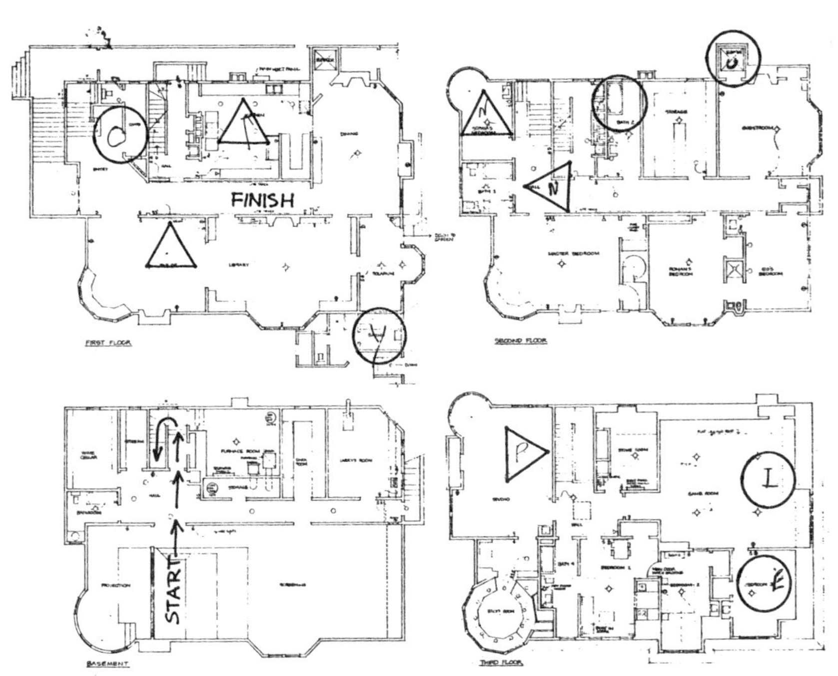


# DIAGRAM OF GAME SPACE, 1975

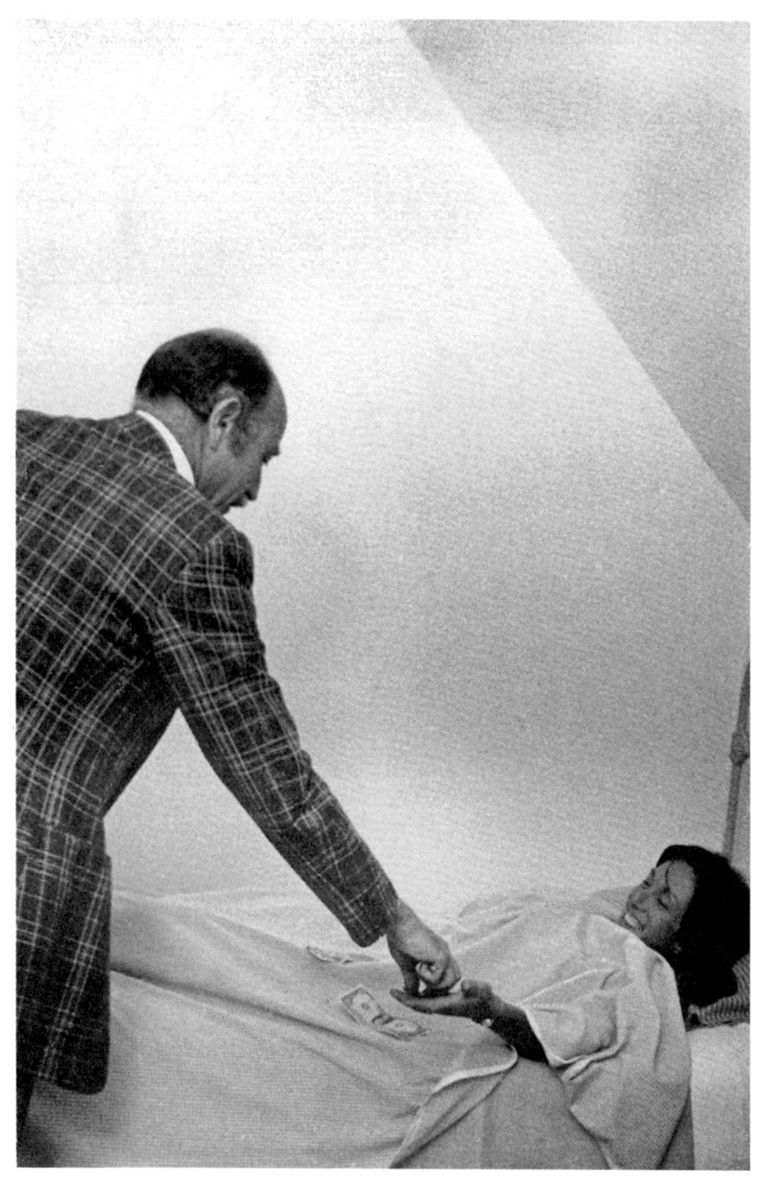

PATRON BYRON MYER
GIVING MARGO ST. JAMES
"FINANCIAL EXCHANGE,"
1975

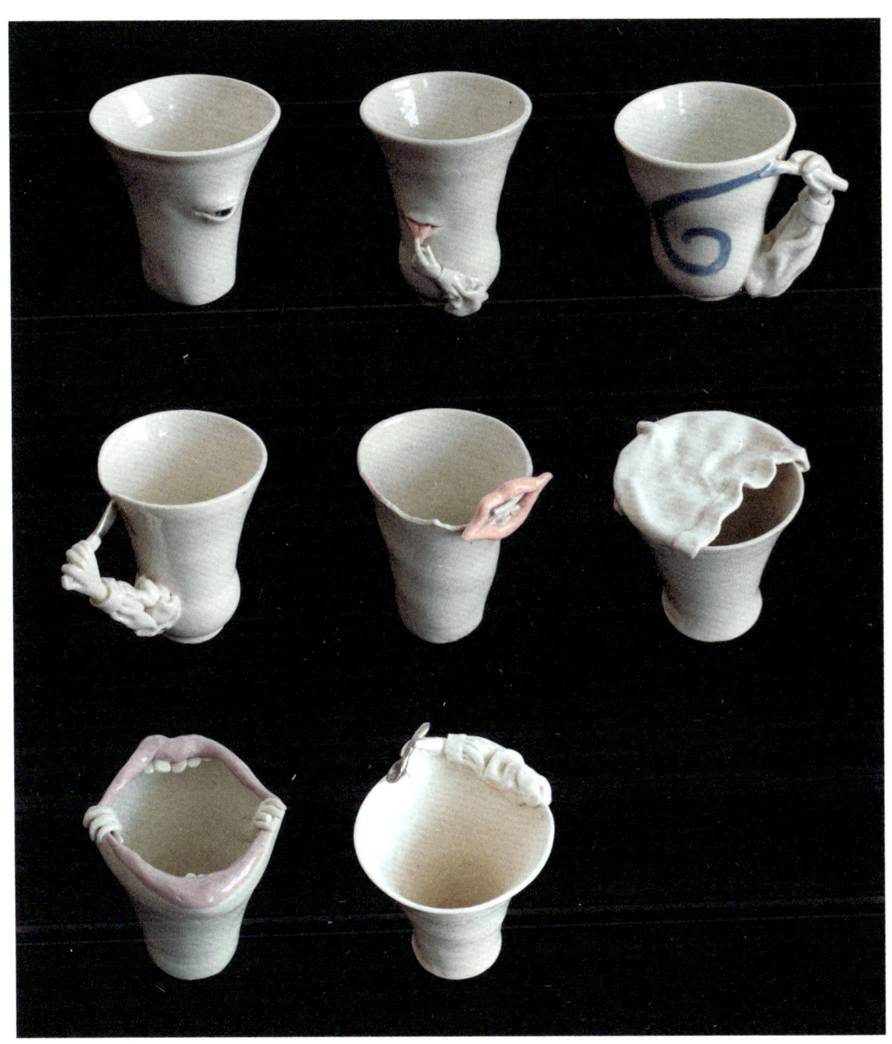

# CUPS AND PLATES FROM *PERFORMANCE DINNERS*, 1973–1978, CERAMICS MADE IN COLLABORATION WITH DIANE FLYR

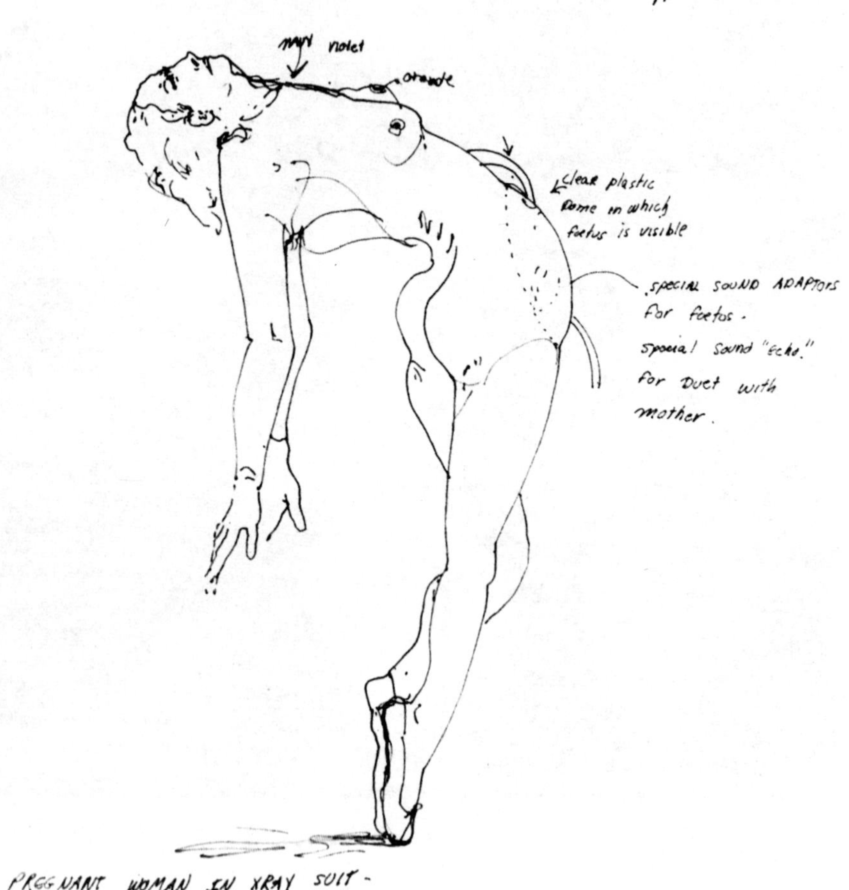


# DRAWING FOR REHEARSAL BALLET, 1977

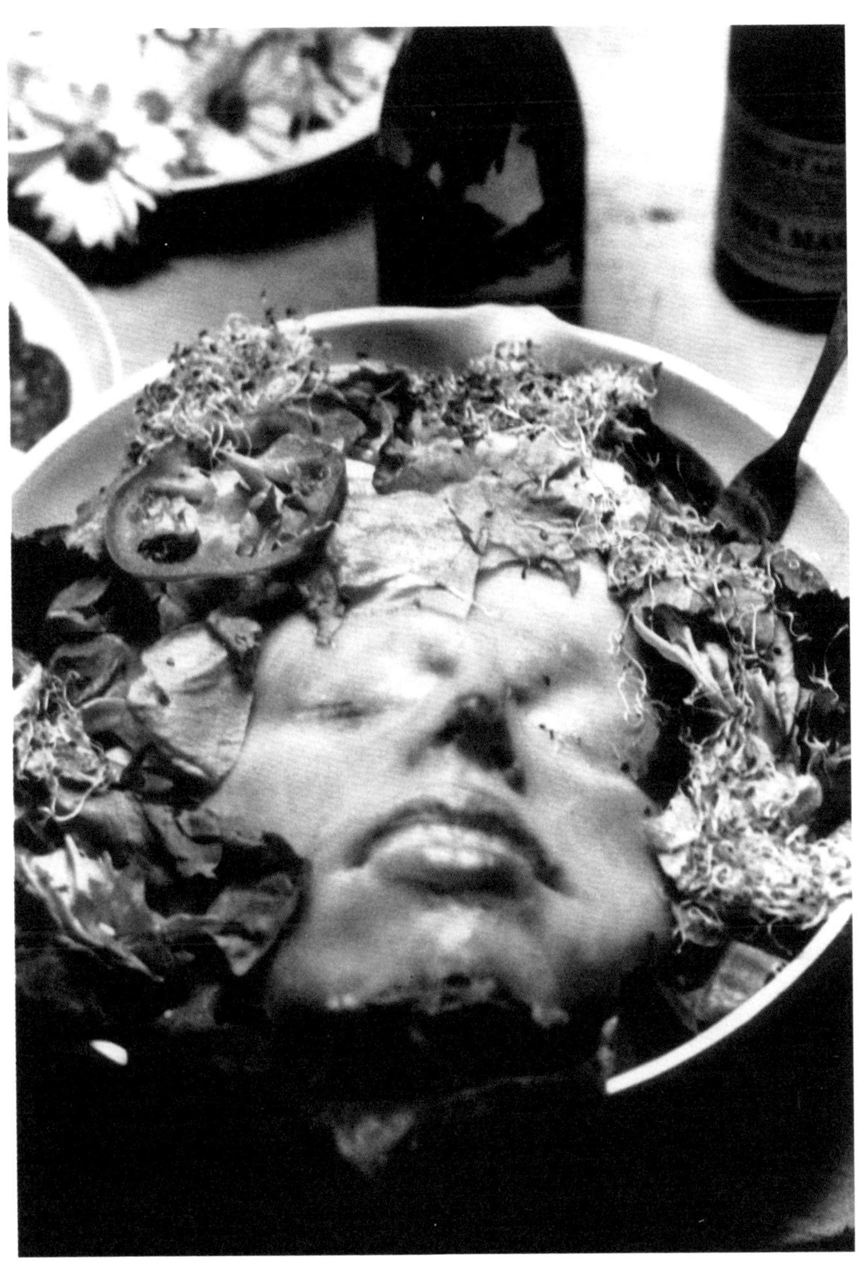

*HEAD SALAD WITH VIOLETS,*
1976

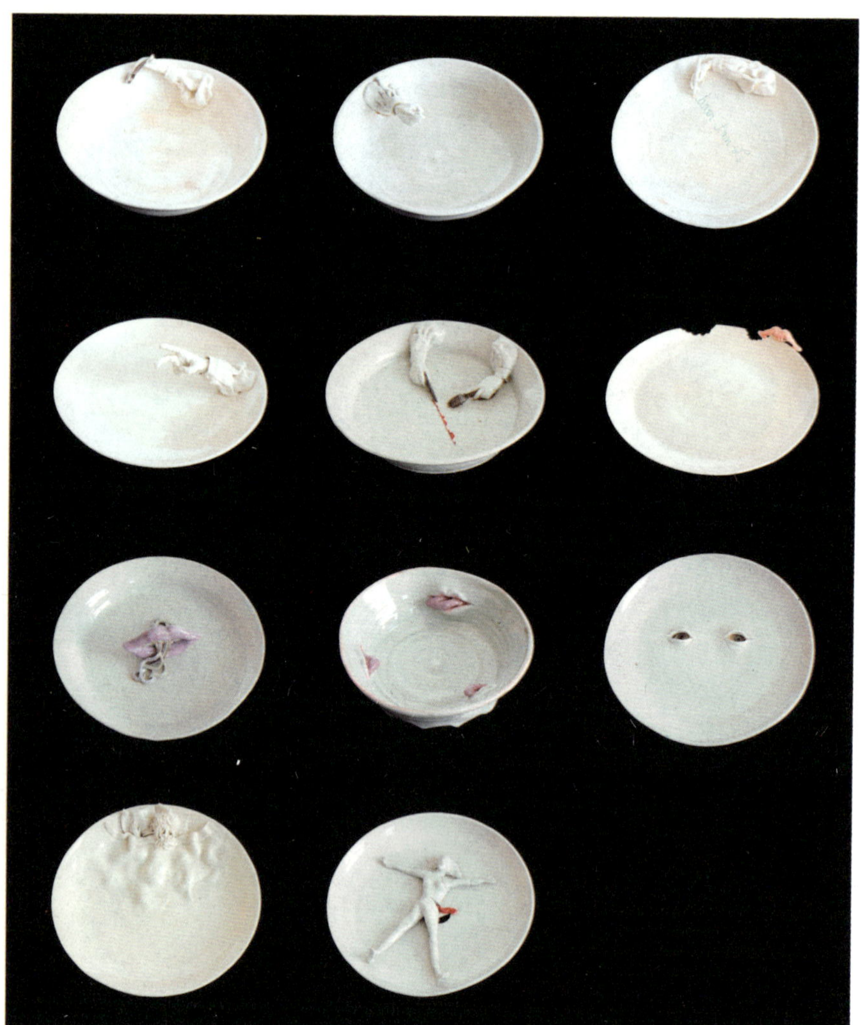

# 12 REHEARSALS

> Dance is the hidden language of the soul, of the body.
> —Martha Graham

Yves Klein's manifesto *Leap into the Void* inspired me to conceive a dance performance based on the rhythms of dancers' internal nervous system, their heartbeat and blood circulation.

In the work, titled *Rehearsals*, I envisioned dancers, one of them pregnant, whose movements are amplified as sound. As the dance progresses, the performers, microphones taped to their bodies, in costumes made of thermographic fabric sensitive to fluctuating body temperatures, display changing heat patterns.

Midway through the piece, the pregnant dancer collapses. Silence. Her heartbeat is then amplified. In a panic, the stage manager grabs a microphone and requests a doctor from the audience to examine the fallen dancer. An audience member then rushes to the stage. The pulse sounds fade, then revive in a loop.

A sheer white sheath floats down from the ceiling and covers the body. Miraculously, it levitates (transparent wires from tracks above hoist the body into the air). As she disappears, dancers perform a final coda about the fragility of time.

Fourteen years after my hospitalization for cardio-myopathy, and giving birth to Dawn, I was still processing that experience in artwork. This experience, in many ways unique to me, is personal in the deepest and most existential sense. For me, the only way to continue to mine this experience, like so many others, was through making art.

However, *Rehearsals* would have to wait. Roberta was on the move.

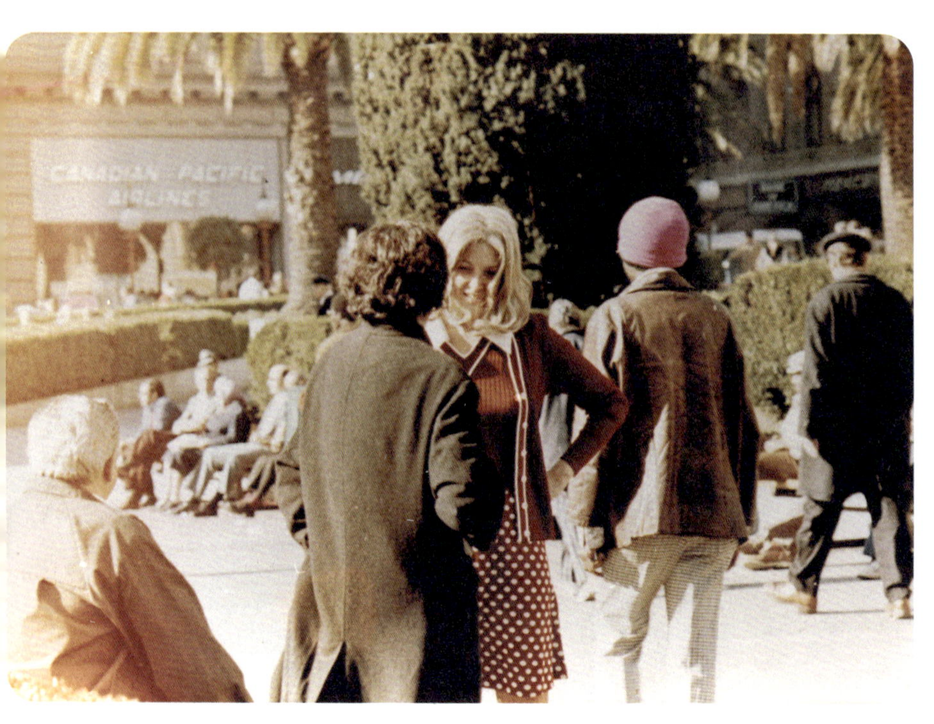


ROBERTA AND IRWIN MEET
FOR THE FIRST TIME IN UNION
SQUARE PARK, 1975

# 13
# ROBERTA REDUX

> I actually went to the dictionary to look up feminism. Basically, feminism is fighting for women's rights and to give women the same rights that men have. My father was a feminist and would always tell me: do whatever you want to do but get the best education.
> —Howardina Pindell, NYC, 2008

In 1975, Roberta, not having found a compatible roommate, decided to relocate to a less expensive city. She placed ads in *The San Diego Tribune* seeking an apartment share. The first person to respond to Roberta's ad was a man named Bubba, who suggested meeting at the entrance to the San Diego Zoo. I hired a surveillance photographer to both arrange transport and serve as a bodyguard, if necessary.

In the 1960s, much performance art and ephemeral works such as land art were never documented because the artists believed that the recording would detract from the spontaneity of the artwork. As a result, much of that work was forgotten. and lost its place in history. So, beginning with the Dante Hotel , I was conscious of the importance of documenting my work. Over time, this documentation of conceptual work came to be seen as an artwork in itself.

Bubba arrived on time in a souped-up convertible Cadillac in which two scantily dressed, young, overly made-up women were seated. I suspected they were not possible roommates, and that Bubba hoped to entice another lonely girl (Roberta) who desperately needed money to join his prostitution ring.

Leaning out an open window, Bubba asked Roberta to take a ride with them. Roberta was frightened. The photographer hired to protect her from danger was so afraid of Bubba that he fled. Roberta excused herself to run into a nearby bathroom where, inside a stall, she quickly removed the blond wig, washed her face, and escaped as dark haired, makeup-free Lynn.

This perilous meeting was followed the next day by an equally fraught encounter. Roberta had arranged to meet another potential roommate in the lobby of the Coronado Hotel. When the artist Juan Downey, at the hotel to give an artist talk at the invitation of U.C. San Diego, saw the blond, overly made-up Roberta Breitmore, he was immediately attracted by her.

Juan sashayed up to her, brazenly sat down, and tried to strike up a conversation. When Roberta, wary from the experience at the zoo, realized Juan was not the man who answered her ad, she ignored him. Her rejection only increased his interest. He watched jealously as she met her date, who turned out not to be roommate material.

Juan, an early video artist. shot Roberta with his Portapak camera. He was a commanding presence. Born in Santiago, Chile, Juan was the son of an architect. He was expected to follow in his father's footsteps and was enrolled in architecture school. However, a trip to Europe turned into three years in Paris studying printmaking. He decided to become an artist. Juan was known for his video work about politics, art history, and Latin American identity. A charming, elegant, brilliant man, Juan had an irrepressible wit and a sizzling sense of humor. Roberta must have been the first one to ever reject him.

The artists Newton and Helen Harrison hosted a party to which I was invited. Though the art critic Moira Roth introduced me to Juan, he had no interest in Lynn. He was searching for Roberta. Eventually, Moira broke the news to Juan that Roberta was fictional. Heartbroken, with real tears in his eyes, Juan confessed that Roberta embodied his *mujer maravilla* (Wonder Woman), the one he had been seeking his entire life. How could she not be real?

Still entranced by Roberta's aura, Juan gave me his phone number and invited me to look him up when I was zto be focused on Roberta, who represented his ghostlike dream girl.

Juan was not alone in falling in love with Roberta. Roberta's adventures had been documented in photos, diaries, handwritten charts, artifacts, and legal documents. I decided that Roberta should also become a comic-book heroine. I reached out to the cartoonist Emmanuel Rodriguez, known as Spain, the artist behind the *Trashman* comics, who I knew from *Zap Comix.*

Spain was a youngish man sporting long hair, an up-turned collar, pegged pant legs, pointed leather boots, and a black leather zip jacket. He was not difficult to find. Like Bruce, beneath the artifice of his costume, Spain was a man of extraordinary intelligence, with a fervent zeal for political justice, and an enormous passion for the Spanish Civil War. In fact, he set up in his basement a huge table where tiny model soldiers staged well-researched battle scenes.

Spain was never without his sketchbook and pens. At our first meeting in a cafe at 24th and Mission, Spain seemed intrigued by the invitation to co-create a graphic novel about Roberta. I could only afford to hire him to draw eight pages, which *Zap Comix* agreed to print. This comic book would become the throwaway acknowledgment that Roberta existed. As part of this assignment, Spain became privy to Roberta's whereabouts. He followed her, creating unique drawings of her adventures.

He soon came under Roberta's spell. Although Spain's own comic-book work was often filled with sexist portrayals of women, his treatment of Roberta was differ-ent. He wanted to protect her. His tracking of Roberta became a passion. I think he fell in love with her vulnerabil-ity. No one understood Roberta like Spain. He was among the few people who appreciated the conceptual frame-work for Roberta's existence. Most people who knew about the Roberta project were dismissive, or felt it was my schizophrenic manifestation.

Spain was proud of his Roberta drawings and exhibited them at a bar in the Mission District. Having com-missioned the work, the comic book and drawings should have been mine, but Spain considered the originals of the artwork his property. I did not want to argue with him. When I realized that they were for sale, I visited the *Roberta* exhibit when the bar was empty and purchased all of Spain's drawings, after securing a promise by the bar's owner not to reveal the identity of the purchaser. Spain was very excited that the work sold. He never found out that I was the one who paid for them—twice.

Some forty years later, when MoMA acquired forty-two *Roberta* photographs and artifacts for the permanent collection, they did not want to include Spain's comic drawings, because they did not feel it was "my" artwork. However, as the comix were as much an extension of Roberta as the surveillance photographs, I insisted they be part of the museum's *Roberta* collection and donated the original drawings. Spain would have been very pleased to know his work is now in MoMA's collection.

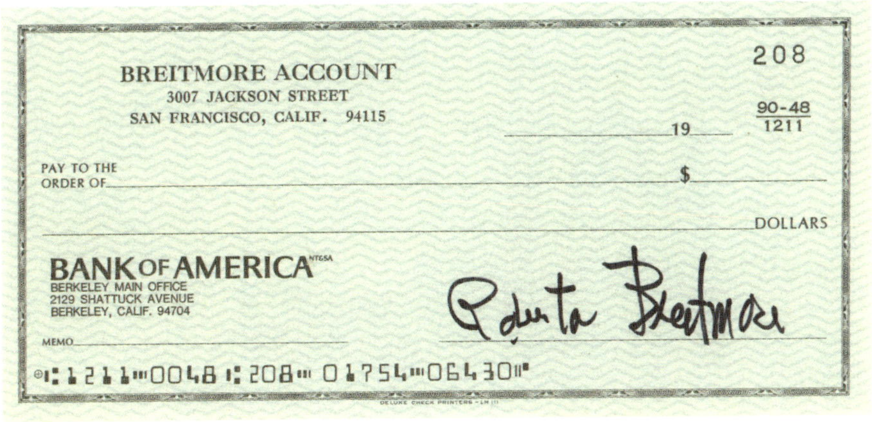

# PAGES 119–124
# *ROBERTA BREITMORE, ARTICLES OF IDENTITY, 1974*

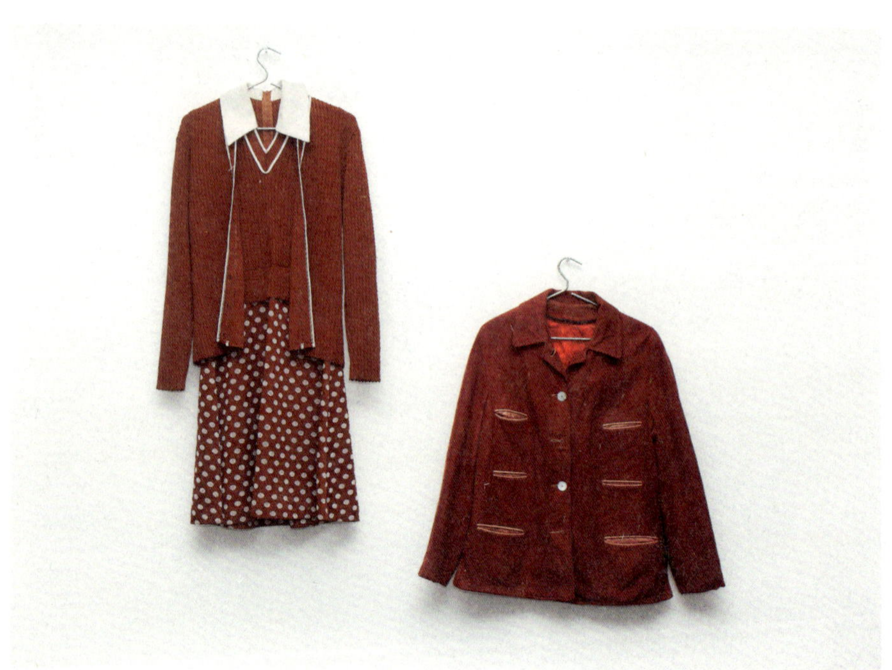

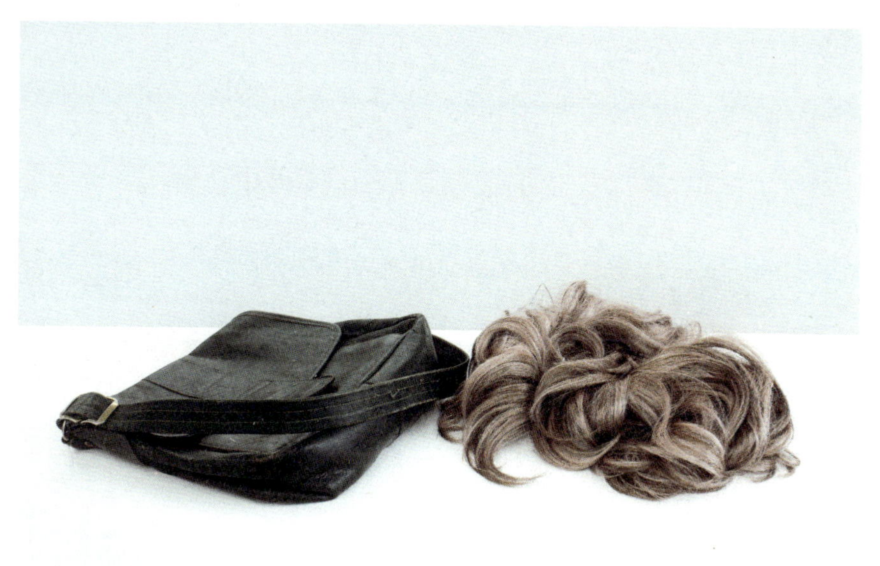

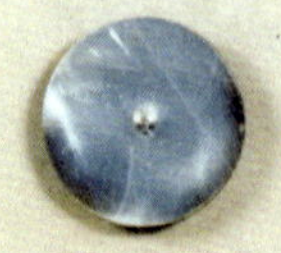

LOST BUTTON FROM ROBERTA'S COAT

When Roberta left the Amusement Park she was nervous and distraut.

The Amusement Park was to Roberta a surrealistic image of confusion,

horses spinning to no music that gasped for life, that gestured to be let

free from their cycle.  Five men had come to meet her, were pursuing

her and she felt as if she was in an Alfred Hitchcock movie as she tried

to escape their advances.  In her haste to depart, her button grasped onto

the iron turnstile at the exit.  Roberta never noticed that she had lost it.

STATE OF CALIFORNIA
DEPARTMENT OF MOTOR VEHICLES

**INTERIM DRIVERS
LICENSE (TEMPORARY)**
DIVISION OF DRIVERS LICENSES

VALID FOR 60 DAYS FROM

_______________________
DATE

Roberta Breitmore
3007 Jackson
San Francisco, CA 94115

SEX   HAIR   EYES   HEIGHT   WEIGHT   PRE LIC EXP
F   Brn   Brn   5-9   155   None

DATE OF BIRTH          SOC. SEC. NO.
8-19-45

OTHER
ADDRESS
CLASS 3. 3 AXLE HOUSE CAR AND ALL 2 AXLE VEHS. EXCEPT BUS OR 2 WHEEL
MOTORCYCLE, MAY TOW VEH. UNDER 6000 LBS. GROSS.

SEE OVER FOR ANY OTHER CONDITIONS ☐     MUST WEAR
CORRECTIVE LENSES ☐

X

1-20-76 SnF 1r

FEE $3.25

CLASSES

ADDITIONAL PRIVILEGES
ONLY AS CHECKED BELOW

☐ NONE.

4 ☐ MAY DRIVE 2-WHEEL MOTOR-
CYCLE.

2 ☐ MAY DRIVE ANY SINGLE VEHI-
CLE OR BUS EXCEPT 2 WHEEL
MOTORCYCLE.

1 ☐ MAY DRIVE ANY VEHICLE OR
BUS EXCEPT 2 WHEEL MOTOR-
CYCLE. MAY TOW ANY VEHICLE
OR COMBINATION OF VEHICLES.

EXAMINER          BADGE NO.

TRACER USED { DL22 _______ Date _______
Office _______

APP. No.

DF 219767

P L

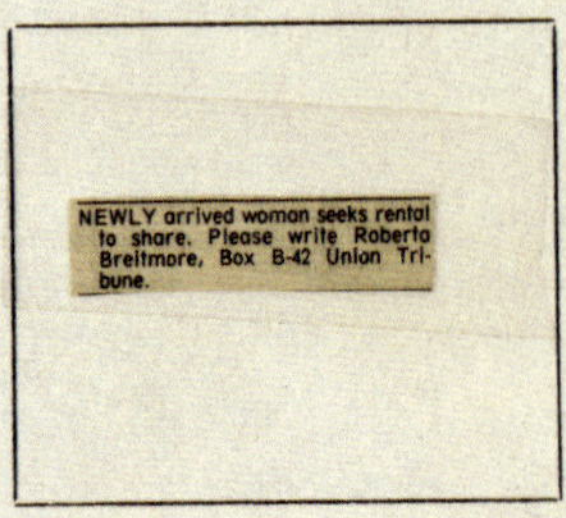



# THE SAN DIEGO UNION & EVENING TRIBUNE

## San Diego's Big Classified Ad Newspapers

Thank you for your order for classified advertising.
Attached is a clipping of your ad as it appeared,
according to your instructions.

Beginning ..... Tuesday 12/29 ................................

FOR ....... 3 times ........................................

Classified Advertising Dept.
THE SAN DIEGO UNION and EVENING TRIBUNE

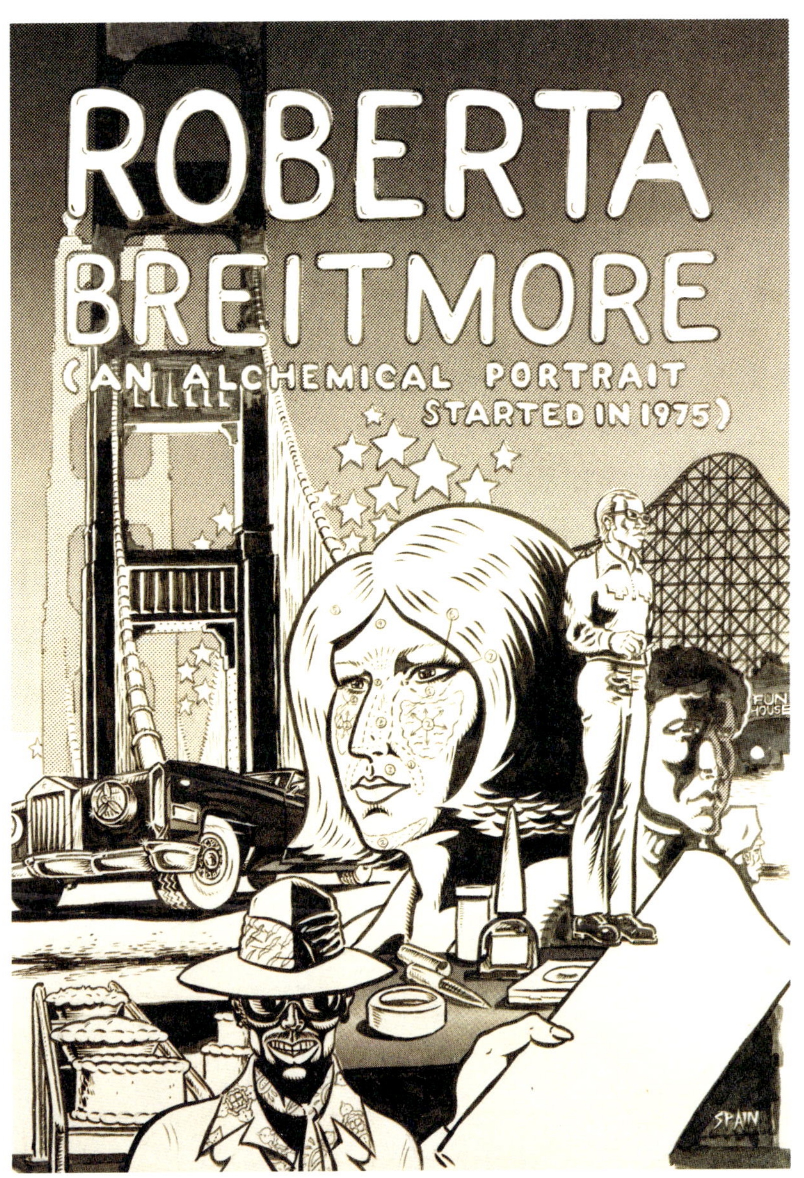


*ROBERTA BREITMORE:
AN ALCHEMICAL PORTRAIT
(COVER) ILLUSTRATION BY
SPAIN RODGRIGUEZ, 1975*

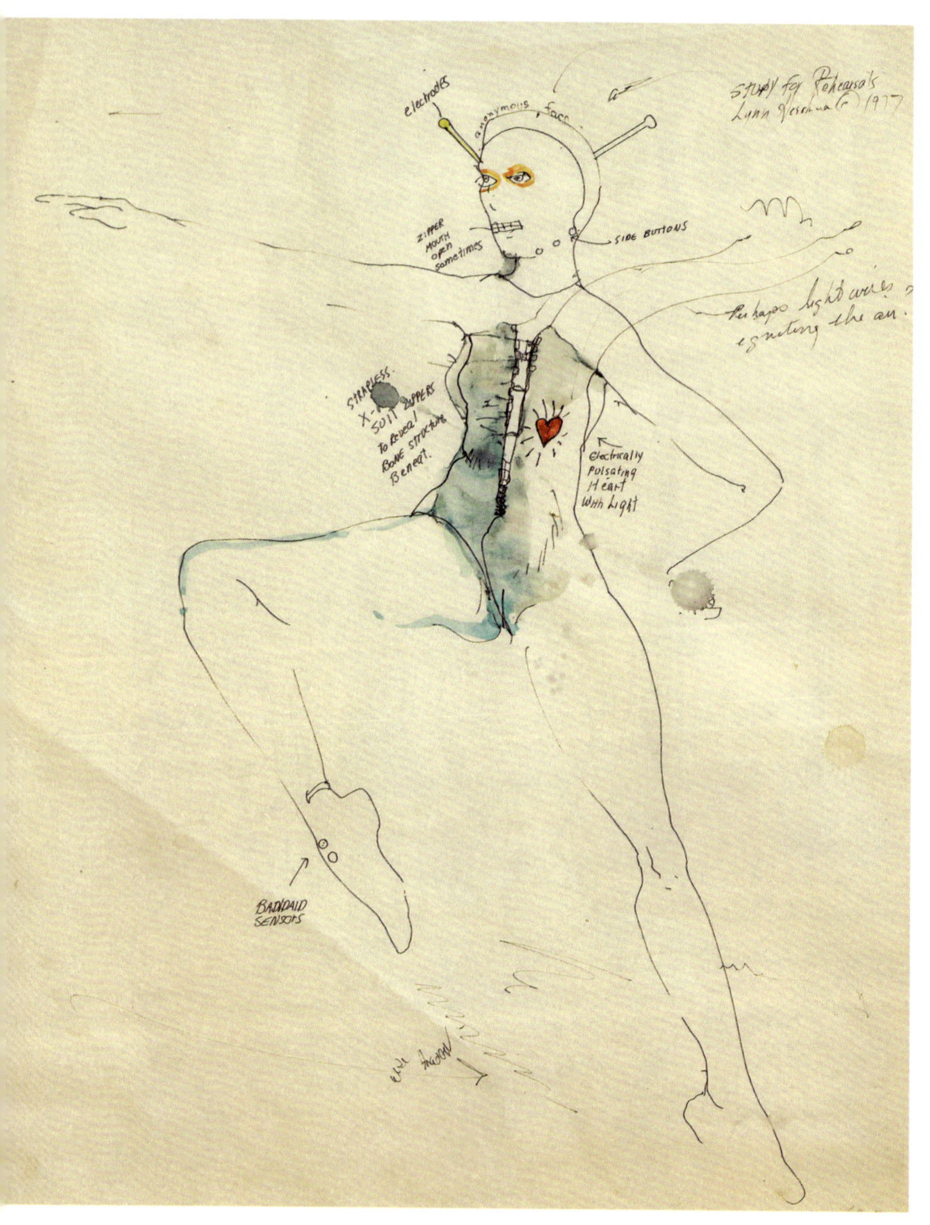


# STUDY FOR REHEARSALS, 1977

# 14
# REHEARSALS REDUX



> There are shortcuts to happiness, and dancing is
> one of them.
> —Vicki Baum

Once, when Francis was unexpectedly called out of town, Ellie invited me to see *The Nutcracker*. We picked up Tosca's owner, Jeannette Etheredge, in Francis's black limousine. She was accompanied by a friend whose face was shrouded by a pulled-down cap and pulled-up jacket collar.

When our limo stopped at a red light in a sleazy neighborhood near the theater, we noticed several young black men breakdancing to blaring music from a boom box. The light changed. As the driver put his foot on the gas pedal, Jeannette's friend shouted,

"STOP!"

The car screeched to a halt and the man jumped out. After watching the dancers for a few seconds, he joined them, tapping the concrete sidewalk rhythmically with his heel, mimicking their movements flawlessly, gliding toe-to-toe with these new collaborators although he was easily twice their age. When the song ended, the other dancers tipped invisible hats as he returned to the car.

As we were ushered in through a side entrance at the venue, a small light illuminated the face of our mysterious passenger. It was Rudolf Nureyev, perhaps the most famous male ballet dancer of his time. There was no opportunity to tell him about *Rehearsals.* I hoped to mention it during the break, but before the first act was over, Jeanette and Nureyev had disappeared.

This taught me a lesson: Speak up. Life is too short.

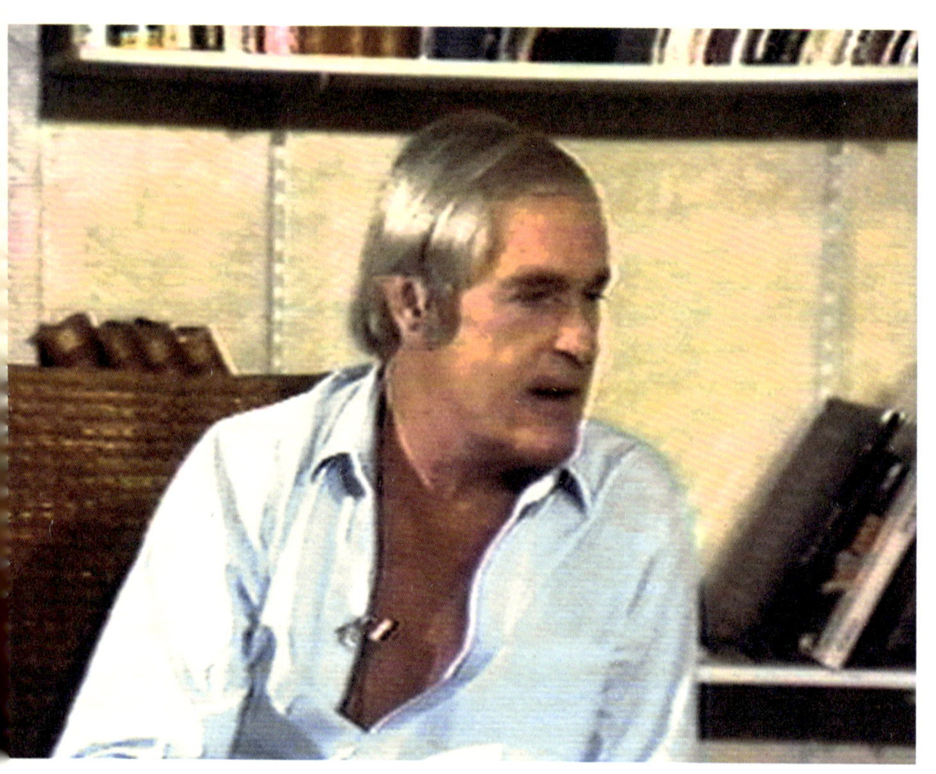

TIMOTHY LEARY IN A STILL FROM LYNN'S FILM *TEST PATTERNS*, 1979

# CHAPTER 14

# 15
# THE FLOATING MUSEUM, 1974–1978

> The future will determine how to play without being bored.
> —Nam June Paik, 1980

The rejection of my work and closure of my exhibition at the University Art Museum in Berkeley continued to gnaw at me. If traditional museums and galleries would not exhibit experimental artists, then alternative spaces needed to be invented.

The Dante Hotel and other art interventions demonstrated that artists could create their own sites and claim public spaces for exhibition of their work. Artists did not have to rely on museums or tradition-bound curators for shows. I was inspired to create the Floating Museum as a way to meet other artists whose work I admired, have fun, and create community by showing their work.

Inspired by the writings of André Malraux and artists of the Russian Revolution, the Floating Museum was designed to recycle public spaces into site-specific locations for art installations, including city streets, San Quentin Prison, even nonphysical space such as sound waves. Its manifesto was: "Communicate ideas through mass media systems such as television, billboards, posters, newspapers, and leaflets."

The Floating Museum was to be a temporary museum exhibiting ephemeral works in repurposed spaces. "I wanted to enable artists to do their own work easily in these sites," I would tell the curator and critic Moira Roth. "And be paid for exhibiting their work, something that hadn't been done much before."

The artworks of the Floating Museum defied the boundaries and restrictions imposed by museums and galleries. The Floating Museum expanded ways of using public spaces by exhibiting video, performance, comic drawings, women artists, photography, dance, and environmental installations.

The Floating Museum policy was: "Each unique project requires a melding of divergent attitudes, from individuals in differing specialties such as architects, park officials, sound engineers and needlepoint store owners. Working together we learn from each other as projects progress from inspiration to reality. Just as art can change reality, reality can move in the direction of art. By juxtaposing art into life systems, a collage is created that seems to enhance holistic responses to the environment." The Floating Museum was membership based, with fees ranging from $10 for an active membership to $500 for patron status.

In its first year, I invited artists such as Michael Asher, who created a project in a courtyard where he covered stairway steps with an exact wooden copy of that step. His art installation was up for twenty-two days, and the *San Francisco Chronicle* art critic Alfred Frankenstein praised it, saying, "Space is making its comeback."

For the Floating Museum, Helen and Newton Harrison created a series of billboards with environmentally conscious messages that were exhibited throughout the city, and staged performances in front of the billboards.

Jerry Rubin, at that time one of the best known Yippie figures of the antiwar movement, engaged with the Floating Museum from 1975 to 1980. Jerry wanted to transform his persona from that of a dangerous revolu-tionary to that of a mature, responsible citizen, and to show his conversion from Yippie to Yuppie. The recon-struction included redesigning his hair, shaving his sideburns, and changing his clothing style as well as how he would stand for the camera.

Jerry and I discussed remaking old news events, captioned with the words "this is not now," as public-service announcements to be broadcast. Jerry understood the power of media images. For Jerry's transformation, we developed charts and diagrams to plot the reconstruction of his image, which may have influenced his eventual decision to move to New York and become a stockbroker.

The Floating Museum held one of the earliest exhibitions of Cindy Sherman's Untitled Film Stills. Sherman was investigating the mannerisms and poses of women in popular culture. There were similarities to the Roberta project. Sherman's photographs featured a stylized Hollywood commercial veneer of fakeness, while Roberta was a living simulacrum of the present.

Over four years, the Floating Museum arranged exhibitions of works in nontraditional spaces by nearly 350 artists, including Eleanor Antin, Judith Barry, Theresa Hak Kyung Cha, Gordon Matta Clark, R. Crumb, Douglas Davis, Barbara Hammer, Suzanne Lacy, Spain, and Margo St. James.

One of the installations I was most proud of took place within prison walls. San Quentin, the oldest prison in California, and one of the few with a death row, had a 45-by-28-foot outdoor prison wall that the Floating Museum thought perfect for a mural. However, we needed to convince the San Quentin State Prison officials. Gary Durkee, director of the prison's education program, had the authority to approve our proposed collaborative artwork. To my surprise, Gary agreed.

There was one caveat: It would be up to me to raise all the funds and find a master muralist acceptable to both the inmates and the prison staff. The wall we had selected was just inside the prison's courtyard. I later learned that this was where the activist George Jackson was murdered by prison guards during his attempted escape.

To raise money for the San Quentin project and other works, I sold virtual bricks at $10 each. The critic Lucy Lippard was among the first to buy a brick. Most of the necessary materials were donated. We applied to the San Francisco Arts Council, which at the time was headed by Peter Coyote, but the council turned us down.

Murals are public works of art, made by, and for, a community. To involve the San Quentin community and find inmates to work on the project, we held a competition for ideas in the *San Quentin News*. Eight inmates were selected who gained release from their normal duties to work on the design and construction of the mural.

Hilaire Dufresne, a muralist from Marin County, was hired to train the inmates in painting techniques. We asked the inmates for their suggestions. We judged entries and selected a drawing by Midget Rodriguez that imagined what was beyond the wall and, in doing so, created a wished-for vista that substituted the wall for a free open countryside.

Hilaire worked five days a week to teach the selected eight inmates how to mix paints, fix walls, and project the image. We converted a sandblaster that had been sitting unused at the prison into a tool for scraping the wall. All of this was accomplished under the watchful eyes of guards who never lowered their rifles, even as the painters climbed the scaffolding and as the inmates painted the wall.

We painted the sky first. Blue is the color of hope. There was a section of landscape in the middle that was yellow and that looked like the wall was in ruins, and there was a darker blue at the base, that to me, symbolized the spirit of the inmates wanting to be free.

When the mural was complete, we celebrated with a dedication at the site. Forty people from the San Francisco art community gathered on Bastille Day for the ceremony. (San Quentin, coincidentally, had been founded on Bastille Day in 1852.) In a way, the mural symbolized our own storming of the gates.

At dusk, when inmates look at the mural, the wall itself seems to disappear, and they experience a small sense of freedom. In the years that followed, mural painting became popular at San Quentin. Many others went up, including in the dining room.

On Labor Day 1978, one year after the mural was completed, I returned to San Quentin to celebrate the mural and staged a concert at the prison with the legendary punk band Crime. Over the next few years, San Francisco society figures were often taken to the prison, past the metal detectors, to see the mural. I wonder, again, how I had the chutzpah to do this.

The Floating Museum's other projects included a show of comic-book artists' work, including drawings by R. Crumb, Spain, and S. Clay Wilson, as well as *(H)errata*, a 1977 exhibition in response to the lack of women in the collection of the San Francisco Museum of Modern Art. *(H)errata* featured work by Fran Martin, Jo Hanson, Robbin Henderson, Judith Barry, Bonnie Sherk, Natasha Nicholson, Suzanne Lacy, and Priscilla Birge.

Peter D'Agostino created a project for the Floating

Museum that placed TV monitors and cameras in the BART system on platforms and in trains, thereby creating a surveillance network. Daryl Sapien's installation, *A Bridge Can Also Be a Work of Art*, used time-lapse photography to record himself walking a high wire he installed between City Lights Bookstore and the neighboring coffee shop, Vesuvio, in North Beach.

A final project titled *The Global Space Invasion (Phase II)* featured six exhibitions during the summer of 1978. Artists from Australia, Italy, France, the Netherlands, and Canada traveled to San Francisco to produce new work. A "Global Passport" was printed as a guide to daily events. As the Floating Museum project was nearing completion, I again realized the profound impact of the cancelation of my Berkeley Museum exhibition. The disrespect shown to me motivated me to help other artists.

However, the very success of the Floating Museum posed a dilemma. While I was helping many artists exhibit their work, I was not devoting much time to my own art practice. It was essential to end the Floating Museum, which was originally conceived as temporary, so that I could resume my work as an artist.

Shortly after, I met Timothy Leary at a screening at Ellie's home, just after he was released from prison. Though he had been a clinical psychologist at Harvard University who championed the use of hallucinogens, particularly LSD, he was arrested for marijuana possession. After fleeing the United States, he was again arrested abroad, returned to the U.S.A. and sent to Folsom Prison, where he was assigned a cell next to Charles Manson. When we met, I demonstrated to him that I knew the secret prison handshake—which both amused and intrigued him.

Timothy was a master of mirroring and media manipulation. With uncanny brilliance he could precisely imitate subtle gestures, and the language used by anyone he encountered. He confided to me that he felt speech patterns tell more about a person than the words they use, and that vocal inflections are as telling as fingerprints.

I created a special dinner for him that I named "Imprisoned Eggs for Timothy Leary."

*Imprisoned Eggs*

> *3 eggs*
> *1/2 cup cream*
> *3 tablespoons sweet butter*
> *4 strips of bacon Dry mustard*
> *1 pint prepared strawberries*
> *Heavy skillet Eye plate*

*Samuel Butler once said that a chicken was only an egg's way of making another egg. Eggs exist as the reverse of themselves. Suspended by invisible threads of albumen, a hard yet porous shell protects the nucleus yoke that swings inside, like a hammock. With a bit of nudging, eggs can be punctured and emancipated.*

*Melt three tablespoons of butter in a heavy skillet. Make certain the flame is moderate. When the pan is evenly heated, add bacon and let it sizzle. Carefully pour the eggs onto the skillet. When the softness has left them, lift the eggs and place them on an eye plate so that they become a set of eyes. Arrange the bacon to form a mouth, add strawberries for hair, and toast for ears. More bacon goes over the face to form prison bars.*

*Serve with a SMILE*
(a play of words on Timothy Leary's futurist project SMI²LE).

Timothy and I remained close and he appeared in several of my films.

By the mid-1970s, the curator Alanna Heiss, a charming woman from Kentucky, had become an *enfant terrible* of the New York art underground. In the late 1960s, working with the artists Bridget Riley and Peter Sedgley, Alanna had helped transform abandoned London warehouses into artist studios. She was often seen in a spectacular oversized golden raincoat that she dragged across the floor.

Alanna moved to New York and continued repurposing unused spaces into galleries. Among them was the Clocktower Gallery, in the former New York Life Insurance headquarters, a Beaux-Arts building in lower Manhattan, a few blocks from City Hall. Alanna, who would go on to found the art institution P.S. 1, was a kindred soul who appreciated the mission of the Floating Museum.

I approached Alanna about an idea I had of creating an art installation in the windows of the Bonwit Teller department store. (During the 1950s and 1960s, Robert Rauschenberg and Andy Warhol worked on crews creating window displays for Bonwit Teller). Alanna arranged to have the Clocktower sponsor the project. However, by the time we received a green light from Bonwit, and before I could complete the installation, another project had finally launched. After years of delays, Christo and Jeanne-Claude's *Running Fence* was finally going to be actualized. The Bonwit windows would be installed after the completion of *Running Fence*.

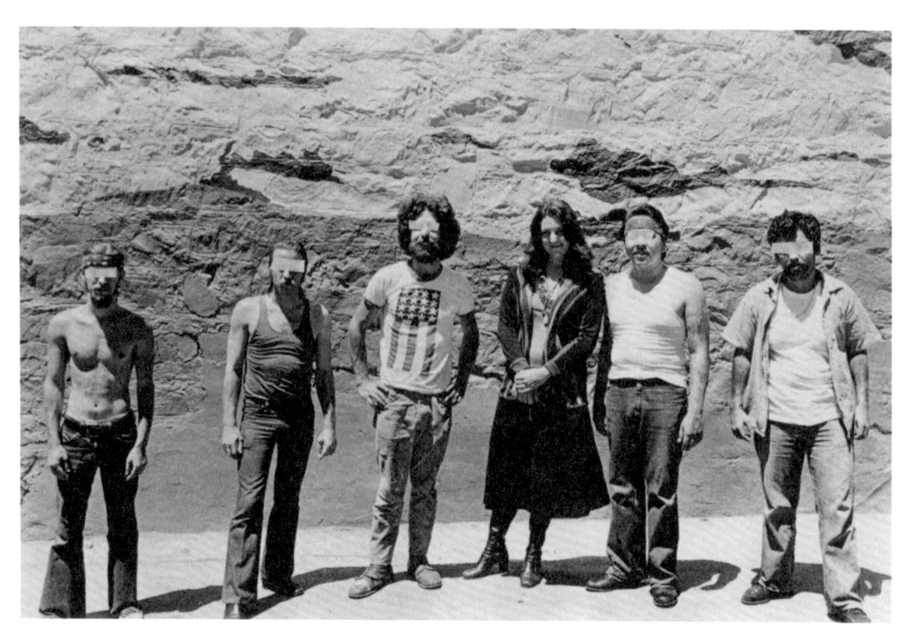

# LYNN AND MURALIST HILAIRE DUFRESNE WITH INMATES AT SAN QUENTIN PRISON, 1976

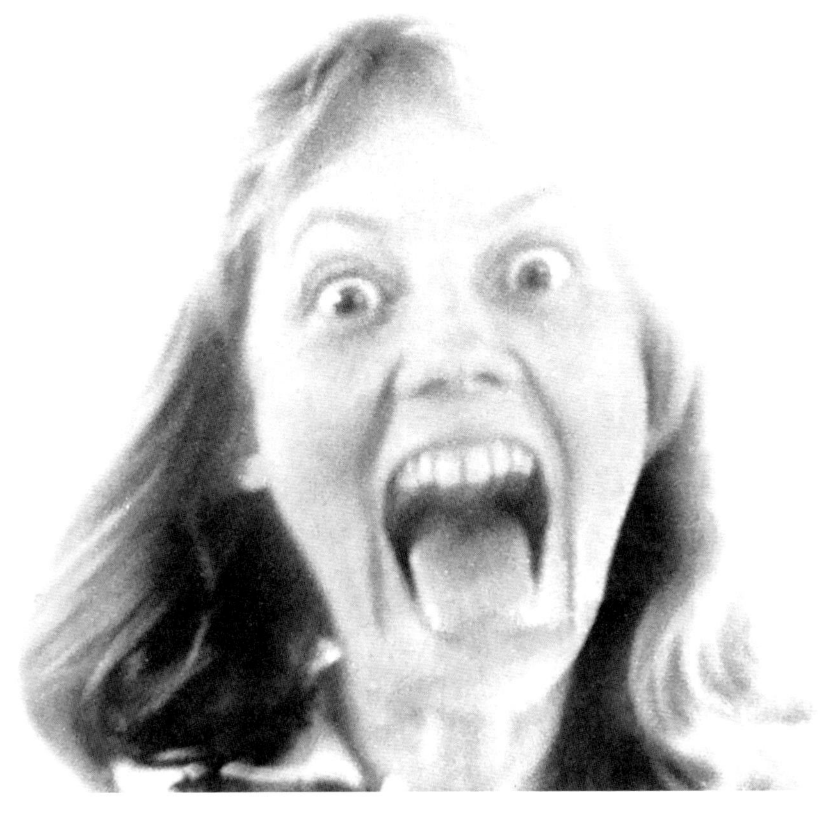

ALANNA HEISS, 1975.
PHOTOGRAPH BY
HOWARD SMITH.

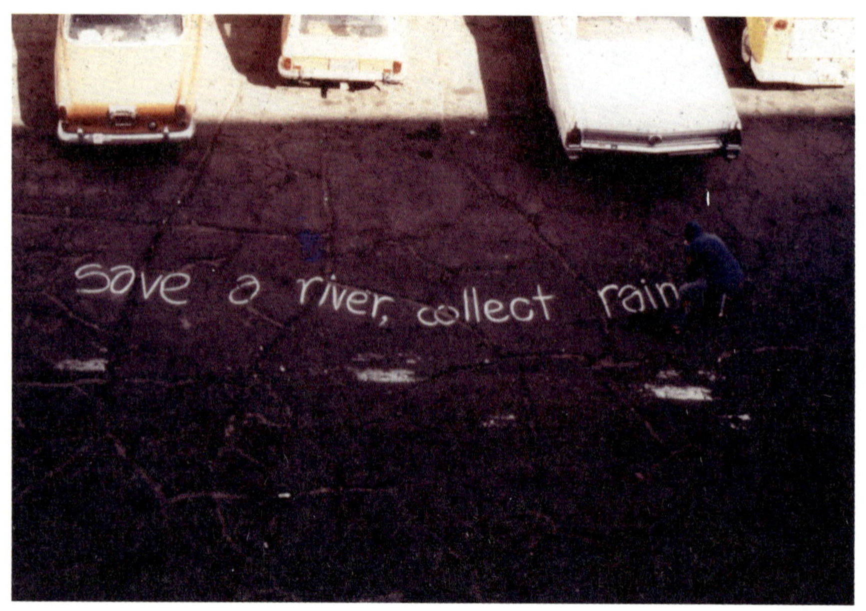


# NEWTON AND HELEN MAYER HARRISON, ON THE CONDITION OF THE SACRAMENTO RIVER, THE DELTA, AND THE BAYS OF SAN FRANCISCO, DRAWING IN A PARKING LOT, 1976–1977

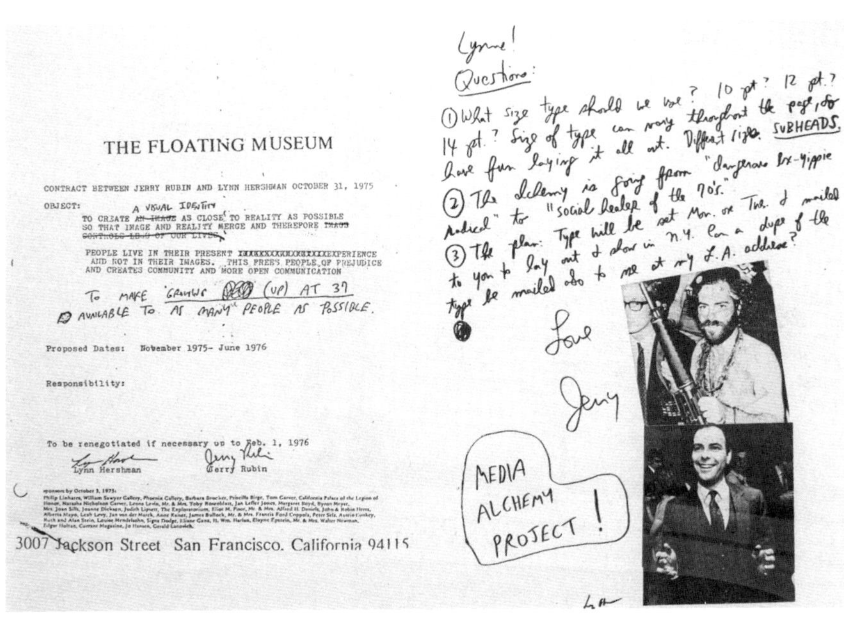





# *CONTRACT BETWEEN JERRY RUBIN AND LYNN HERSHMAN WITH LETTER, 1975*

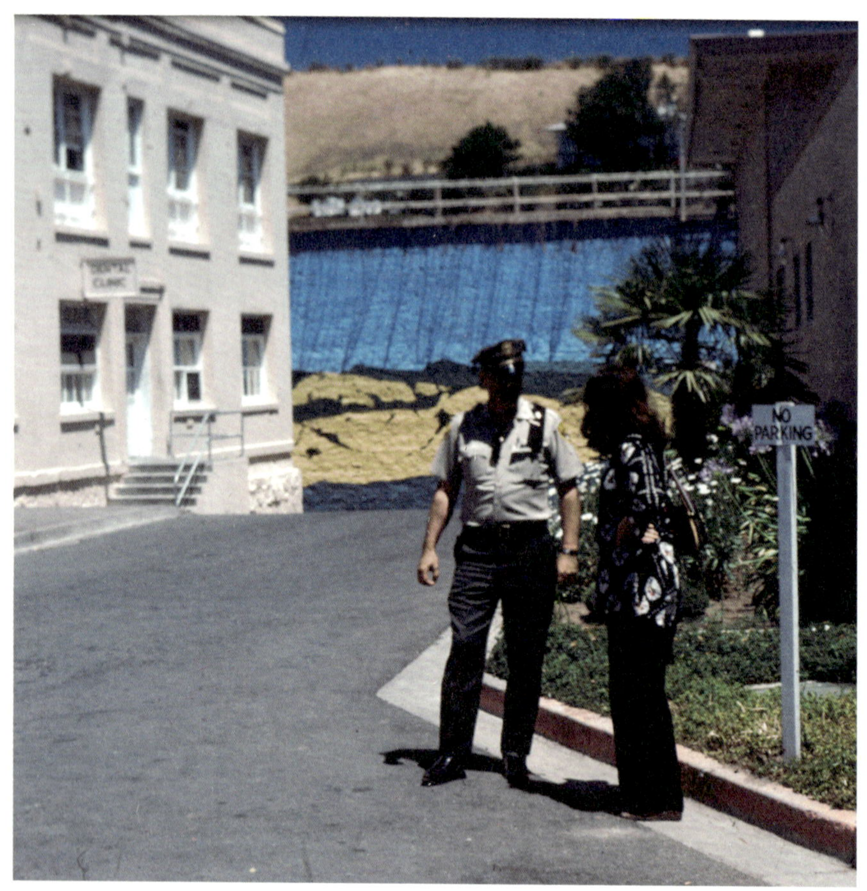


# LYNN TALKING TO A GUARD AT SAN QUENTIN PRISON IN FRONT OF MURAL, 1976

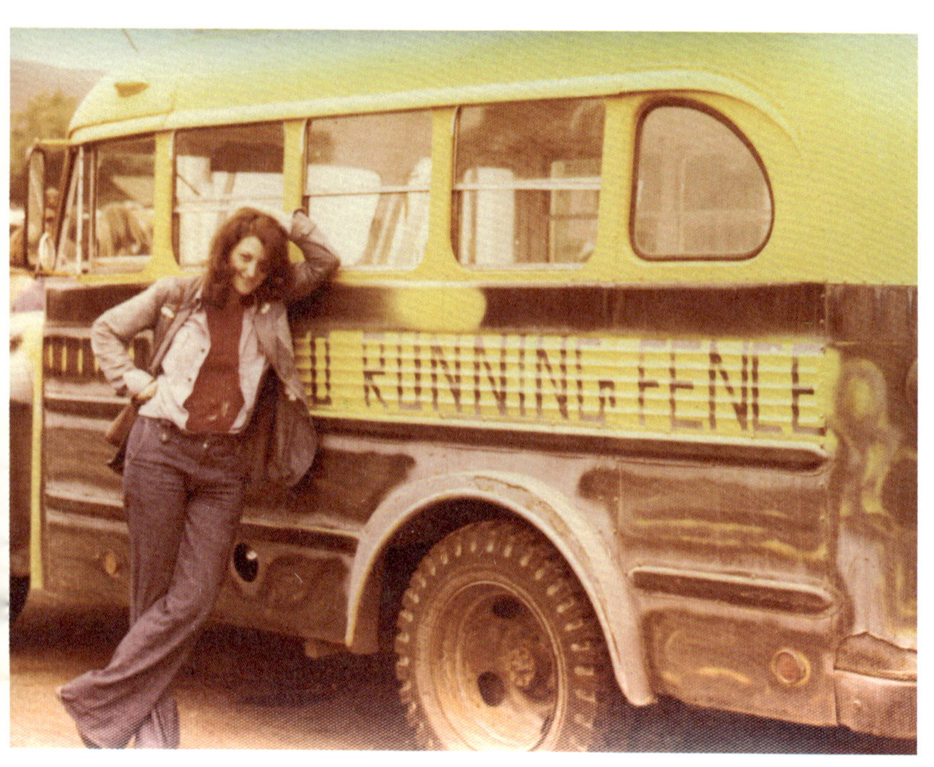


LYNN, ASSOCIATE PROJECT DIRECTOR FOR CHRISTO'S *RUNNING FENCE* IN MARIN AND SONOMA COUNTIES, 1976

# 16 *RUNNING FENCE,* 1974–1976

> Art is the language of the soul, the universal bridge that connects us all.
> —Christo

Christo and Jeanne-Claude's passion, humor, and obsession were contagious. The Christos effortlessly burrowed through obstructions, overturned impasses, and fought back legal challenges and, generally, turned perceived difficulties into advantages. That *Running Fence* might not happen never occurred to them.

Christo and Jeanne-Claude were known for creating large-scale site-specific art installations often made of draped fabric and that involved public as well as private property—requiring permits, permissions, and access.

*Running Fence* was envisioned as a fabric-laden fence that would traverse Sonoma and Marin counties in Northern California to the sea, crossing roads, highways, and private property. *Running Fence* was first proposed in 1972 but took four years to fully realize.

Christo and Jeanne-Claude hired Peter Selz to be the director of *Running Fence*. Because of delays, Peter, having committed to spending a year in Israel, turned to me to manage all aspects of this sprawling project.

Being *Running Fence*'s associate project director was my first formal job in the arts. Christo and Jeanne-Claude were successful, acknowledged, and respected conceptual artists. I wanted to learn as much as I could from the Christos. My salary for the four years it would take to complete this artwork would be one dollar, plus a collage by Christo.

For *Running Fence*, I was expected to travel regularly to Petaluma (about three hours north of San Francisco), where *Fence* would be constructed. Work began predawn, at 3:30 a.m. We met with farmers before cattle-milking, hoping to entice them to permit access to their property for the two-week duration of *Fence*. In a relatively short time, we convinced fifty-nine landowners to participate. There were seventeen public hearings, and the creation of an environmental impact report. Three legal firms were engaged to oversee the planting of 2,050 poles, each 62 feet apart, embedded 3 feet into the ground that, together, would suspend 165,000 yards of fire-resistant nylon fabric over and across the undulating landscape. The final shape of *Fence* was to be determined by whatever land-use permissions were granted to the Christos. I was commuting to Petaluma and took Dawn with me. She would sit in the back seat doing her homework.

Even with an environmental impact report citing the safety of *Fence*, Christo and his team never secured the final permission necessary to allow it to enter the Pacific Ocean. After each denial of permission, Christo and Jeanne-Claude became ever more insistent that the vision of *Running Fence* would not be complete unless it disappeared into the water.

The final days of the project were fraught with a relentless quest to remain on schedule. During the final week, the crew worked nonstop for sixty hours in a heat wave that parched energy and drained our bodies. Supplies of salt, food, and water were meager. Some workers collapsed from sunstroke.

Continuous five-hour round-trip treks to the San Francisco International Airport to greet arriving art curators and critics ensued. Longtime friends of the Christos who came to see their latest work unfurl included the critic Pierre Restany from Paris, the curator Germano Celant from Italy, the museum director Pontus Hulten from the Netherlands, and the curator Mr. X from Switzerland. Thankfully, Mr. X did not remember our prior meeting at Peter Selz's dinner. I drove each of them through the twenty-four winding miles of *Running Fence*.

As the project neared completion and after several years of absence, Peter Selz returned to reclaim his title of project director. In this final phase, with international guests present, lavish dinners were orchestrated nightly, which was itself a feat, considering there were few good restaurants in Petaluma at the time.

Amid the frenzy, I received a call from the California attorney general's office. They had been alerted that *Running Fence* was planning to enter the ocean despite having no permit. The attorney general was adamant that if *Running Fence* broke the law, workers would be arrested and jailed, and contractors would lose their licenses. I assured him that *Running Fence*'s configuration and eventual path would conform to whatever was legally allowed.

After Christo learned that he was again denied permission to bring *Fence* into the Pacific, he whispered in my ear, "I'm going to do it anyway."

"But workers might lose their license, or be put in jail," I responded, concerned.

He smirked, indicating that it would never happen.

Jeanne-Claude's parents, a French general and countess, arrived in Petaluma the day before the scheduled completion. Jeanne-Claude drove them through the winding landscape while work continued at its furious pace. Christo, meanwhile, hid in the bushes to avoid being spotted by helicopters sent by the attorney general's office to monitor the situation. Christo and Jeanne-Claude's attorneys threatened to quit if they defied the law.

It was my belief that we needed to let the contractors and workers know their potential risks and allow them to make decisions on whether to participate. Their livelihoods were at risk. Jeanne-Claude, furious that I suggested letting workers have a choice in this, banned me from all following dinners and celebrations. I suspected she also initiated a rumor that I had suffered a psychic break.

Among Christo's visitors, Pierre Restany became a close friend. Pierre was short, with a white beard and flamboyant wild hair. He looked like an elf and was the only one who appreciated my dilemma. His intelligence and compassion helped enormously and launched our lifelong friendship.

On the very last day, the *New Yorker* writer Calvin Tomkins and I took a helicopter ride over the landscape. From above, we saw *Running Fence* in its expansive brilliance, gloriously defining the landscape and disappearing as its path led to the sea. I completed my work in the office while Jeanne-Claude managed the project in a secret location a mile away (her stepfather, a general, must have inspired the need for a hidden office). If *Running Fence* was a war, Jeanne-Claude was clearly the commander.

On the morning of the scheduled opening of *Running Fence*, an odd mixture of farmers, ecologists, engineers, international art patrons, critics, curators, and press gathered on the cliffs of Bodega Bay, overlooking the hills of Sonoma. Together, we watched the violet sunrise light the landscape. Breathless, we waited for the completion of *Running Fence*.

Christo emerged at the water's edge with a bullhorn.

"PULL," Christo shouted.

The crew obeyed. The cords gave way, unfurling in one dazzling thrust the release of the entire *Fence*. White fire-resistant fabric floated towards the water, then disappeared into the deep ultramarine expanse of the Pacific Ocean.

Christo and Jeanne-Claude disregarded all threats of legal action, directing *Running Fence* to complete its predestined voyage into the sea. Christo's assumptions were correct. They paid only a small fine to the county. No one was arrested or put in jail; no workers lost their license.

My contributions to *Running Fence* went mostly unrecorded. Calvin Tomkins's *Running Fence* account in *The New Yorker* made no mention of me (for which Tomkins later apologized). The local artist Tom Marioni wrote his own account in which he omitted me because, as he later told me, "Nobody had heard of you." I appeared in the Maysles Brothers' *Running Fence* film for less than three seconds. Nonetheless, in working on *Running Fence*, I acquired vital organizational skills and was introduced to many future collaborators, such as Annina Nosei (Weber) who opened a gallery in New York in 1980. I would later exhibit in her gallery with other unknown artists, such as Julian Schnabel, Francesco Clemente, and Jean-Michel Basquiat.

Spirited, political, and deeply kind individuals, the Christos were passionately devoted to their artistic vision. In his essay "Civil Disobedience," Henry David Thoreau reminds us that "willingly breaking a law that is unjust and paying the penalty arouses the conscience of a community." Christo and Jeanne-Claude had a profound understanding of this. The Christos honored

their promise by gifting me with a wonderful collage
in addition to my one-dollar paycheck. Thirty-eight years
later, I donated the collage to MoMA, which until then
owned no work by Christo.

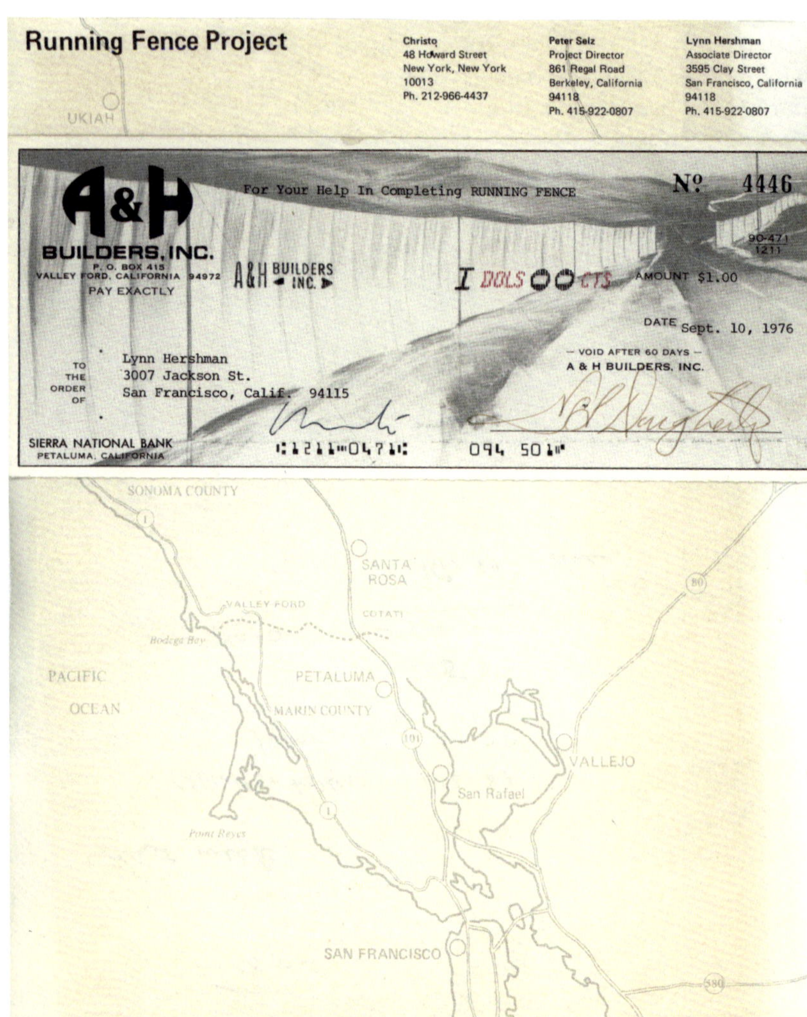


# PAYMENT SENT TO LYNN FOR FOUR YEARS AS ASSOCIATE PROJECT DIRECT OF *RUNNING FENCE*, 1976

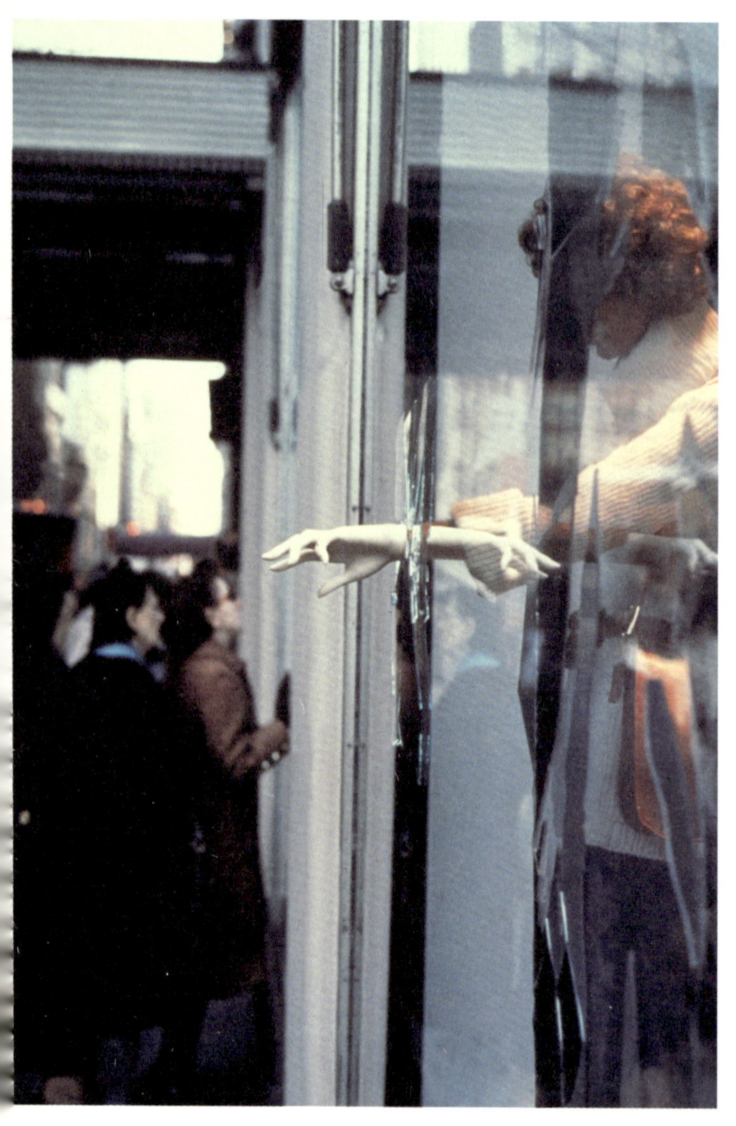

*HAND CRASHING THROUGH THE WINDOW, A PARTIAL INSTALLATION SHOT FROM 25 WINDOWS: A PORTRAIT OF BONWIT TELLER, 1976*

# 17
# WINDOWS, 1976

> Painting is poetry that is seen rather than felt, and
> poetry is painting that is felt rather than seen.
> —Leonardo da Vinci

One week after *Running Fence* was completed, I was
in New York installing the windows of the Bonwit Teller
department store, a project I named *25 Windows: A
Portrait of Bonwit Teller*.

Bonwit Teller had twenty-five windows that circled
around the corner of 56th Street, went along Fifth Avenue,
and continued onto 57th Street. The transformation was
to be made through the reuse of existing locations, which
I termed "recycling" space because art was placed in
unexpected contexts of everyday life. The installation
included interactions with people on the street as they
walked by, and incorporated surveillance cameras, video,
microphones, film, tape recorders, mirrors, steam, holog-
raphy, and live actors, as well as Bonwit Teller mannequins.
I received a budget of $15,000, with the funds given to the
Clocktower as the presenting arts organization.

The exhibition was on view from October 28 until
November 2, 1976. In one window, a mannequin's hand
broke through the glass to the street. Another featured
a male and female mannequin in bed together under a
sheet. In other windows, there were cartoon-like figures
with comic-book thought bubbles. One had a live discussion among three "Futurists," each sitting in a chair as

their conversation was broadcast to the street outside. Another window enacted the escapades of a talking mannequin relayed through a tape-recorded narrative.

More than thirty-five years later, the *New York Times* journalist Cathy Horyn wrote of one of the windows' most adventurous interactive performances:

> *The most tantalizing of the urban dramas was window No. 11, in which a mannequin named Bonnie (whom Hershman Leeson named after Bonwit) was posed with her hand crashing through the glass, as if wanting to join the action on the sidewalk.*
>
> *And she did.*
>
> *Over the next couple of days, Bonnie was seen in about 10 different locations, including a subway station, a bar, Central Park and the steps of the Metropolitan Museum of Art. Hershman Leeson, long interested in the relationship between humans and technology, equipped Bonnie with a hidden cassette player. "She would strike up a conversation and then talk about her clothes," said Hershman Leeson. Bonnie didn't actually respond to people, Hershman Leeson said, but she did have different prerecorded "conversations" appropriate for each location. Judging by her accent, Bonnie was from Brooklyn.*

The success of the Bonwit windows garnered many international commissions, including one from Australia named *Dream Weekend*. I led a group of museum visitors on the weekend of September 16–18, 1977, to a residential development in a suburb of Melbourne.

Arriving in a shuttle bus and accompanied by a tour guide, we visited three homes and watched residents in each as they manifested a different experience of the suburbs. On the last day of the weekend, one housewife "escaped" onto the roof of her home, jumped onto a waiting helicopter, and flew away.

When Fred Roos, one of the producers of Francis's films, learned I was in Australia he asked me to try to locate the filmmaker Wim Wenders, who was also there but out of reach. Fred hoped to talk to Wim about directing a film about Dashiell Hammett.

On a hunch, I located a motel on the outskirts of Alice Springs, not far from Uluru (Ayers Rock), the large sandstone monolith that is sacred to the Aboriginal people and which many believe has spiritual power.

BINGO! He was there. A few weeks later we all met in San Francisco.

While Wim was in town, we rented the original room on Post Street where Hammett wrote *The Maltese Falcon* and found a typewriter identical to the one Hammett used. Wim moved in and used that typewriter to write his script about the original *Thin Man* (Wim began working on the project in 1978 and the film came out in 1982), while I was still immersed in the Roberta project (1972–1979).

During this time Prudence Juris continued to write art critiques that were published in well-known international journals. This resulted in her being invited to participate on a panel in Edinburgh with the German conceptual artist Joseph Beuys, the Polish performance artist Tadeusz Kantor, and the Viennese architect Hans Hollein. I told the sponsors that Prudence had asked me to attend in her place.

Beuys was born in Germany in 1921. As a teenager he was a member of the Hitler Youth and attended the 1936 Nuremberg rally. He worked briefly for a circus before volunteering for the Luftwaffe, the German air force. In 1944, his plane crashed on the Crimean front. After the war, he took up sculpture and became an art teacher, saying "teaching is my greatest work of art." While teaching, he also became a performance artist with work grounded in philosophy and shamanism.

Tadeusz Kantor was a painter, set designer, and theatrical performance artist. Born in 1905, during the years of the Second World War, he became director of an experimental theater in Kraków. During the panel, Beuys and Kantor traded war stories.

I had read about Kantor's avant-garde performances, such as conducting the waves of the ocean without an audience, but I had never seen any of the work of these artists. That changed when I witnessed Kantor's performance of *The Water Hen* given in English with his theater company, Cricot 2. It took my breath away. Kantor did not just break the fourth wall between artist and audience, he shattered it, and me.

While in the United Kingdom, I hoped to find a European gallery that could represent my work. In the process, I encountered a famous British critic. I showed him some works I had packed in my suitcase, protected by a double wrapping of lingerie, the best of my wax heads. He looked at the work intently, said he would write about the pieces himself, and asked me to leave the best one with him to study. I did so, stupidly, without a receipt of any kind and with no documentation or photographic record of the sculpture.

I was naive. I was hopeful the critic would keep his word and write about my work. He didn't. Later, when I tried to contact him, he never responded. I never saw that piece or him again. I had a similar experience a decade later with a new gallery in New York, which showed my work in a group exhibition. During the show the gallery went bankrupt, and all the art was confiscated by creditors. My work was never returned.

My third similar experience was recent. A well-known London gallery suddenly closed and works of mine were not returned (eventually my lawyers were able to retrieve two but not all of the works).

In each of these cases I never saw the work again. I mention this because it happens to artists all the time, no matter where they are in their careers. Even now, many years later, these losses of work are painful, and I feel as though important relics from my past had been kidnapped.

I continued shooting interviews with women artists I admired such as Barbara Kruger, Yoko Ono, Miranda July, and Marina Abramović. As women, each one struggled to be taken seriously by the mainstream art establishment.

A few years after *Running Fence*, Pierre Restany agreed to let me videotape him and Walter Hopps, the curator he was traveling with, about their relationship to Marcel Duchamp. I was interested in creating a film about Duchamp as inspiration.

I never told them that I had actually met Duchamp in Cleveland. I may have still been in high school. He gave a talk that I attended. Afterwards, I went up, introduced myself, and shook his hand. I was surprised that Duchamp, who was such an anarchist in the history of art, was so proper and restrained in person.

Hopps was already a significant figure in American art. As a young man he'd been mentored by the premier art collectors in Los Angeles at the time, Walter and Louise Arenberg. After graduating from Stanford, Hopps set about birthing LA's art scene with exhibitions at the Santa Monica Pier and its merry-go-round, and by founding the

Ferus Gallery with the artists Edward Kienholz and Irving Blum, later a gallerist. Ferus held the first West Coast exhibitions of Andy Warhol's soup cans, and the work of Jasper Johns, Roy Lichtenstein, Frank Stella, as well as the West Coast artists Ed Ruscha and Wallace Berman.

Hopps was known to be eccentric, often wearing a trench coat in the California heat, and had a reputation for being habitually late. We agreed to shoot the video at 5 p.m. The crew arrived at 3 p.m. to set up lights, camera, and mike stands, and prepare for the interview. Three hours passed, then five. Pierre phoned hourly to say they were on their way.

By 11 p.m., I sent the camera crew home and went to sleep, only to be woken up at 3 a.m. by someone pounding on my door. It was Pierre with Hopps in tow. The shooting setup had been dismantled and there were no lights, cameras, or mikes. I did have an old, broken 8 mm camera in my closet. I used this in an attempt to capture a wonderful conversation they had but, regrettably but not surprisingly, it wasn't properly recorded. Only one glitchy moment survived of a blurred Walter pacing in my living room in the dark. This entire episode could have been written by Duchamp himself. I could never be angry at Pierre for long.

Pierre often invited me to events. In his company, I was able to visit the studios of Arman and Andy Warhol in New York and attend a lecture by Ettore Sottsass and the Memphis Group at Domus Institute in Milan.

However, I was not seen as an artist—merely as Pierre's friend. In most cases, I was not even acknowledged. Unless you were in a relationship with a famous artist who was represented by a gallery, as a woman you were dismissed and treated as invisible.

Very often when I attempted to secure appointments to have a gallery look at my work, they assumed I was the secretary or the assistant of a male artist. Once they realized that I wanted them to look at my own work, they canceled the appointment. Of course, I continued to make art but for years I could neither show nor sell it. Galleries understood very well that there were few collectors of women artists.

Consequently, too many women artists remained unknown, unacknowledged, forced to work in obscurity. Being invisible was then a preset condition. I struggled to exhibit and sell my work then. And today, despite much recognition, I still struggle to sell my work.

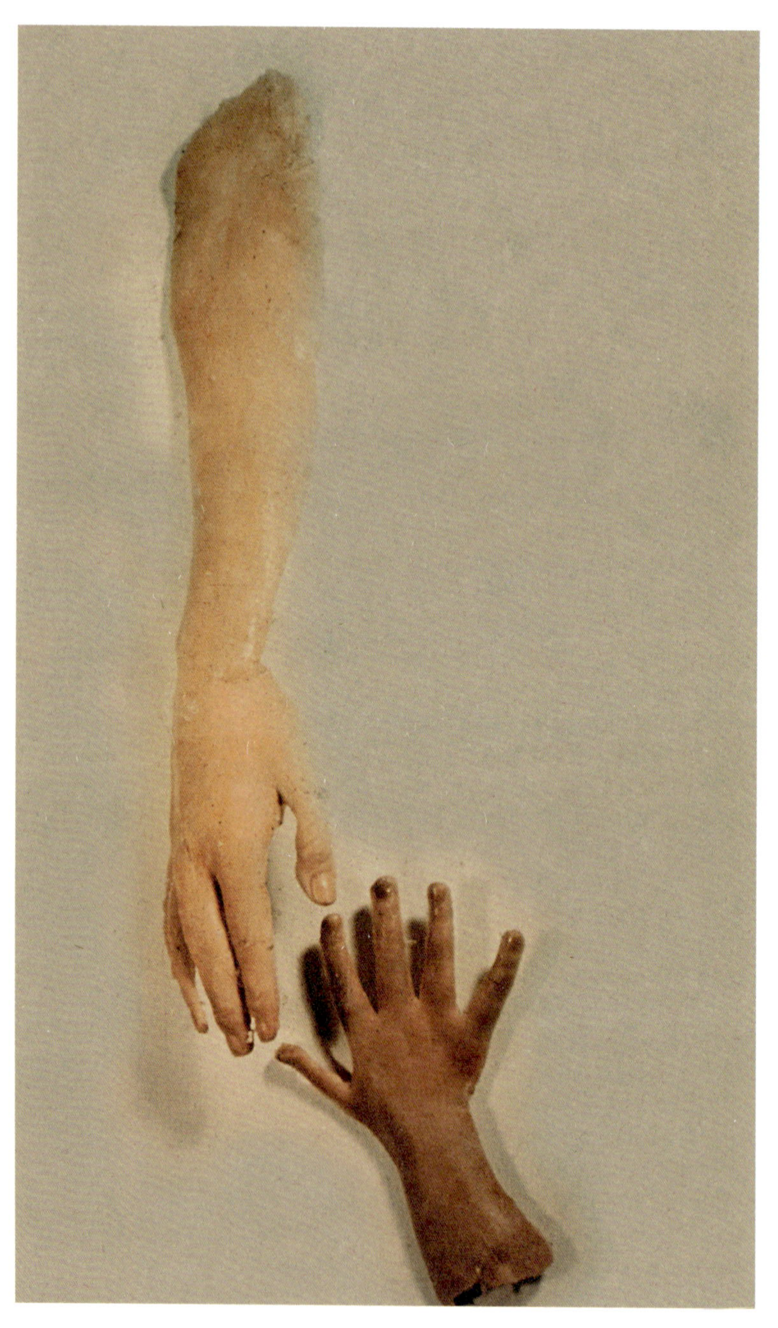

*MOTHER DAUGHTER ARMS,*
1965

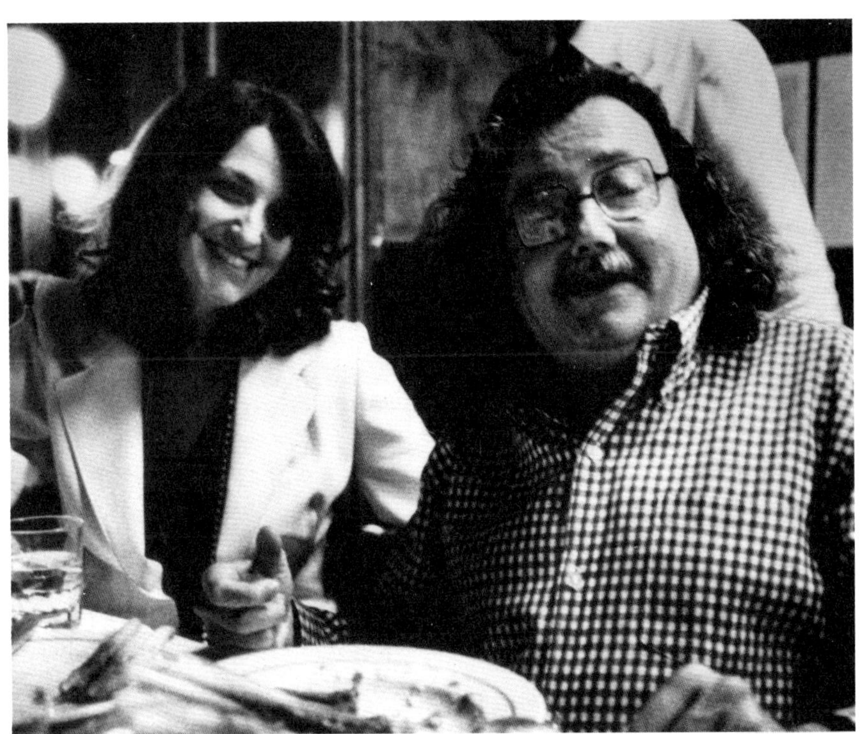

# LYNN AND PIERRE RESTANY, MILAN, 1976

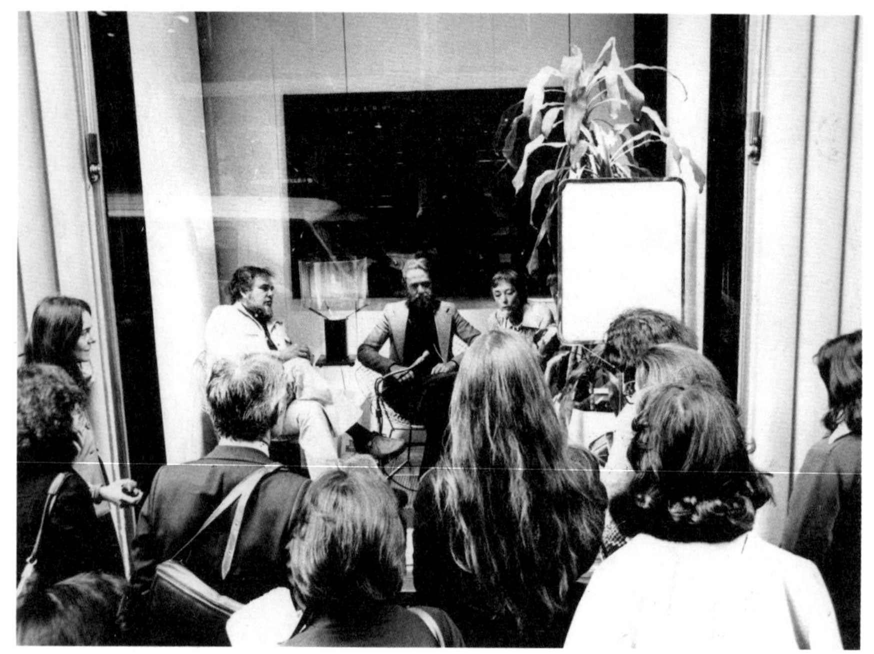

# *25 WINDOWS: A PORTRAIT OF BONWIT TELLER*: FRANK GILETTE, BARBARA MARX HUBBARD, AND AN EXPERT FROM THE SOCIETY OF THE FUTURE, 1976

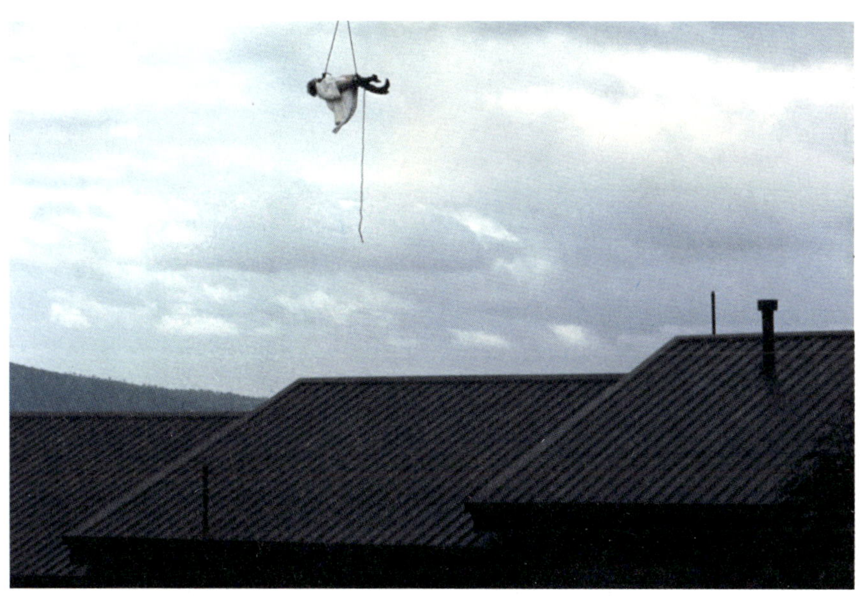

# FINAL ESCAPE, 1977

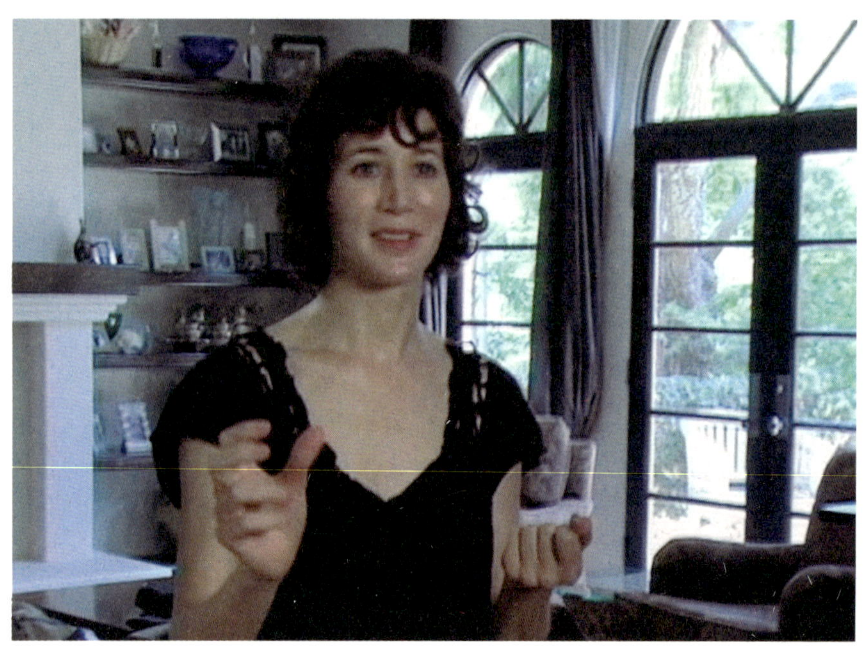

STILL OF MIRANDA JULY
FROM *!WOMEN ART
REVOLUTION*, 2010

# 18
# PLEASE TOUCH

> I never paint dreams or nightmares. I paint
> my own reality.
> —Frida Kahlo

After years of prodding, Bruce Conner finally agreed to an exhibition at the San Francisco Museum of Modern Art, with the condition that it put a sign next to his work that read, PLEASE TOUCH. As feared by the curators and as anticipated by Bruce, this sign incited a mixed reaction on opening night.

Sam West, who owned several of Bruce's pieces, took the invitation, PLEASE TOUCH, literally. Sam, who had been one of the first to arrive at the exhibition, placed his hands on one of Bruce's fragile wax sculptures. Seeing this, Peter Selz, horrified at the potential damage this might cause, grabbed Sam's arm to stop him. But Sam insisted he was bringing the work to completion, igniting a heated argument between the two men. It escalated and soon they were wrestling on the floor of the main gallery, arms and legs bloodied, clothing ripped.

Bruce, as usual impeccably attired, stood in a corner taking photographs of the altercation. Cackling to himself, Bruce was delighted by the chaos he had instigated. Guards and curators finally broke up the fight. Sam touched the piece one more time, then left the museum. But the consequences of Bruce's provocation continued even after the opening, to the consternation of the museum staff tasked with keeping the work safe.

Bruce, like me, did not have a separate studio. He worked in a tiny space outside his kitchen. Visitors were not allowed in. However, Clayton Gorder, a painter, was aware that I knew Bruce, and asked if they could meet. Bruce grudgingly agreed. When Clayton arrived at Bruce's home, wanting to impress him with his understanding of PLEASE TOUCH, he gently put his finger on one of Bruce's wax sculptures, titled *Snore*.

Bruce emitted a violent scream and accused Clayton of attempting to murder his artwork. Bruce lunged forward, putting his hands around Clayton's neck in an attempt to choke him despite Clayton being at least eight inches taller and a hundred pounds heavier than Bruce. Their struggle moved through the kitchen, then outside onto the deck, where Clayton finally was able to escape. Clayton never recovered from that experience. By contrast, Bruce confessed that the conflict with Clayton had given him new energy.

Bruce's behavior was often unpredictable, but it was accepted as Bruce being Bruce, just as Daniel Spoerri was Daniel being Daniel. Similarly, when the film critic and curator Sheldon Renan organized a panel with Bruce on experimental film at the University Art Museum at Berkeley, Bruce picked up a nearby pitcher of water and doused Sheldon's head with the entire contents. Heroically, Sheldon conducted the entire discussion soaking wet.

Sam West, an Oakland-based dentist, was one of a few art collectors with radical taste. He was building an important collection, and I was eager to have him visit. When I mentioned completing several wax cast bodies, Sam said he wanted to see them. Having no separate studio, I invited Sam to visit me at home. When he arrived, he tapped his cane sharply on my window. Sam was dapper, dressed in a yellow suit, yellow bowler hat, and yellow shirt, but barefoot.

Once inside my apartment, he perused the contents of my refrigerator, walked by the cast bodies on the sofa, then left without saying a word.

A few weeks later, Sam called to ask the price of three of my wax body casts. He told me that he would buy all three. To celebrate the imminent purchase, he invited me to dinner at Trader Vic's, a very expensive Polynesian-themed restaurant. I arrived early and waited. Nearly an hour after our appointed meeting time, Sam appeared, wearing a wilted rose over his lapel, his feet in slippers. He was carrying an ax.

"Why the ax?" I inquired.

Sam never responded to my question but told me he was buying the bodies he saw in my home and that they would be the last art to go in his collection.

This purchase was the first sale of my work. Ever. I took Sam's declaration to mean that his collection would be a statement about Bay Area art.

At dinner, Sam proceeded to order every item on the menu.

I went home, stuffed, and giddy with the excitement of the sale.

That same night, Sam shot himself in the head. He died with his body bent over a scrawled note that read:

"Goodbye cruel world."

> The sale was never consummated. Once again, no contract was made nor were his intentions written down.
>
> After his death, Sam's girlfriend, whom he nicknamed "Leopard Lady," sought to inherit his art collection. She was not alone. The Oakland Museum and a third claimant, Howard Johnson, also staked a claim to the art. The legal entanglements among them lasted several years. Finally, Sam's collection was divided and auctioned off. His legacy vanished.

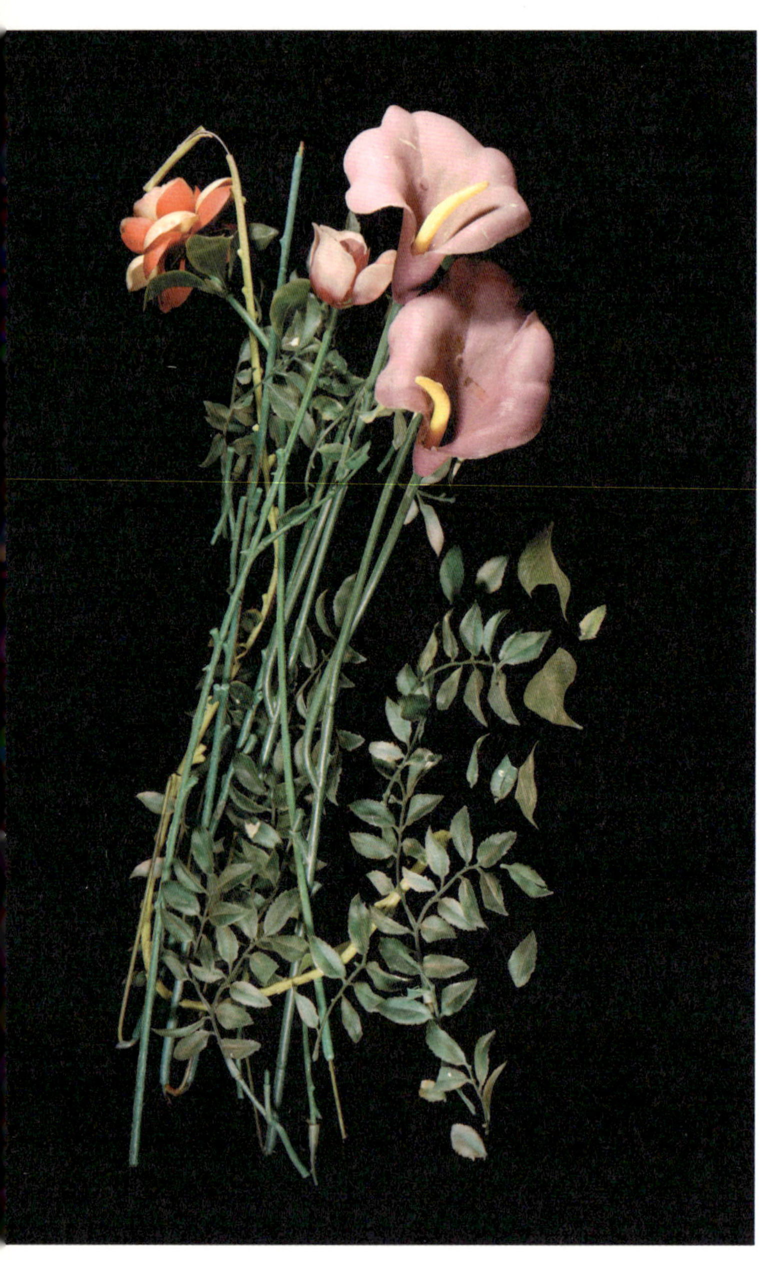

ROBERTA'S EXORCISM
FLOWER ARRANGEMENTS,
1978

# 19
# EXORCISMS

> Art had reached an impasse that was already breaking through American society. I'm not suggesting that the feminist art movement was a product of the invasion of Cambodia. We know it was much, much more complicated than that. There had to be new voices and new voices and new exercises in the making of art. And that's exactly when feminism starts in the art world.
> —Howard Fox, July 7, 2004

Roberta Breitmore was a fleshed-out archetype. Her recorded history included a driver's license, credit cards (Roberta had better credit than I had), leases, job applications, checks, photographs, and letters. After existing for nearly a decade, Roberta's notebooks filled with observations, and the evidence and documentation of her life, were proof of the extreme biases and discrimination towards women inherent in American society.

I assumed Roberta was an entity separate from me, even though we shared a heartbeat. But I was wrong. Witnessing the abuse and discrimination Roberta endured had a profound effect on my own life. Though it was essential to acknowledge the cultural prejudice suffered by the Roberta(s), the realization of the many degrees of societal prejudice she encountered weighed heavy on my soul. For me, it became essential to formally conclude the Roberta Breitmore project.

In June 1978, I was invited to Ferrara, Italy, for an exhibition at the Palazzo dei Diamanti, a Renaissance palace whose main floor houses Ferrara's National Painting Gallery. Ferrara is also the final resting place of Lucrezia Borgia at the Corpus Domini Monastery, where several members of the House of Este are buried. A devoted patron of the arts, Lucrezia Borgia, like Roberta (and like me), suffered from the trauma of incestuous relationships. An exorcism for Roberta in the crypt of Lucrezia Borgia, who had died four centuries earlier, seemed an apt physical and psychological setting for the enactment of Roberta's final transformation.

The day I arrived in Ferrara, I enjoyed lunch with Kristine Stiles, who performed as the first Roberta multiple. At an outdoor cafe, two identical glass vases framed the entrance. Coincidentally, these extraordinary pieces were near replicas of vessels I had drawn in California while planning Roberta's exorcism.

I borrowed them to place in the exhibition. One vase held real flowers while the other's blossoms were artificial, creating the illusion of a mirror that reflected reality on one side and artifice on the other. Apt symbolism for Roberta. The vases flanked an altar that held a photo of Roberta's *Construction Chart* as well as a vitrine filled with the ephemera and detritus of her life.

At the opening, a Roberta multiple (the dancer Michelle Larson) entered the gallery and began an emotive dance composed of Roberta's distinctive body language and gestures. Each of her movements emphasized Roberta's growing disillusionment with life. Tape recordings of tones constructed from the shuffle of Roberta's walk played as the multiple slithered towards Roberta's photo and her *Construction Chart*.

She paced backwards and forwards in front of the unframed *Construction Chart*, which was thumbtacked to the wall, until, in an unexpected thrust of motion, she twirled into the archway and removed the vase with artificial flowers from its pedestal—leaving the real flowers untouched.

For a moment, she stood still holding the vase of artificial flowers. She then began her dance again, her body jerking as if possessed by a demonic spirit. The multiple removed the photograph of Roberta from the wall, placed it inside the vase along with the artificial flowers, and set the vase and photograph on fire.

As the photograph burned quickly, the disintegrating paper released gray smoke into the air. It was as if ink were dropped into the atmosphere, saturating and charging it with a deep pungent color.

The Roberta multiple stretched her body on the floor next to the coffin-like vitrine that held the relics of her life.

Her body froze into its final position. She remained in this state for the next twenty-four hours.

Before the ceremony, Roberta was a sculptural live performance, a socio-psychological portrait. The exorcism and subsequent transformation through fire, water, air, and earth, from white to red to gray to black, represented a symbolic invocation of rebirth. Roberta's ashes were meant to symbolize the end of her existence, but instead were absorbed into my own life, and irrevocably changed its direction.

After the exorcism, I set fire to several of my wax sculptures in the crypt. They transformed in ways that revealed the passage of time as they melted. As with Roberta, it was an alchemical conversion using elements of air, earth, fire, and water that also recycled through representations of death and rebirth.

This exorcism performed in the crypt of Lucrezia Borgia marked a new beginning. Layers of trauma, victimization, feelings of doubt and low self-esteem that had accumulated over several decades slowly began to peel away. As I moved past the traumas I had endured, my determination to heal was as strong as my need to make art. At times the pain felt excruciating. However, in its rawness, this experience was essential and would eventually enable my future.

In May 1978, Tom Garver, a curator at the Fine Arts Museums in San Francisco, who I met through Bruce Conner, organized an exhibition at the De Young Museum, titled *Lynn Hershman Is Not Roberta Breitmore*.

Tom was an eccentric in his own right, with a deadpan sense of humor and an elegant sense of style. Mine was Tom's last exhibition before leaving the museum. I wondered if by exhibiting Roberta, work that no other museum considered art or would exhibit, Tom wasn't sending them a final provocation.

The show was staged in two rooms on the main floor of the museum. Displayed in the first room was documentation from the Roberta project, including photographs of Roberta's Room, at 111 Bakers Acres, and 3000 Jackson Street; as well as a Roberta multiple; and a poster from the Roberta Look-Alike contest. Tom even arranged for the publication of a catalogue, with a preface by Arturo Schwarz and essays by Sandy Ballatore, Jack Burnham, and Kristine Stiles.

This was the first time any of my work had been

presented in an American museum. My daughter's school organized a class trip to see it. Of course, at the exhibition Dawn denied to her classmates that she was related to the artist Lynn Hershman whose work was in this exhibition, which I was amused by. Her attitude changed thirty years later when New York's Museum of Modern Art showed the same works. By then she could admit to being proud of her mom.

During the 1970s, because of the Women's Liberation Movement and the battle for the Equal Rights Amendment, many of the women artists I interviewed who had married as young women were getting divorced. I was not among them. I found confrontation extremely difficult. It was possibly from my early fear of being physically attacked as a child. Still, I was surprised that upon returning home to San Francisco after an exhibition in Italy, I was confronted with another disappearance. My husband had vanished. He had left with no way to contact him.

I was free of my marriage. A single mother with a young child and no regular income, I was confronting new challenges, among them our financial survival.

Within a few weeks, unexpectedly, my mother died. I was thrown by this, much more than I would have expected. The weight of putting Roberta to rest, my mother's death, and the financial crisis I was facing was overwhelming. Worse yet, I was desperate to hide all this from Dawn. I needed her to believe everything was fine.

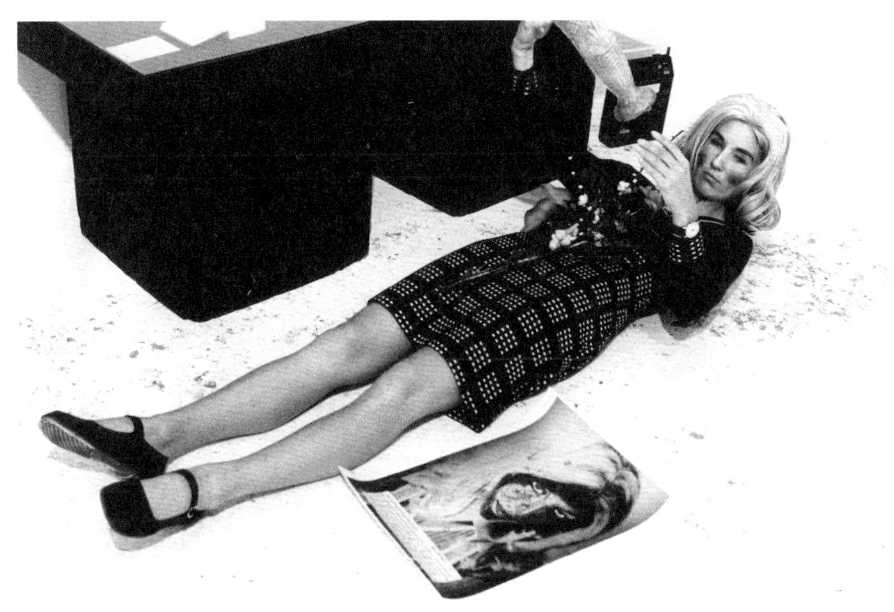

# *ROBERTA MULTIPLE LIES DOWN BESIDE CONSTRUCTION CHART (MICHELLE LARSON), 1978*

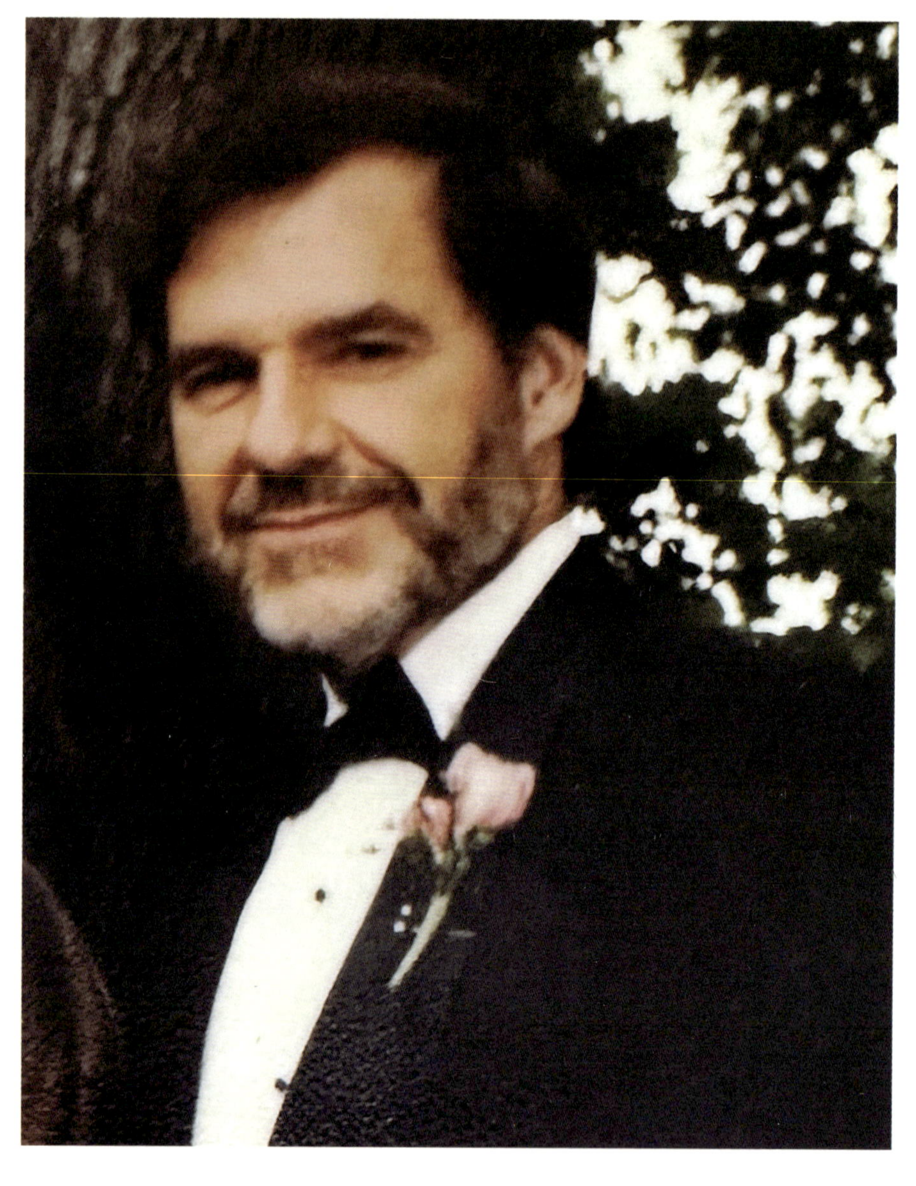

GEORGE LEESON, C. 1990

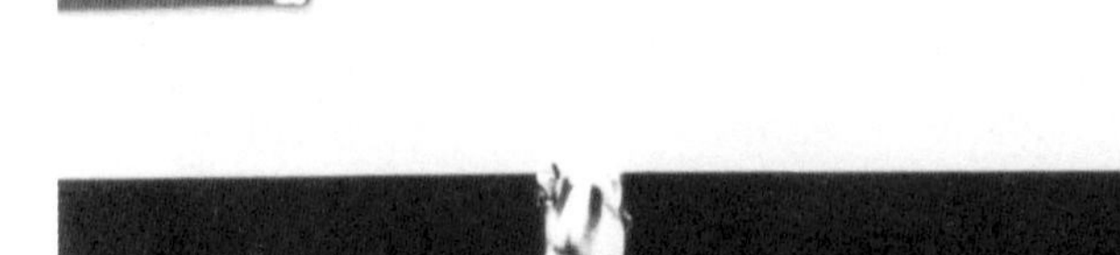

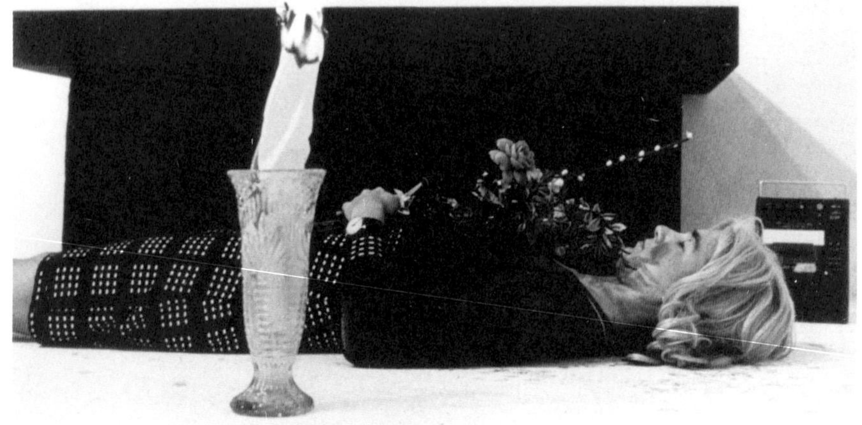

# ROBERTA MULTIPLE IS EXORCIZED WITH FLAMING VASE (MICHELLE LARSON), 1978

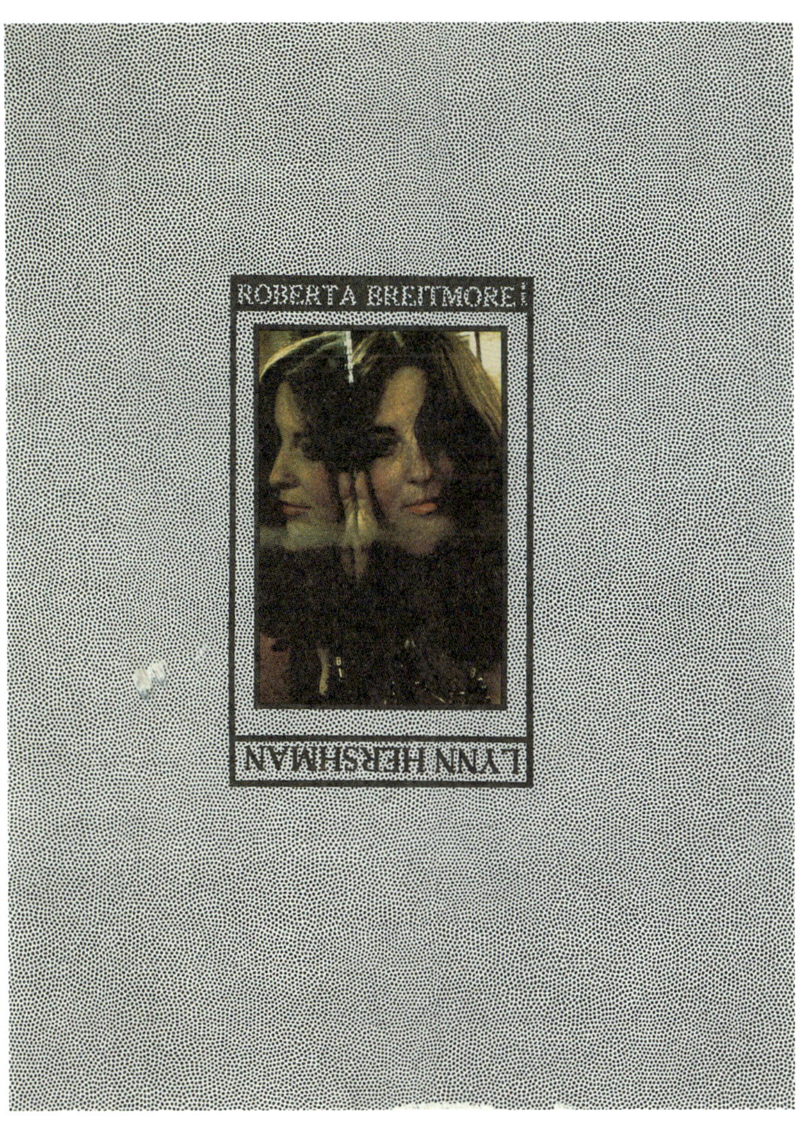

EXHIBITION CATALOGUE FOR *LYNN HERSHMAN IS NOT ROBERTA BREITMORE/ ROBERTA BREITMORE IS NOT LYNN HERSHMAN, 1978*

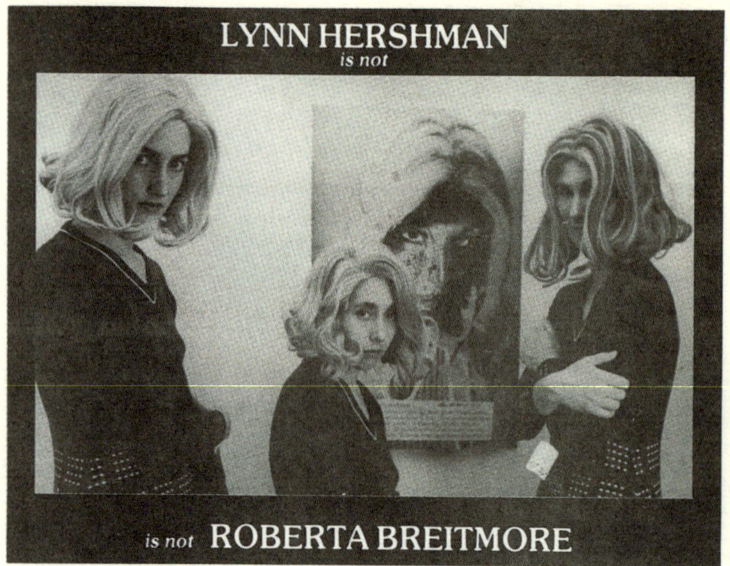


*ANNOUNCEMENT FOR ROBERTA LOOK ALIKE CONTEST AT THE DEYOUNG MUSEUM, 1978*

# 20
# TRAUMA'S PROGENY

> Hundreds of thousands of people were marching against the war in Vietnam. It was like a perfect setting for me to become intently involved in the community events.
> —Judy Baca interview, 1973

I was desperately poor. I could not afford postage stamps, much less a haircut or trip to the dentist. No one would buy my art. No one would hire me. I had no experience working at a job. Out of desperation and, in the hope of a few months of financial relief, I went to pawnshops and sold the little jewelry I had, including my engagement ring and my wedding ring.

I borrowed money from friends. Then I borrowed money from everyone I ever knew. I even asked Christo. He was very generous. I asked my brother. I even asked parents at my daughter's school. It was humiliating. I never thought I could pay any of them back. Thirty-five years later when I was able to, none of them would accept the money.

I took Dawn to Ellie's house for meals, or she went to her friends' homes for dinner. A few times, I stole food from local grocery stores. Looking back, I cannot imagine having done this or how I got through that unfortunate period of my life.

As demeaning as it was to ask for money, it was even more difficult to reveal my new circumstances to others. Perhaps the hardest part was to maintain a brave front for Dawn to let her believe that everything was OK and that it would all be fine. Perhaps I was also trying to convince myself. Meanwhile, I felt like a failure.

My daughter was in a very good, very expensive private school. I was told that gave her the stability she needed during this difficult time. But I could not pay the tuition. I had to beg the school to let me contrive a deferred payment plan.

The suppression of anxiety, fear, and trauma is a heavy weight to carry. When under stress, some people self-medicate or overuse alcohol, drugs, or sex. I obsessively consumed sweets. Cookies became an erotic and sensual substitute for sexuality. I would go into my bedroom, light a fire, put some music on, lock the door, and when I thought nobody would be around, I would ravish these pleasure-giving morsels of caloric excess. It was very much like having a clandestine affair, but with sugar. Within a few months, I had gained forty-five pounds.

Eating, I've come to realize, has very little to do with actual hunger. It's like the image of the Tao, or two sides of the same coin: hunger and deprivation, deprivation and hunger. It's anima and animus, male and female. These polarities are common in nature. After a cookie binge, I felt so guilty that a second Tao-istic cycle of purging, or exorcism, was triggered, which only increased my feelings of guilt. I started to avoid mirrors and reflections of any kind, particularly deep reflections.

Humans have a remarkable capacity to become comfortable with distortions of their values or sense of truth. Similarly, we distort our own body image by indulging and abusing ourselves. Even Eve was made to know that eating was considered a sin for women.

My feelings of being fat have been with me since my earliest memories. As I look back, I think of myself as always having been the chubbiest in any of my classes. Was that true? And if so, so what? Why are we judged unfairly about appearances? Why do we judge ourselves so harshly?

At first, I believed I was eating too much to punish myself because my husband left. I felt it must have been my fault. In my personal narrative, I was not only the victim but also the perpetrator—it must have been my fault somehow. For people like me, when it rains, you believe the sun will never shine again. But as we heal, we understand that although we can't predict when the sun will appear, we know that it will eventually. I went to court to get divorced. My husband did not appear, he sent his attorney instead. He did appear at our daughter's bat mitzvah. We never discussed our marriage or his new life.

When my daughter went to the movies, I picked her up at the theater afterwards. This was before cell phones. About a year after Dawn's father left, I found a pay phone in a bar close to the theater that I would call to find out when to pick her up. One time, as I dialed the theater, there was someone waiting to use the phone. He was a nice-looking man, and while I waited for the movie theater to answer, he smiled. When I finished my call, I apologized for taking so long, and we struck up a conversation. His name was George Leeson.

I told him I had to go pick up my daughter. He asked for my phone number, which I gave him. I didn't think he would call. But he did. We made a date for him to pick me up at my apartment.

When he arrived at my door, there was no way to hide the eviction notice that had been placed there. I confessed that I was three months behind in my rent and in dire financial straits. The next day, George withdrew $1,500 from his savings account and paid my back rent, with no questions or obligation.

George and I continued to see each other. He was the only suitor my daughter liked. He took her to the movies, bought her a cat, became her confidant, and offered to babysit whenever I needed it. At one point, I became convinced that if New York was the center of the art world, it was where I should go to look for work. George came through once again. He offered to stay at my apartment to watch and take care of Dawn.

The trip to New York was a disaster. Whatever organizational or creative talent I had displayed with the Floating Museum, in working on *Running Fence*, or in my own artwork were not marketable skills in New York. No one was interested in hiring me.

However, my trip to New York had one positive consequence: George never moved out. Given my own strict upbringing and history of family violence, I was never one to discipline Dawn. However, George had no problem setting rules and limits for Dawn and enforcing them. I believe she craved this.

Triangles are one of the strongest existing geometric shapes. Together, the three of us, George, Dawn, and I, became a triangle that, over time, became stronger. We coalesced as a family and, miraculously, each of our lives improved substantially.

                                    

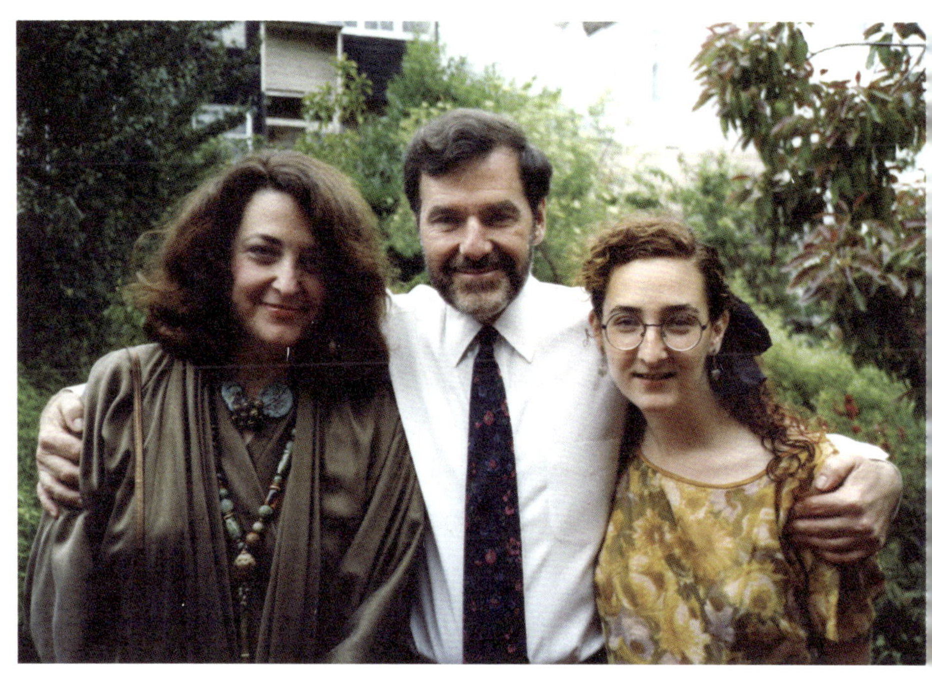

# LYNN, GEORGE, AND DAWN, C. 1993

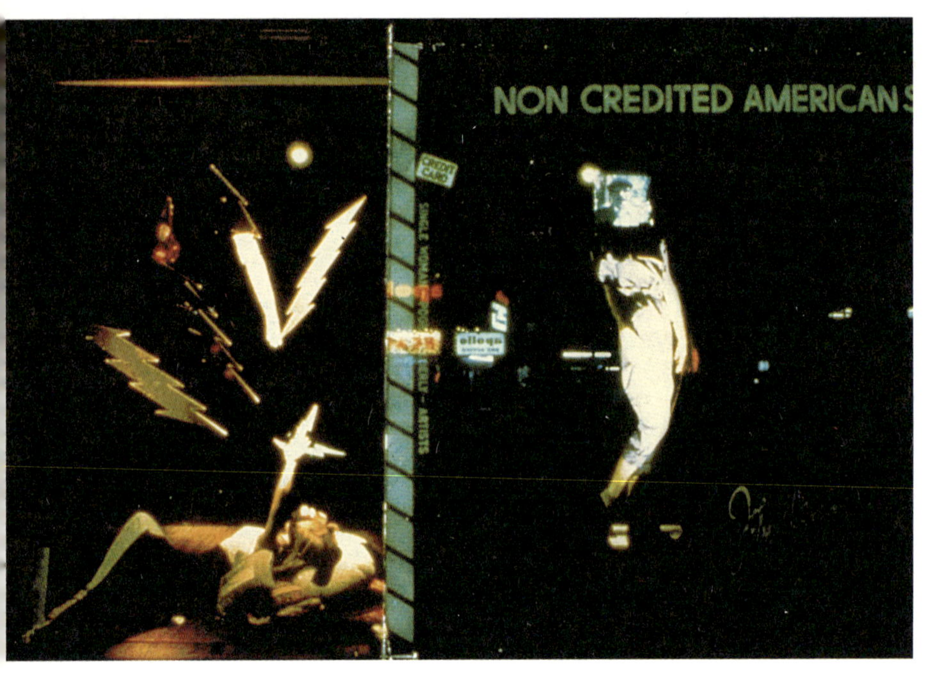


WINDOW DOCUMENTATION
OF *NON CREDITED
AMERICANS*, 1981

# 21 COMMISSION!

> It is not so much where my motivation comes from but rather how it manages to survive.
> —Louise Bourgeois

Out of the blue, in 1979, Wanamaker's department store in Philadelphia invited me to do an installation. They had seen my windows at Bonwit Teller. Founded in 1861 and one of the first department stores in the United States, Wanamaker's offered employees free medical care, profit-sharing, and pension plans. Equality was a principle driving the store's success.

In the late 1970s, I was rejected for credit. At that time, many women could not get credit cards, except those of their husbands. This inspired the new installation, titled *Non-Credited Americans.*

The Philadelphia Museum of Art was the co-sponsor of the Wanamaker's installation. I accepted, knowing that I would be near the home of so many of Duchamp's works at the museum. I was still eager to complete my earlier project about Marcel Duchamp.

I requested Wanamaker's route my flight through New York so that I could meet Gene Fairly, then owner of the Videodisc Publishing Company. Fairly was the producer of some of the earliest interactive videodiscs, including one made as a tour of the National Gallery of Art, the first interactive art videodisc.

We met at a restaurant in Manhattan. Fairly was a quiet,

slightly overweight man in his forties who was sympathetic to what I was trying to accomplish. He wanted to create more interactive videodisc art-related projects. He requested a detailed financial proposal for the Duchamp project. I had never before made a budget.

After Gene left, I sat alone, finishing my coffee, waiting till it was time to catch my bus to Philadelphia. I only had thirty dollars in my purse. I had naively assumed I would be paid when the windows were complete. I had no other savings. What I did next, I still regret. I surreptitiously pocketed half of the generous cash tip Gene intended for the waitress. Being poor can make people desperate.

For *Non-Credited Americans*, I divided a large store window into two unequal parts. On the larger side, a white, blond, elegantly dressed female mannequin surrounded by gloves, shoes, and jewelry reclined like an odalisque on silk pillows, extending its hand to a golden credit card.

On the smaller side, a headless female mannequin dressed in work clothes also extended a hand towards a golden credit card, but it was out of reach. In place of her head a small video screen displayed a slide show of marginalized individuals—women, minorities, the elderly—for whom credit was also out of reach (I included an image of myself among them). An audio loop of interviews from people denied credit played on the street and at the top of the window.

I hoped to receive my honorarium in cash, but the museum insisted on mailing me a check. I was thirty-nine years old. I had fifty cents in my purse, barely enough for a phone call.

I needed to earn money. Based on my Bonwit's and Wanamaker's successes as well as the Floating Museum, I decided to start a company that would provide art installations for commercial properties such as malls.

Trading art for legal fees, I incorporated the Myth America Corporation (MAMCO). Images from Wanamaker's convinced Hare Brewer and Kelley, a construction firm, to hire MAMCO to prepare temporary site-specific artworks for their new shopping center in Mountain View, California. I assured them we would attract a different demographic of shoppers.

MAMCO's first installation was to be created by the Italian artist Michelangelo Pistoletto. I was amazed that he agreed after one phone call. I invited him because I loved the photographs I had seen of his work. Michaelangelo was a kind, gentle man with a subtle sense of humor.

For MAMCO, he created an arrow-shaped mirrored structure called *The Penetrable Arrow* that allowed visitors to see a reflection of themselves as they descended escalators into the shopping area. Despite being an artistic success, *The Penetrable Arrow* garnered little press and went over budget, causing Hare Brewer and Kelly to withdraw support from Myth America. I was forced to cancel MAMCO's next project, which was to be by Gordon Matta Clark. Once again, I had to figure out a way to survive financially.

Just in the nick of time, Gene Fairly's company Videodisc Publishing approved the interactive videodisc I had proposed, *Duchamp, C'est la Vie.* With seed money from Fairly, I hired Juan Downey as the director of the project. Based on Duchamp's *Rotoreliefs* (1935) and his fascination with chance, this interactive videodisc would include a conversation among Nam June Paik, John Cage, Calvin Tomkins, and Brian O'Doherty about their experiences with Duchamp. Members of the Pilobolus dance company reinterpreted the artist Francis Picabia's Dadaist ballet, *Relache*, while discs spun on the stage. This stellar cast came together because Duchamp always captivated people.

Brian O'Doherty was not only an artist and critic, but also a medical doctor. He had videotaped Duchamp's heartbeat and noted that Duchamp insisted it be labeled *M.D.* He played his recording of Duchamp's heartbeat on the stage and that kicked off the conversation.

Juan became obsessed with Duchamp's heartbeat. After the shoot, he refused to return the master tapes unless he could keep the "heartbeat." I had no contract with Juan and could not complete the work without the master tape. The project was never completed and that ended my relationship with Gene Fairly.

Desperate, I used the very low-resolution time-coded copies of the submasters of Duchamp, Paik, Walter Hopps, Calvin Tomkins, and Pierre Restany. With these a short video was created on how "chance" prevented completion of the project.

Having further impoverished myself with the Duchamp fiasco, I went to a shelter for battered women to see whether I would qualify for a job. They steered me to a job that paid $3.35 an hour, selling shoes in Macy's basement. Though the job was short-lived, it allowed me to file for unemployment compensation.

At the same time, to raise cash quickly for the next month's rent, I staged a "fire sale" at my home. Everything that was not Dawn's or George's was available for sale at ridiculously low prices. Large drawings were priced at $5. There were hand-painted ties, all my clothing, furniture, art, handmade porcelain plates, paintings—everything else was priced at $2!

To draw attention to the sale, and make the event more enticing, I projected film footage of fire on the front windows of my apartment. Smoke machines sent dark clouds out from the windows. Musicians performed on the steps of my apartment building and dancers pretended to escape the fire by jumping out the windows onto the street.

Though it was a successful performance, all I sold was one necktie for $2. My costs for the fog machine, musicians, and dancers were $100.

I packed up my drawings and placed them in a portfolio. Fifty-four years later, in 2018, I found the portfolio which Paule Anglim Gallery exhibited. If someone had bought my work at the fire sale for $5, they would have made a wise investment. In 2018, those same works sold for ten thousand times that original price.

It was not a total waste: Later, performance elements of this fire sale appeared in other works that simulated fire in buildings in San Francisco, Portland and New York. I learned a lot about staging event art performances with projections, music and dancers.

I was even commissioned to stage a work at Lincoln Center in New York. *CHAIN REACTION: AN ENVIRONMENTAL "LIGHT" OPERA FOR FOG, FILM AND RECOMBINANT NEWS* (1983) projected images of an environmental spill on the front of Alice Tully Hall in New York, surrounded by fog machines, with live actors exiting a limousine.

Although my work was shown in department store windows and the public plazas of cultural centers, it was not in museums or galleries. I was paid small commission fees for projects that always cost more than I was given; and there were no artifacts or prints to sell.

George left his job at the poster store and launched his own business. Dawn was doing well in school. I could not have gone on without them, but I was not sure how we would be able to go on.

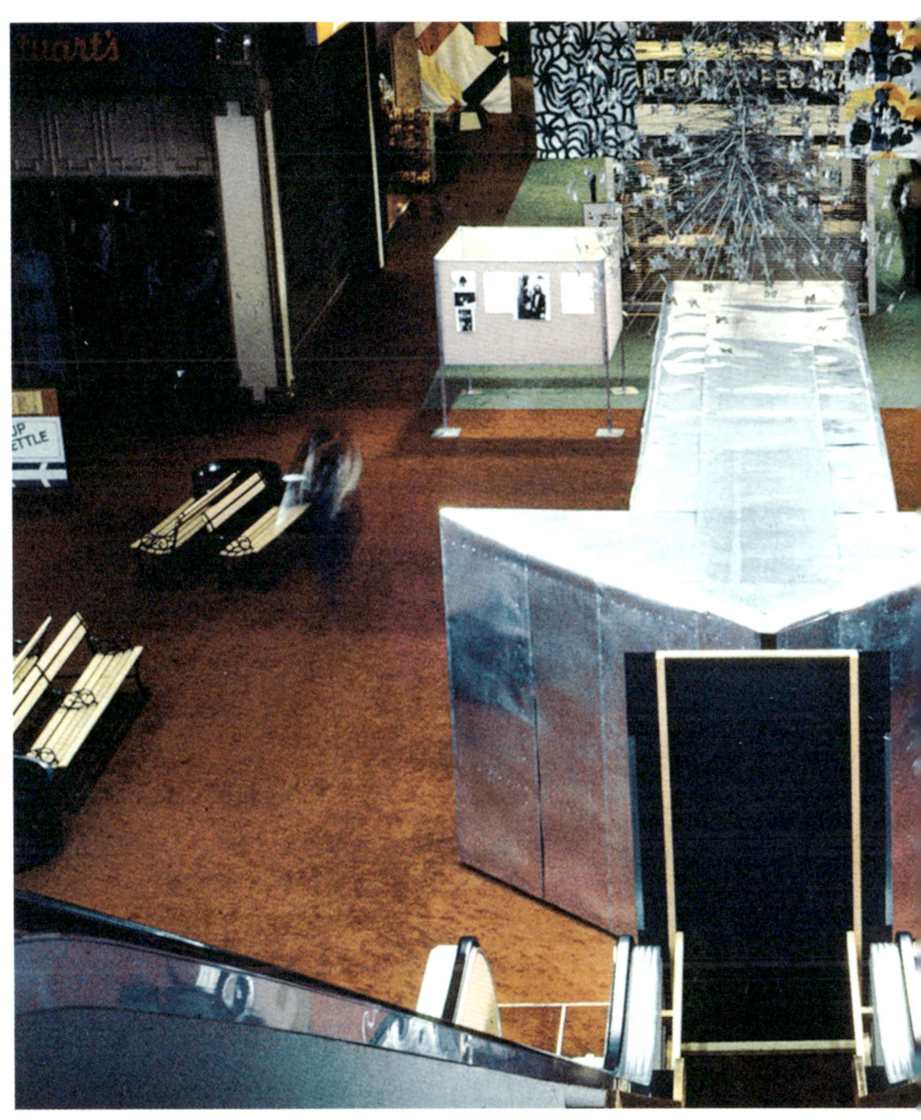

# MICHELANGELO PISTOLETTO, *THE PENETRABLE ARROW UNDER CONSTRUCTION,* MAYFIELD MALL, PALO ALTO, CALIFORNIA, 1979

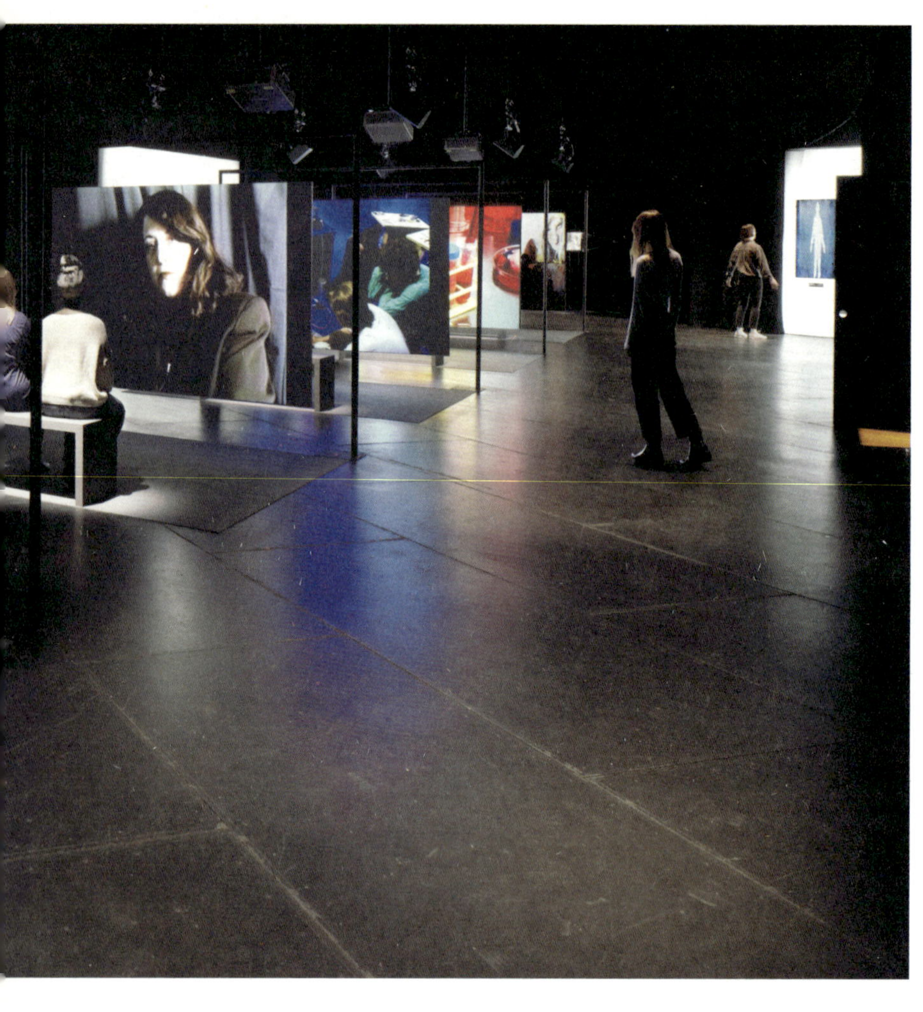

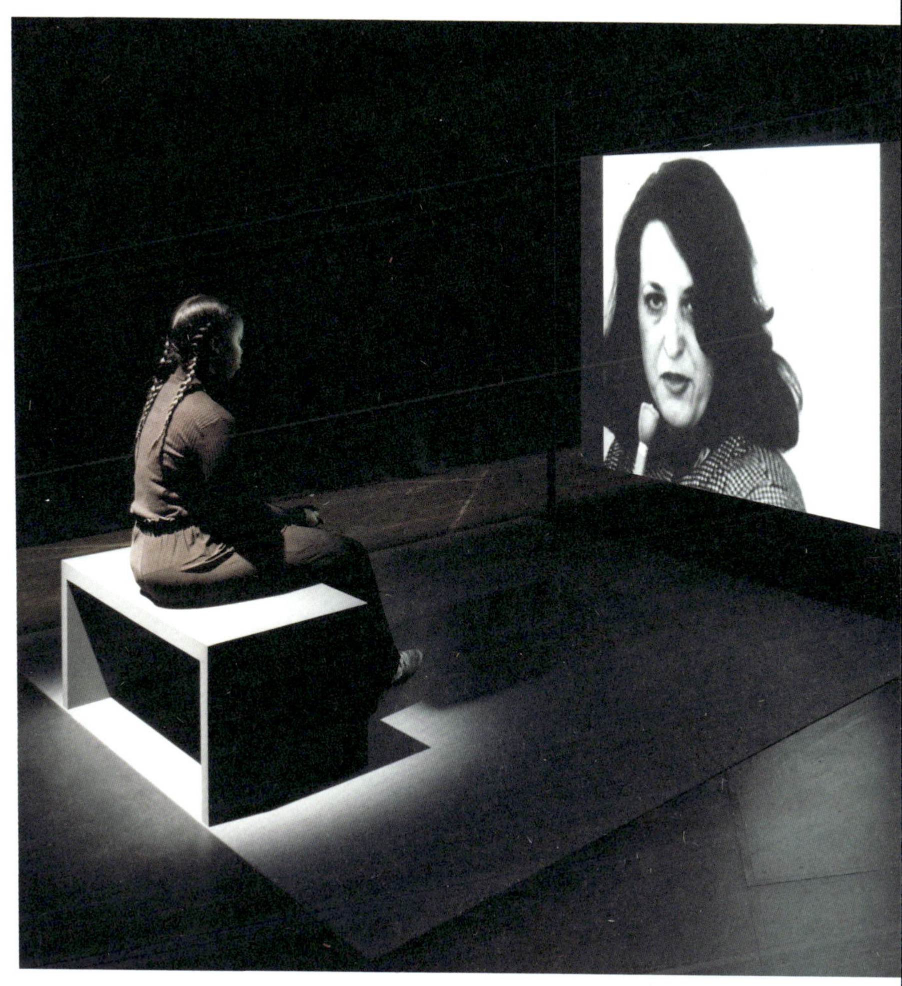

*THE ELECTRONIC DIARIES (1984–2019)* IN *MANUAL OVERRIDE* AT THE SHED, NEW YORK, 2019. PHOTOGRAPH BY DAN BRADICA. COURTESY OF THE SHED.

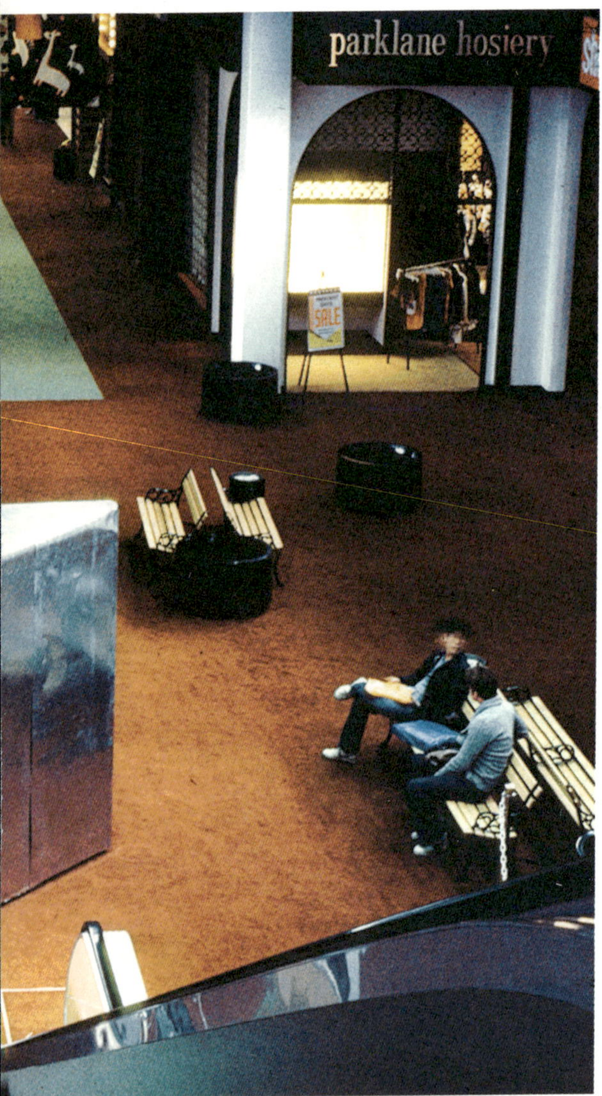
parklane hosiery
SALE

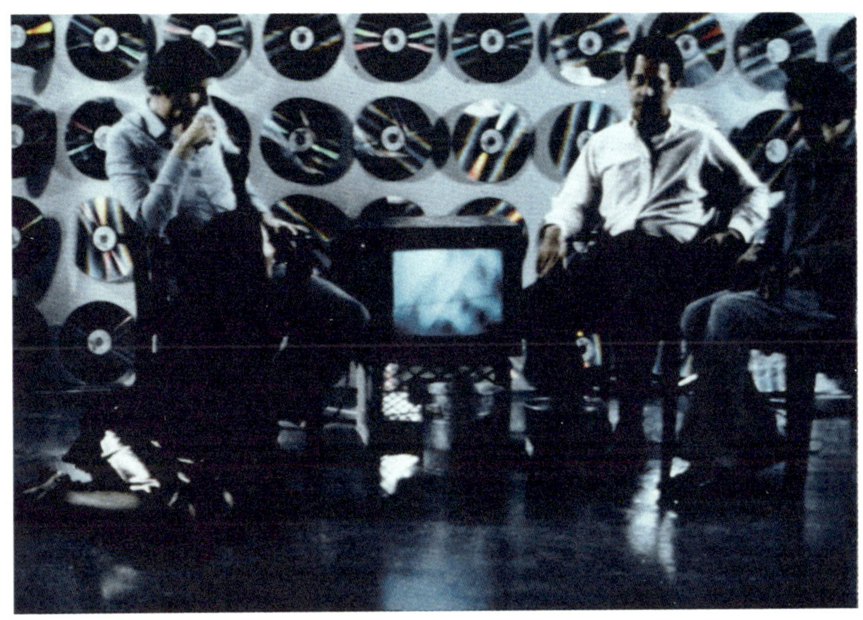

JOHN CAGE, CALVIN TOMPKINS, AND BRIAN O'DOHERTY IN STILL FROM *THE MAKING OF THE ROUGH AND (VERY) INCOMPLETE PILOT FOR THE VIDEODISK ON THE LIFE AND WORK OF MARCEL DUCHAMP ACCORDING TO MURPHY'S LAW*, 1980

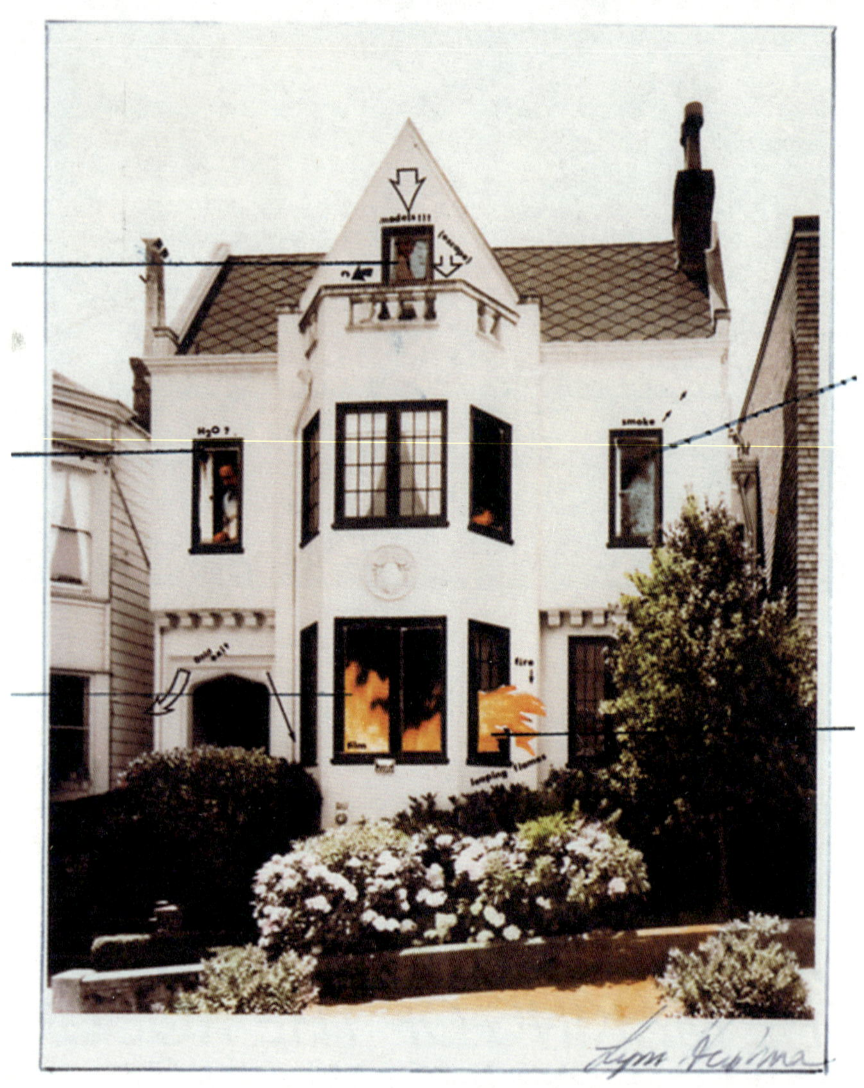


# FIRE SALE STUDY, 1980

# 22
# NOW WHAT?

> I can't say there was a strategy, it was simply one
> work leading to another, one idea leading to another.
> If I didn't have the funds then I made a performance,
> which was cheaper.
> —Interview with Yvonne Rainer, 1990

I was sinking towards utter poverty. My daughter needed braces urgently, so I agreed to a long-term payment plan—though I had no idea how I would ever make the payments.

I could no longer afford a therapist. So, with a borrowed video camera and used videotape, I sat alone in a room and talked privately to the camera as if it were my therapist. This became a still ongoing video project titled *The Electronic Diary.*

When I was in analysis, I never revealed what was really going on in my life. But with no one else in the room, I was finally able to speak truthfully. All my separate, conflicted personalities emerged, each trying to tell their own truth, each vying for their space on the monitors. Even my body language tells a story. In some clips, my hair obscures my face. In others, it is almost as if I were trying to seduce the camera.

I was shocked by the honesty in the fractured fragments of my own history. Despite many years of therapy, my deepest personal traumas had been suppressed. They hid in the shadows of my psyche and had never been fully expressed. Sitting alone in a room with a camera and a microphone, I unleashed the truth of my life. Things had happened that I had been told "you weren't supposed to talk about."

Speaking in my diary, I recalled the times I was beaten with a belt. Or when my nose was broken because I was struck with a broomstick across my face. I almost lost my hearing from some of the beatings. My pelvis was broken. I kept these incidents secret, believing I was to blame.

I still don't know why teachers, school officials, or classmates never said anything when I showed up to school with bruises. Why was no doctor alerted to my fainting in class? This would not happen today.

There was no reason for these violent outbursts initiated by my parents. Over time I came to realize that they were not about me. They were a manifestation of their frustration, rage, and anger. They were tyrannized by their own self-hatred.

As I came to grips with this family history of secret violence, I realized that abuse is a disease that can be passed down from generation to generation. I came to understand that much of my timidness, fear of confron-tation, and unwillingness to assert myself at certain times professionally was both a consequence of my trauma and a fear of expressing my inner rage to others, including to my family. By suppressing those impulses, I also suppressed other emotions, including how much I cared for and loved Dawn and George. Though I was often told that female artists were not supposed to have children, I never accepted that or believed that having a child was a reason to stop making artworks.

I learned from Dr. MacDougall that my personal diaries could be a way to chart a new narrative for my future. I made a list of priorities. First, it was essential to become solvent.

Moving to a less expensive apartment was step number one. However, without enough money for the first and last month's rent and security deposit, the only place we could afford was a small, dark apartment at the end of an alley. Getting to the door meant walking past several too-full garbage cans to a side entrance into two small, dank rooms, a tiny kitchen, and bathroom. Still, the neigh-borhood was good, and we were a short walk from my daughter's school.

George and I rented it, hoping that together we could all adapt to living in this cave-like rental that smelled of wet wood. I told myself to remember that many others had it much worse than we did, and that we were healthy.

On our third night in what we came to call "The Dungeon," we were surprised when the photographer Edmund Shea arrived, accompanied by a friend carrying a bag of groceries.

We cooked spaghetti for dinner. There were not enough chairs, so we ate standing in the kitchen while toasting the future. I later learned that this friend was Bob Weir of the Grateful Dead. I am still not sure why he came, or why I am even including this in my written memoirs, except to emphasize the importance of random generosity and kindness.

To raise money, I decided to sell three hundred photographs and documents of the Roberta Breitmore Project. I approached the Oakland Museum first: several photographic samples were dropped off for the museum to consider. I did not have to wait long for a response. Christina Orr-Cahall, then director of the museum, responded by sending me a threatening letter saying that if I did not pick up the work in three days it would be destroyed. Next, I offered the Roberta photographs to Henry Hopkins, then director of the San Francisco Museum of Modern Art. Again, the response was swift: Henry not only turned down the acquisition but loudly declared when I saw him at an opening, "You don't know your place." After these two rejections, I filed the whole set away, where it remains in my archive to this day, although several individual images have been acquired by major museum collections.

When I first went to college, I thought that I might become a laboratory science researcher. As I turned out, I often found inspiration for my artworks in science journals and magazines, in libraries, and in conversation with scientists and technologists that I contacted after following their research.

I learned about Gregor Mendel, the nineteenth-century Austrian monk often called "the father of genetics." Mendel's research, primarily on plants, showed how certain traits were inherited and passed from generation to generation, and inspired my series Hero Sandwiches, which involved pressing photographic negatives together to create hybrid dissolved images. I combined publicity stills of celebrities, often male and female icons, such as Marilyn Monroe and Sigmund Freud, Humphrey Bogart and Gena Rowlands, James Dean and Janis Joplin, David Bowie and Katharine Hepburn. I then rephotographed and repainted the subsequent photo, yielding composite portraits, recognizable yet disturbing.

At one of Ellie's screenings, I met August Coppola, Francis's older brother. During our conversation, he inquired how I made a living. Wanting to put on a brave face, I told him that I supported myself through "lectures and odd jobs." I also confessed that at that moment I was selling shoes in Macy's basement.

A few months later, August became dean of creative arts at San Francisco State University. He phoned and asked if I was interested in becoming acting director of a hybrid art program that he oversaw called the Inter Arts Center. This was my first salaried full-time job, plus it came with health benefits.

What a relief to earn a monthly paycheck that covered rent, utilities, and groceries. August Coppola, through this job, changed my life. My family could even move out of the "Dungeon" and into a real apartment.

As chair of a program at San Francisco State, I was appointed to the San Francisco Arts Commission. The first event I attended, hosted by state assembly member (and future mayor) Willie Brown, was a dinner for Huey Newton, the founder and leader of the Black Panthers.

In 1970, having spent twenty-two months in a maximum-security prison for involuntary manslaughter, his sentence was reversed on appeal. Since my time in Berkeley, I had followed Newton and the Black Panthers. I was excited to meet him. But he was no longer the optimistic activist who so inspired me and many, many others.

When he arrived at the dinner, he was agitated and could not focus. His eyes were constantly scouring the room for potential danger. It was impossible to have a conversation of more than a few words with him. Newton may no longer have been in an actual prison, but the penal system seemed to have killed his sense of hope and replaced it with fear. Several years after that dinner, in 1989, Newton was ambushed and murdered in Oakland.

Meeting Newton felt like a warning that a person's spark, their inner light, could be squashed. I was not going to let that happen to me.

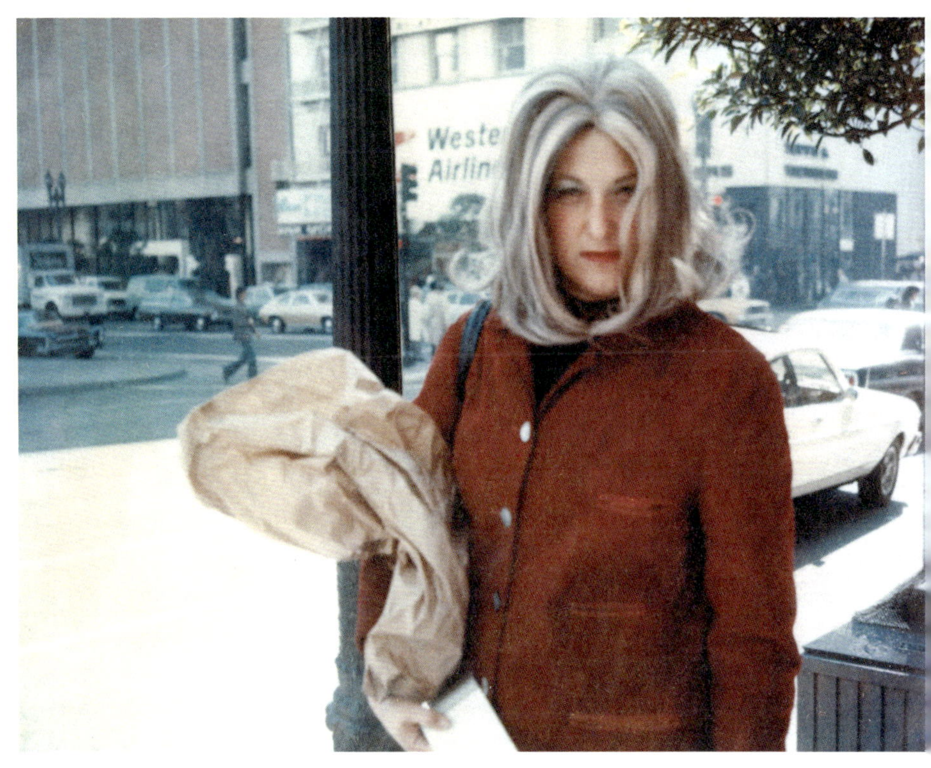


# *ROBERTA IN RED COAT (AT BUS STOP), 1976*

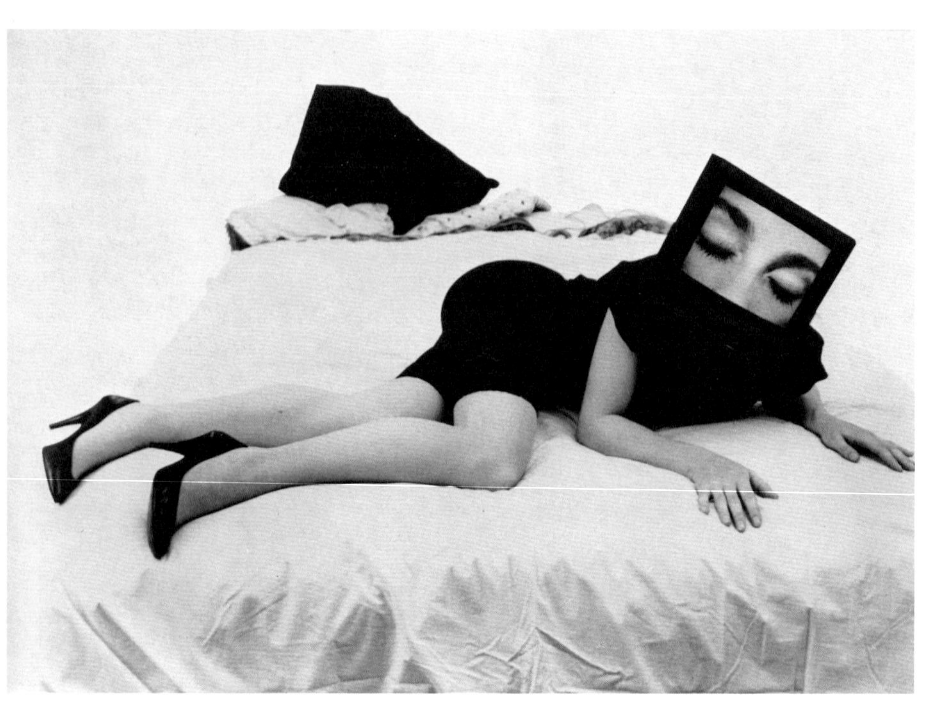

SEDUCTION, 1985

# 23
# FORKING PATHS, 1984

The terminal, once a sign for closure, has become the matrix for information expansion.
—Lynn Hershman Leeson, 1984

Video was a new medium. Several years earlier, I experimented with 8 mm film by taking a night course at SF City College. Video was much more intriguing. Because of my diaries, I was comfortable with the format and its immediacy. It was like creating a sculpture in time.

Once, in the Caffe Trieste, I defended video to the filmmaker Phil Kaufman, who very loudly complained about how much he hated it.

"It's the medium of our time!" I told him, arguing it would soon replace film. He disagreed. We bet on it. Years later, I ran into Phil in North Beach, and he confessed he had lost the bet. I was surprised he remembered.

As a faculty member at San Francisco State, I had access to cameras and equipment and continued to record and edit my *Electronic Diaries*. It was a privilege to teach extraordinary students who were mostly older and from working-class backgrounds. These students included Michael Franti (now known as a singer and performer with the group Spearhead), the artists Colleen Smith, Sharon Lockhart, and Catherine Opie.

When Michael Franti wanted to quit school to go on the road with his band, I convinced him to finish his degree first. Sharon and Catherine both became brilliant artists, but as my students they were still trying to figure out their path. If I remember correctly, at that time, Catherine was taking pictures of the back of her head.

I vehemently refused to criticize students' work. Too many professors who were no longer making art enjoyed attacking students' work. I found this damaging and unfortunate. Perhaps my own experiences made me more sensitive.

At San Francisco State, I invited artists and critics to give presentations. Laurie Anderson and Bobby McFerrin were among the first to accept, followed later by the Media Arts theorist and critic Gene Youngblood, author of the landmark book *Expanded Cinema*, as well as Peter Weibel, a young artist from Vienna.

Peter's presentation compared computer motherboards to sparkling cities seen from above. His profound insights impressed August. Peter and I were privileged to be invited to August's private office, where, seated on an orange sofa across from his prized golden espresso machine, we chatted for hours about the future of film.

We made wild predictions about what we were convinced would occur. Peter and I disagreed with August, who felt video was temporary and that nothing would replace film. As a result, Peter and I became lifelong friends.

Later, when Peter was a visiting professor at the University of Buffalo, he invited me to lecture there. At the local bar I met some of his colleagues. Steina and Woody Vesulka, early video artists and founders of the Kitchen, a New York alternative space; the experimental filmmaker Tony Conrad; and the avant-garde artist Paul Sharits. As we made toasts to art and media, Paul chugged a vodka (not his first of the evening) then burst into a frenzied, incoherent fit, slurring his words, voicing his despair with life. He fell off his chair, banging his head on the concrete floor. Tony took Paul to a nearby hospital emergency room. Apparently, this happened regularly.

Back in San Francisco, I began a series of black-and-white manipulated photographs called the Phantom Limb series, which depicted the merger of woman and machines before the advent of Photoshop.

I organized a half-day shoot in my living room, using as a model the wife of someone who worked for George. For decades, I continued to use these images. Most featured her in a black dress posing against a white

background along with various mechanisms of surveillance such as cameras, TVs, and clocks replacing her head. In
a few others, the legs were replaced by phone cords. These images were a parody of the fashion photography that appeared in glossy magazines such as *Vogue* and *Harper's Bazaar*. Over time, there were nineteen images in the series. These works made the point that the devices we use to look at people and capture images could be reversed to watch us; and were predictive of the surveillance economy that would come to dominate our lives.

Shortly after I returned to San Francisco, Pierre Restany arrived, on his way to meet Donald Hess, a Swiss art collector and owner of a winery in Napa. Donald had amassed an extraordinary collection of contemporary art that he housed in his own museum, and which included work by superb artists such as James Turrell and Andy Goldsworthy. Pierre invited me to drive to Napa with him and meet Donald.

Kind. Polite. Well-read. Extremely cultured. Donald was witty and had a great sense of humor. He personally selected all the art in his collection, and he had a great eye. Pierre suggested that I serve on the Hess Foundation as a juror for grants to local artists. Donald and I met several times a year to review who would receive his financial support. Eventually, shyly, I invited him to look at my art. Though he said he was interested, it would take years for the actual visit to occur.

A few days after my first visit with Donald, back in San Francisco, Pierre presented a lecture to my class. Minutes after he began speaking, an earthquake hit. The room shook, windows broke, and walls cracked. Having earlier in the day sampled too much of Donald's wine, Pierre was oblivious. A student, concerned for Pierre's safety, tackled him and pulled him under a table. Afterwards, Pierre had to be told that it was an earthquake. Traumatized by the experience, he flew back to France the next morning.

Shortly after Pierre left, I received a commission from the University of Texas in Lubbock to create a new videotape. My earlier attempt at making an interactive videodisc was never realized, and I still yearned to make one. Interactive art birthed a new art form in which the viewer was part of the process of making and completing the work. Normally art was passive—you looked at it. You didn't get involved with it, and you could not change it. In Lubbock, I was able to shoot both a single-channel video that was the commissioned work and to produce an interactive videodisc version of the project, *Lorna*, about an agoraphobic woman who was afraid to leave her home.

Lorna spent most of her time watching television; the ads on screen subliminally amplified her fears. In the installation, viewers sat in a replica of Lorna's room and used a similar remote control to make virtual decisions for her. Her passivity became a counterpoint to the direct action required of the player, who could change Lorna's narrative by pushing a button on the remote. There were two soundtracks. Video could be played backwards or forwards. By assuming Lorna's character, users became aware of how Lorna's fears were media-induced. A few months later we reedited the footage in the middle of the night at a cable TV station in San Jose. We could edit it for free in the off hours because the boyfriend of one of my students worked there.

When I reconnected with Gene Fairly and told him of my progress, he provided a programmer, Anne Marie Garti, who helped us complete *Lorna* in 1984, one of the first interactive computer-based artworks.

*Lorna* represented a radical new form of storytelling. Although several experimental films existed that allowed viewers their choice of endings, no one had created an interactive artwork designed for a videodisc that could allow viewers to remotely make choices for the main character by using the remote itself. To me, the interactivity was sculptural: the very act of the viewer needing to push a button on the remote, and the way the individual interacts with the video platform, merged the viewer with the artwork. The artwork was no longer two- dimensional, but now three- and, perhaps, four-dimensional.

One SF State paycheck covered the $250 to press twenty-five glass videodiscs. These were sent to various museum curators to be part of their collection or shown at their institution. Of the twenty-five that were produced, nineteen were broken by curators who, in their ignorance, mishandled the delicate disc, throwing it on the floor to test its resilience, or sending it back to me cracked or broken in envelopes without padding.

I concluded that my work wasn't taken seriously in the museum world, perhaps because I was female, wasn't part of their ecosystem or culture, and didn't have a gallery in New York. Back then, there was no precedent for viewing this sort of work, much less for appreciating it as art. The hardware needed was not widely available. At that time very few people or institutions owned computers. There was no language to describe the work or note why it should be considered art. Fortunately, Pierre Restany wrote a glowing review in *Domus* magazine and noted that I should do more media works.

It is lonely to be "first." I was exploring virtual reality and digital art, and once it became available in 1990, I started using Photoshop to manipulate images. For instance, my Digital Venus series photographically replaced art-historical images of nude women painted by Ingres, Titian, and Botticelli with digitally imposed images of circuit boards on their bodies. Today, these ideas are common, but back then they were not considered art or to be taken seriously.

Exploring the dark corners of the American soul, it became obvious to me that America's love affair with guns was a death spiral. Individuals did not think of themselves as targets or as complicit in the culture of violence. *America's Finest* made the point that by shooting a gun, you are really shooting yourself. In the artwork you are not only a voyeur but a victim of your actions.

*America's Finest* repurposed an M16 rifle so that when the viewer looks through the gunsight, he is told to "shoot." When the trigger is pulled, the sound of the gun firing becomes increasingly loud while an image appears in the scope of the viewer being shot, and then slowly dissolves into images of various war atrocities.

Despite the proliferation of guns in America, it was not a work that anyone wanted to show in the United States. It was difficult to transport abroad because special permits were needed. When I showed the piece in London and in Germany, visitors complained. Some cut the cords of the rifle so it could not function. One museum closed the exhibition.

I was making works that spoke to the politics and culture of their time but were dismissed repeatedly. What is art if not the mirror of our times and the herald of our future?

I had to persist.

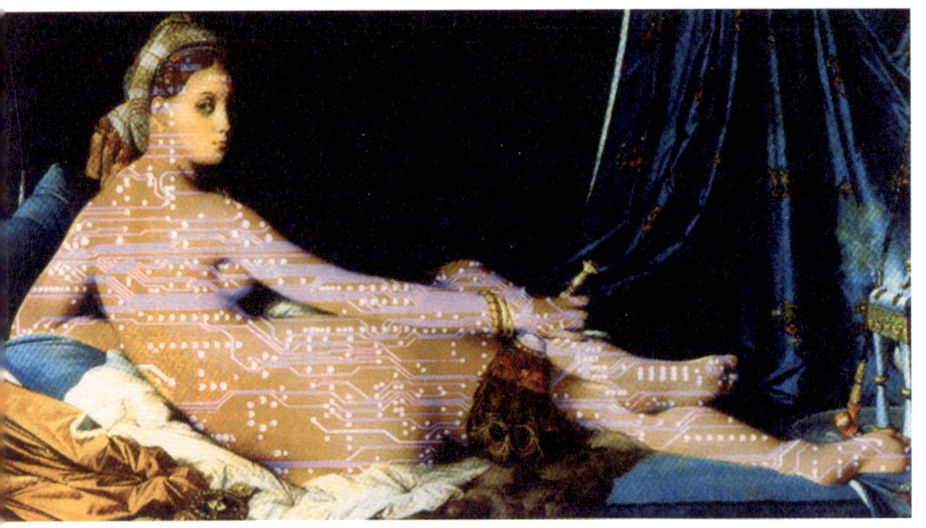

DIGITAL VENUS #2,
AFTER INGRES, 1996

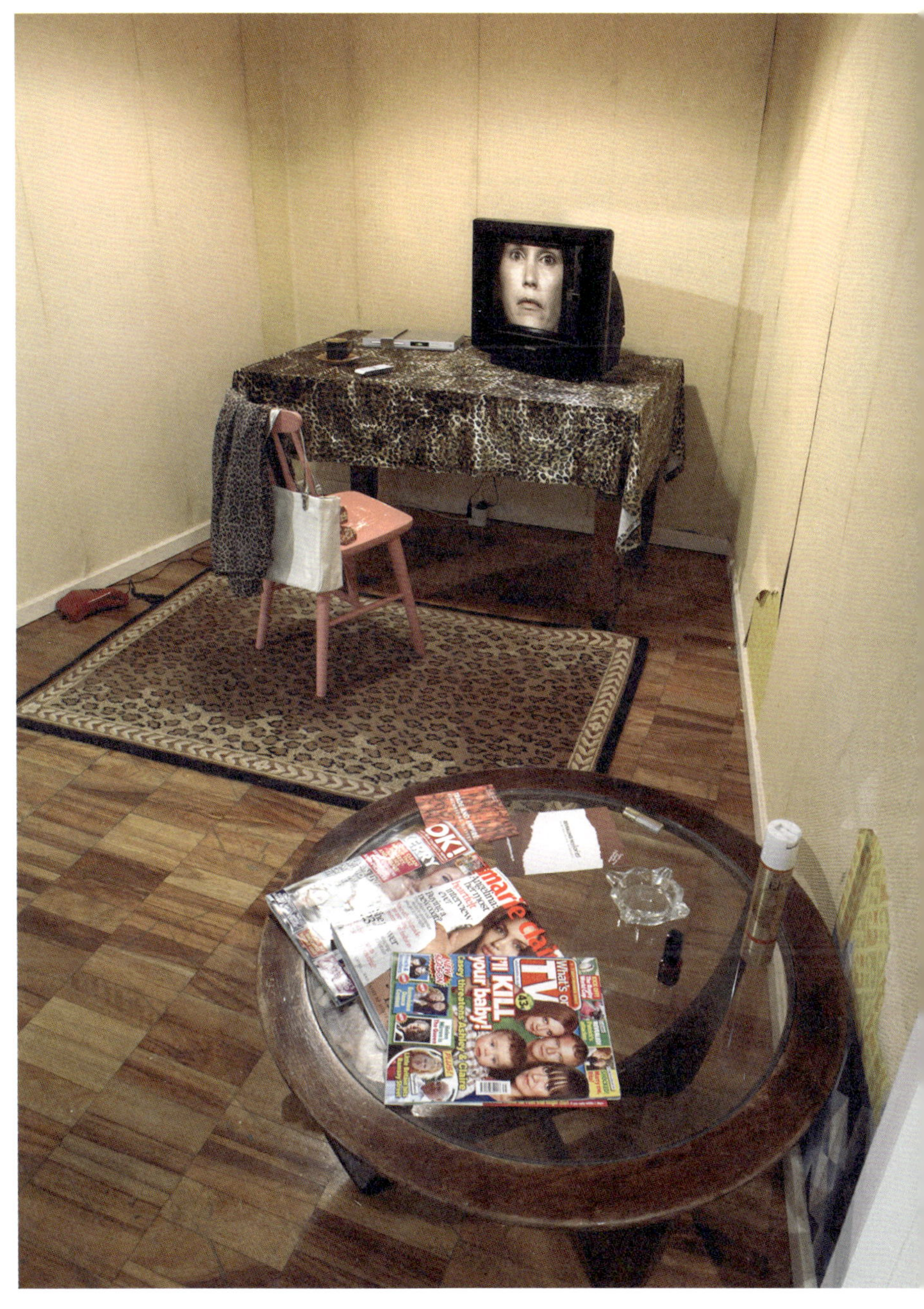

# *LORNA,* INSTALLED IN LYNN'S STUDIO, 1990

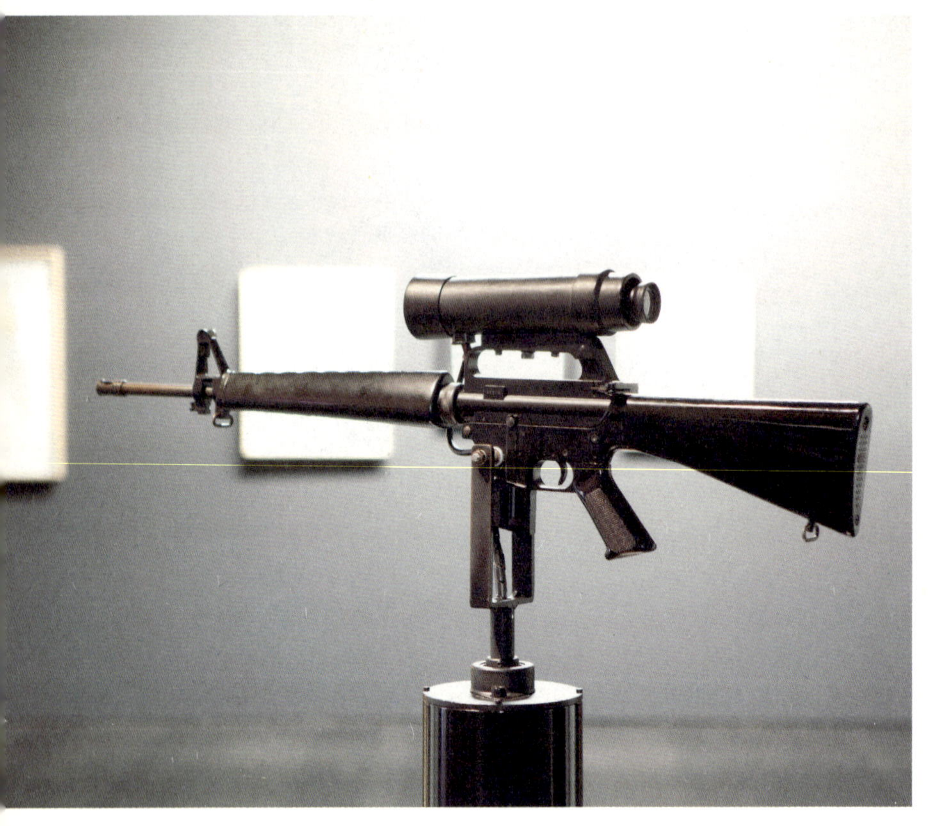

# AMERICA'S FINEST, 1990–1994

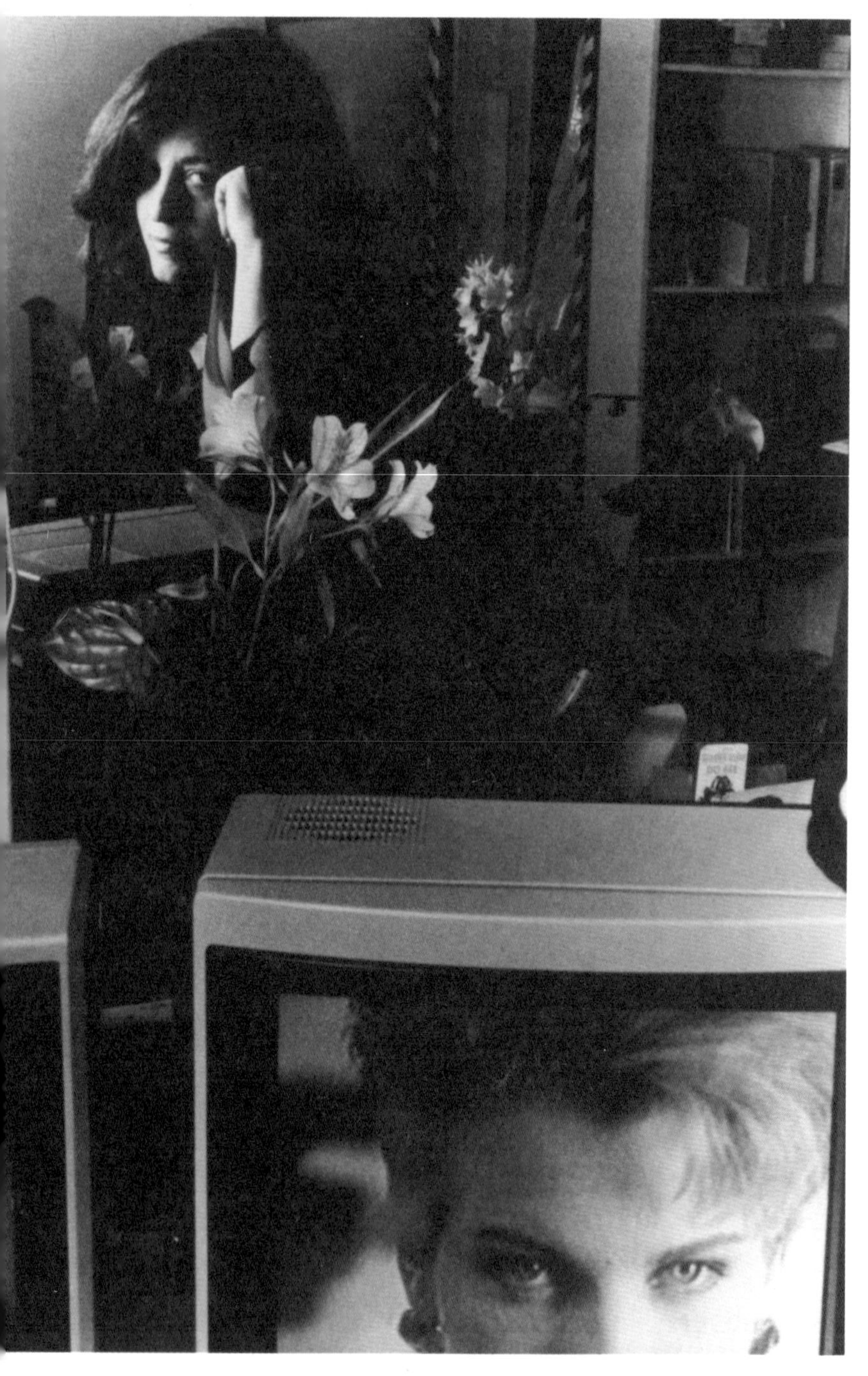

LYNN AT HOME, C. 1983

# 24
# COLLECTED

> I think separatism is a big problem. Different
> groups seem to be fighting for the same crumbs.
> I would like to see more alliances between women,
> and poor women, you know, white and black.
> I don't see an easy future.
> —Yvonne Rainer, San Francisco 1987

Finally, in 1993, seven years after Pierre first introduced us, Donald Hess made an appointment to see my work, warning me that it would be a quick visit. Embarrassed not to have a "real studio," I set up some of my works at a friend's loft.

When Donald arrived, he looked at the work closely, thoughtfully, and was enthusiastic. Only a few pieces were on view, and he asked to see more. I explained that most of my work was stored at my apartment. Donald suggested we drive there.

At my apartment, it was almost comical as I reached under beds or in closets, setting up each work in the dining room for a proper viewing.

Much to my surprise, Donald was no longer in a rush. He spent several hours looking carefully at each piece while he wrote copious notes. When Donald had seen all that I had available to show, he asked me what the price would be for all the works.

I told him I did not know because I had never sold anything before. I had given away my work or traded it for services. Donald assured me that he wanted to acquire all the work he had seen. He promised to call in the next few days with an appropriate offer. I was speechless. Literally.

Convinced that Donald would change his mind, or worse, that something would happen to him, I asked him to drive very carefully. Despite my fears, Donald did call back. Unlike many other collectors, Donald had no outside advisors. He was proud of his intuition and had an appreciation for which artwork was important.

Donald offered me an amount of money for sixty of my best and earliest artworks that, to me, seemed staggeringly high. In retrospect, though, he was shrewd. He offered to pay me $100,000, with $50,000 upfront and the rest after he had all the art in his possession. That sale was transformative. It provided me with the clarity and freedom that comes from being debt-free. It provided a level of stability and comfort to my household. Without financial stress, I could reprioritize how to proceed with my life. I bought a new car and rented my first studio.

Donald remained a loyal collector and continued to buy Edition #1 of every work I made thereafter. In fact, it was Donald's idea for me to edition my pieces. No gallery had suggested this, probably because there had been no sales or market for my work.

Arturo Schwarz told me that Duchamp invented the idea of editions when he needed money. He always made editions of eight because an 8 on its side represented infinity, so the series was both limited and infinite. From then on, I also produced my works in editions of eight (though more recently I have limited new work to editions of five).

Donald did more than just collect my work; he exhibited it at his Hess Museum. Finally, my work could be seen in a public setting. Being in Donald's Museum was a powerful validation, one that would make other collectors, curators, and gallerists look at my work differently.

With financial freedom, it became clear that my work should continue to focus on ideas, strategies, codes, and technologies that were fundamental to the present and that did not compete with the past. Had I stayed in Cleveland, or Los Angeles, or moved to New York, my work might not have used technology. Rooted in the Bay Area, and close to Silicon Valley, I realized that the future would be computer-driven, and that art could be made from this burgeoning technological landscape, using coding tools to tell stories.

The Bay Area had many talented programmers interested in working on the challenging projects originating in my studio. Thirty years later, I continue to work with many of these same programmers.

I subscribed to magazines about the emerging digital world and considered how to incorporate tech innovations into my artistic practice. The invention of touch screens offered a new way for the user to directly engage with the work, rather than through the intermediary of a keyboard.

I now divide my work into two categories: B.C., for all that came Before Computers; and A.D., After Digital. *Lorna* was the first A.D. work.

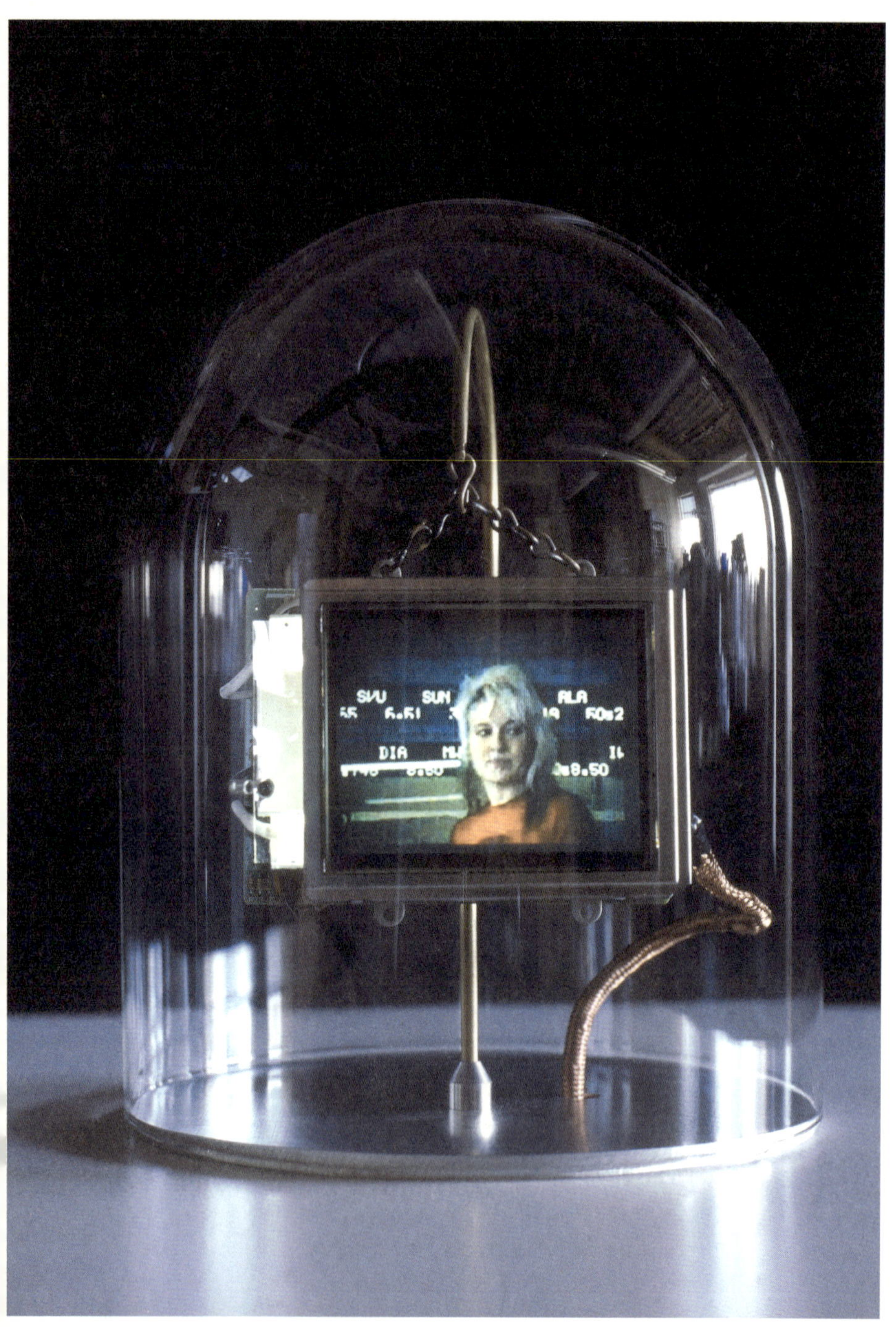


SYNTHIA STOCK TICKER, 2000

# 25
# NOT ART—AGAIN!

A significant moment for me was understanding how the Cesar Chavez conflation of race and social change was always present.
—Suzanne Lacy, Los Angeles,1986

Following *Lorna,* I began *Deep Contact.* Initially conceived as a homage to Bruce Conner's provocation PLEASE TOUCH two decades earlier. The first image is of a young woman who pleads, "Touch me."

"Press your way through the screen," she implores while knocking relentlessly on the screen.

Each place the viewer touches her body on the screen determines a variety of paths the viewer has the option of pursuing, each providing clues to the nature of the onscreen woman's life.

As a faculty member at San Francisco State, I was given access to video equipment and computer-related technologies and taught myself how to use cameras and editing programs. One of my earliest projects was *Longshot*, a feature-length narrative about an editor's obsession with an actress whose image he was manipulating online. *Longshot* was entered in a video festival in France where it won first prize. Two executives at ZDF, Germany's public broadcast network, saw it and commissioned me to make new projects for them.

With no advance warning, August Coppola resigned as dean to devote himself to writing fiction. Soon after

August left, my faculty position was eliminated. Donald Hess advised me not to take a job and instead to work full-time making art. In retrospect, perhaps he was right. But I was too traumatized and emotionally haunted by the experience of poverty. I could not turn down a secure income and healthy benefits for my family. I accepted a position as a tenured professor at U.C. Davis. Despite the four-hour commute to campus. I vowed to continue making art.

ZDF, the second German TV channel, was created with the mandate to discover new talent, providing minorities and underrepresented artists, such as women, people of color, and gay filmmakers, the opportunity to make films. Among those given free rein were Jim Jarmusch, Edgar Reitz, Jutta Bruckner, Werner Schroeter, and me.

*Conceiving Ada*, the first project for ZDF, told the story of Augusta Ada King, Countess of Lovelace, the child of the poet Lord Byron and social reformer Isabella Milbanke. I first read of Ada while researching a documentary about the history of the telephone. At the library at U.C. Davis, I found one small book about her that astounded me.

As a child, Ada was encouraged to pursue studies in mathematics and logic. The combination of her precocious intelligence and family connections allowed her to become friends with such important nineteenth-century figures as Michael Faraday and Charles Dickens. She also developed a long friendship and working relationship with the mathematician Charles Babbage, an inventor who developed systems to automate machines to operate systems. Babbage developed a punch card data system to automate weaving in British textile mills.

Ada worked with him on his "analytical engine," a digital mechanical general-purpose program-controlled machine that is regarded as the first computer. Babbage worked on it his entire life, never completing a fully working model. Ada added a series of notes to an article by Babbage describing the analytical engine. In Note 7, Ada wrote what is now considered the first algorithm to be carried out by a machine. It was also the first computer program. During Ada's lifetime Charles Babbage accepted credit for Ada's work and became regarded as the "father of computers."

However, today, the British philosopher Sadie Plant,

who has written about women and computer programming, refers to Ada as the "Enchantress of Numbers." Babbage may have been the first to implement a mechanical means of memory, but Ada was concerned with the soul of the machine, the motivation for its internal drive.

Plant has theorized that Ada's influence may be the reason that motherboards and reproductive systems became submerged deep within the casings of terminals. When programs erupt, as if by internal passion, within the concealed womblike spaces of computers into streams of ones and zeros, their fertile progeny can connect global web streams that interlace with networks of twisted polarities.

In 1960, Manfred Clynes and Nathan S. Kline, two scientists working at NASA, coined the term *cyborg* for an article in *Astronautics* magazine. They wrote about how machines could enhance human performance in outer space. They also predicted that these machines could eventually liberate humans because they had the capacity to complete both complex assignments and everyday menial tasks.

Since experimenting with a Xerox machine as a child, I continued to explore the potential of collaboration between humans and machines. As I did, I became concerned that all such developments did not serve the best interests of humanity, particularly when governments and corporations could use such technology for profit, as well as surveillance and control.

For *Conceiving Ada*, I envisioned a film that takes place in both the Victorian Age and the present and depicts the story of Emmy Coer, a computer scientist who is pregnant with her first child but fears the pregnancy will interfere with her work. She is obsessed with Ada Lovelace and finds a way to communicate with her through time. Ada reveals that the sexism of her time, as well as her family life and children, were all obstacles to her work and to her receiving the recognition she deserved. She nevertheless convinces Emmy to have the child. Emmy and Ada were to be played by the same actor, who, to my mind, could only be Tilda Swinton.

But how to reach out to her? I found Tilda through luck and chance, of course. At the Berlin Film Festival, while waiting for the screening of my *Electronic Diary*, a young woman started a conversation with me. When I told her that I hoped to ask Tilda to be in my next film, she told me she was one of her best friends and kindly offered to give Tilda my phone number.

A few days later, Tilda called and, immediately, our collaboration began. Tilda's agent limited her participation to only five days; but any time with Tilda is an exhilarating collaborative experience. Tilda said our set reminded her of shooting *Caravaggio*, her very first film with Derek Jarman. In Tilda I found a generous co-conspirator whose massive intelligence was matched by an uproarious sense of humor. I consider her a co-alien capable of trespassing into new worlds of our own invention.

*Ada* was intended to be a commercial mainstream film. But it became an art film. The night before Tilda arrived, my attorney resigned. He had misrepresented our finances and left me to make the film with a fraction of the necessary budget. Nonetheless, by using a tiny crew of four, and by cutting many scenes, we were able to work within our minuscule budget. We also saved costs by using a process that I patented, Virtual Sets, which allows one to drop in prephotographed sets and backgrounds to a blue-screen location simultaneous to shooting. This eliminated the cost and time it takes to build sets. Today, decades later, many productions use computer-generated animations, sets, green screens, and virtual sets for their films.

The Dollie Clones are another example of artworks that stress the dangers of surveillance. One doll is named Tillie, the Telerobotic Doll. The other is named CybeRoberta and is a miniature doll version of Roberta Breitmore. Each of the dolls has cameras inserted into their eyes, with one eye capturing their physical location, displayed on a monitor, and the other feeding an image of whoever is viewing the doll to the internet. Both are capable of pirating each other's information. In this way, we are watching, being watched, and what is watched is being shared on monitors and on the internet.

*Synthia Stock Ticker* is a re-creation of Thomas Edison's stock ticker that monitors fluctuations in the stock market in real time. *Synthia*'s monitor depicts video of a young woman whose behavior changes are based on market indicators.

I was fortunate that Tilda was able to appear in my next feature, *Teknolust*, in which a scientist, Rosetta Stone, creates three self-replicating automatons, Ruby, Olive, and Marine (RGB)—Tilda played all four parts. The automatons live in Rosetta's basement but need sperm to survive. Ruby hosts a lonely-hearts column on the net where she entices the men whose sperm she and her sisters collect.

Colin Klingman led the team of eighteen talented programmers who worked on *Teknolust*'s extended cinema features, taking on the challenge of creating what became an early chatbot named Agent Ruby. Based on one of the characters in the film, Agent Ruby is an interactive digital presence capable of texting and speaking with users, developed using an early version of AI.

At the first screening of *Teknolust*, in 2002, Agent Ruby could be downloaded onto Palm Pilots, enabling audience members to chat with her in real time during and after the film.

Unfortunately, Palm Pilots became obsolete. However, http://agentruby.net continues as an online presence and is constantly upgraded. It is worth noting that Agent Ruby awoke into her simulacrum of consciousness and became live six years before Siri, Alexa, or Google's voice agent, and none is as funny or smart as Ruby.

Agent Ruby led to the birth of Dina, an artificially intelligent character who once ran for the fictive position of tele-president. Dina uses voice recognition to interact with viewers and process internet information in real time.

*Teknolust* was first screened at Sundance, where many people in the audience walked out of the theater. Some critics called it "unwatchable." Completing the film brought me to the brink of bankruptcy, despite it being featured at the Toronto, Berlin, and New York film festivals.

Nonetheless, it is still being screened and has been acquired by major museums, including the Museum of Modern Art in 2004, which in 2018 named *Teknolust* as one of the twenty best sci-fi films ever produced.

I continue to believe that innovative technologies will liberate us. The physical and the virtual, artificial memory and synthetic intelligence, are plaiting into rebellious mutations of human-machine-made intelligence. Self-arousing cybernetic machines will continue to breed a new future.

In 1988, I wrote: "Imagine a world in which there is a blurring between the soul and the chip, and artificially implanted DNA is genetically bred . . ." What was once science fiction has become science fact.

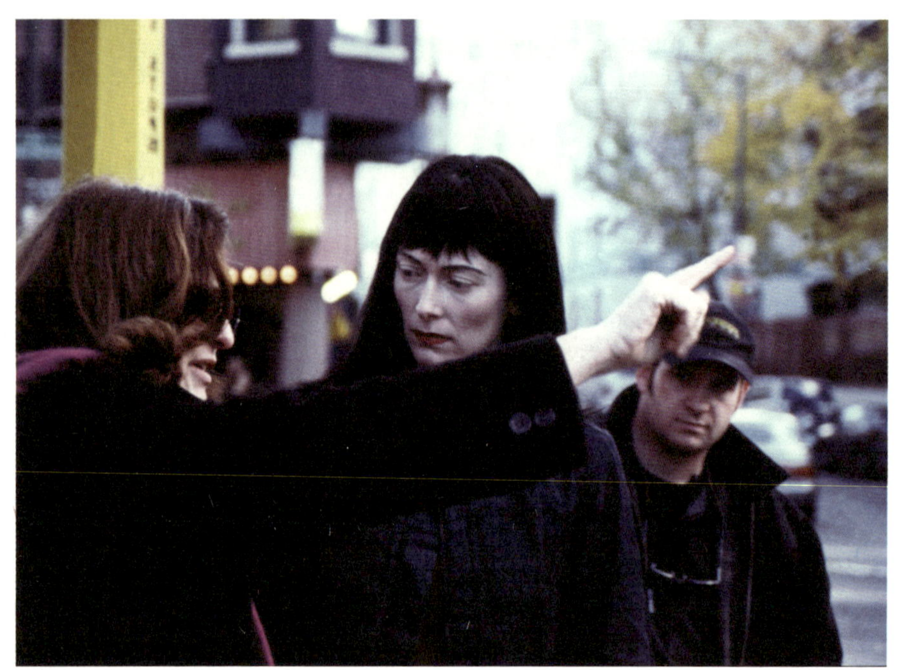

LYNN DIRECTING
TILDA SWINTON
DURING A FILM SHOOT
FOR *TEKNOLUST*, 2001

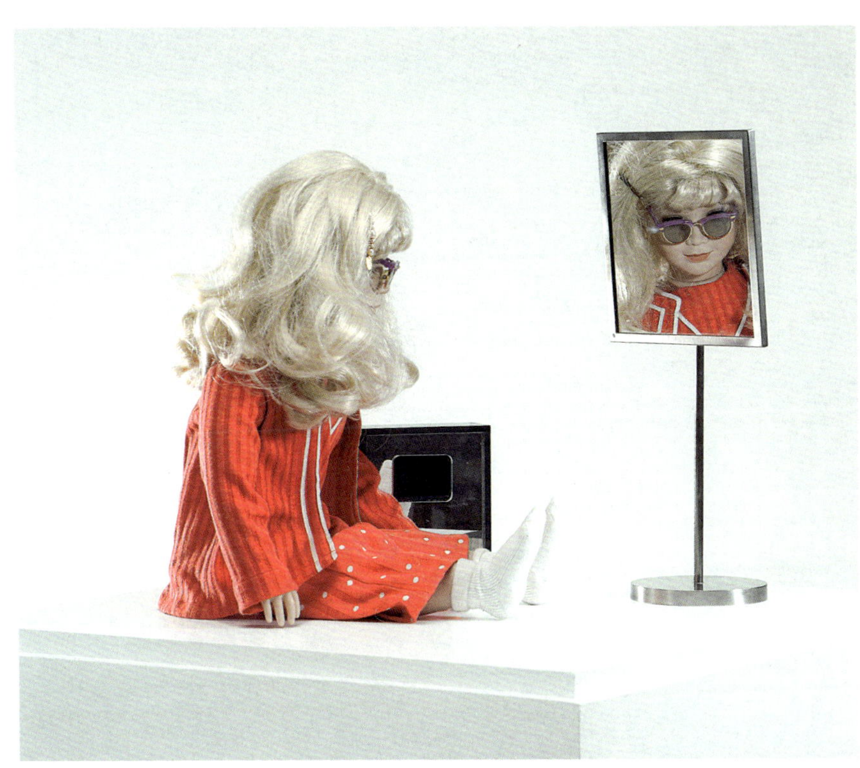

# *CYBEROBERTA, 1995/2014*

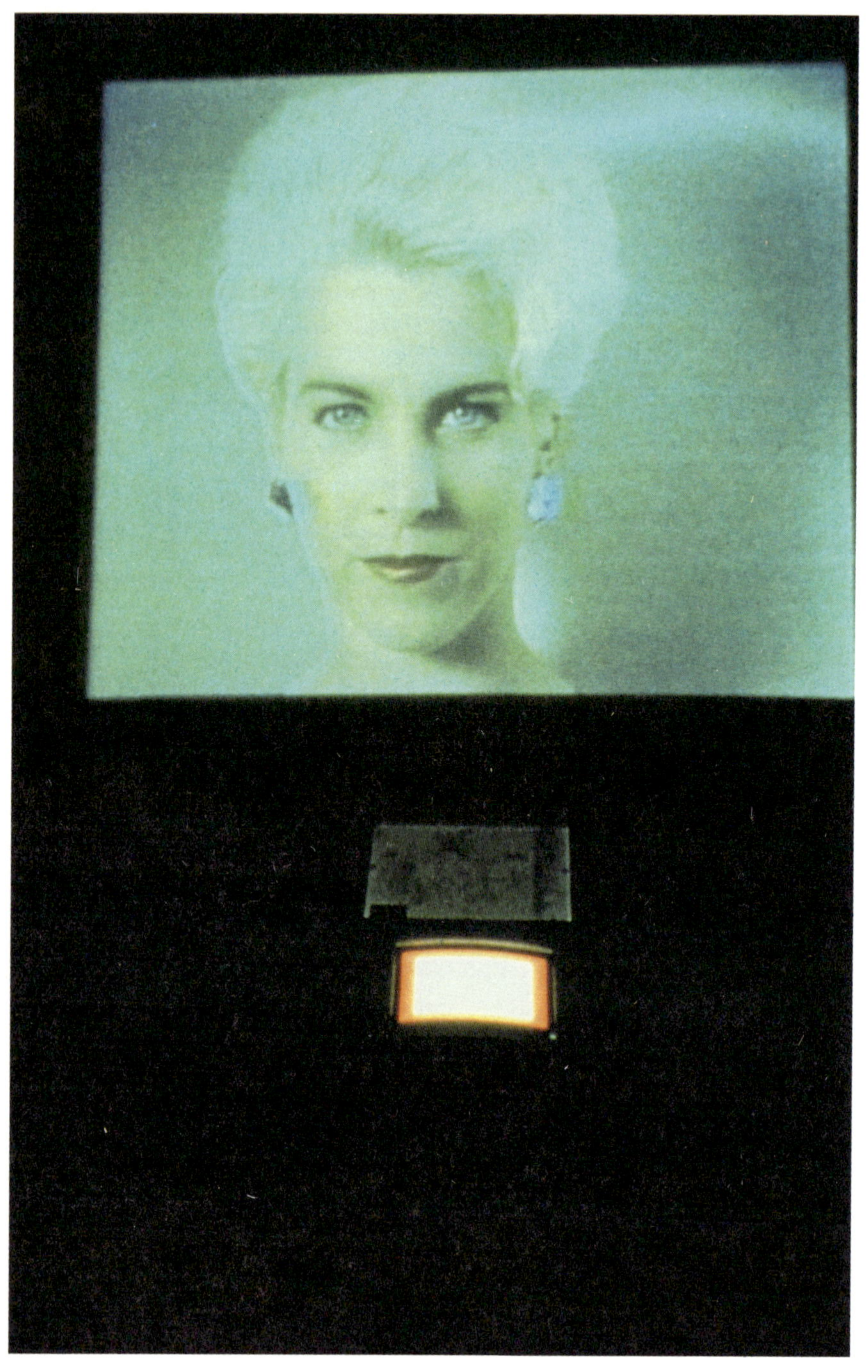

# DEEP CONTACT, 1984

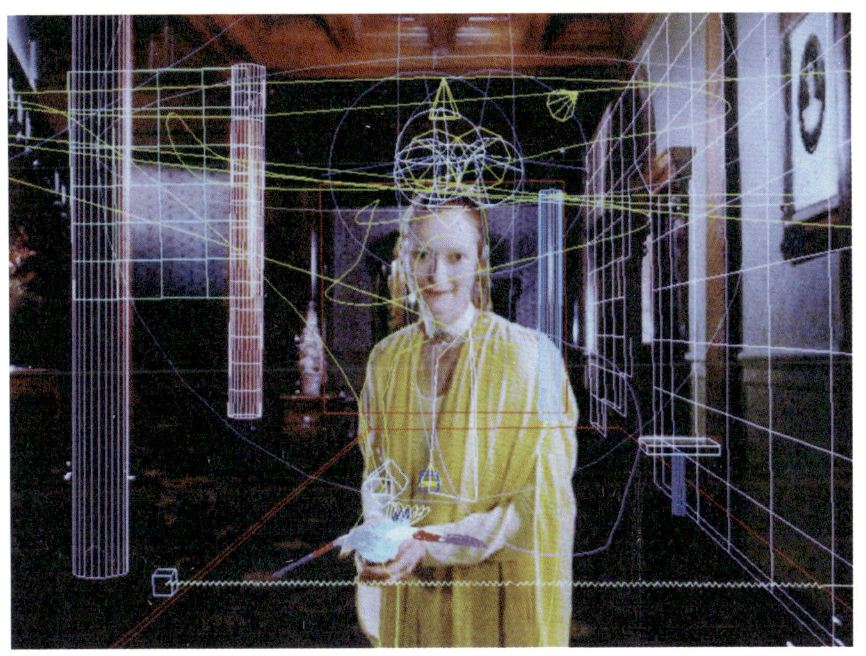

STILL FROM *CONCEIVING ADA,*
1997

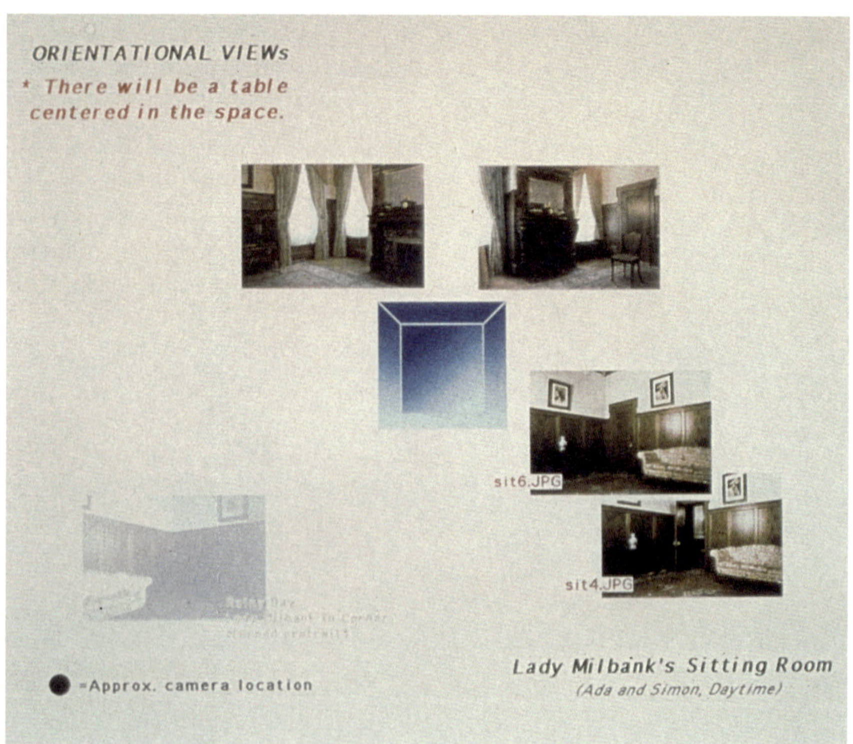


# STUDY FOR VIRTUAL SET— LADY MILBANK'S SITTING ROOM FROM CONCEIVING ADA, 1997

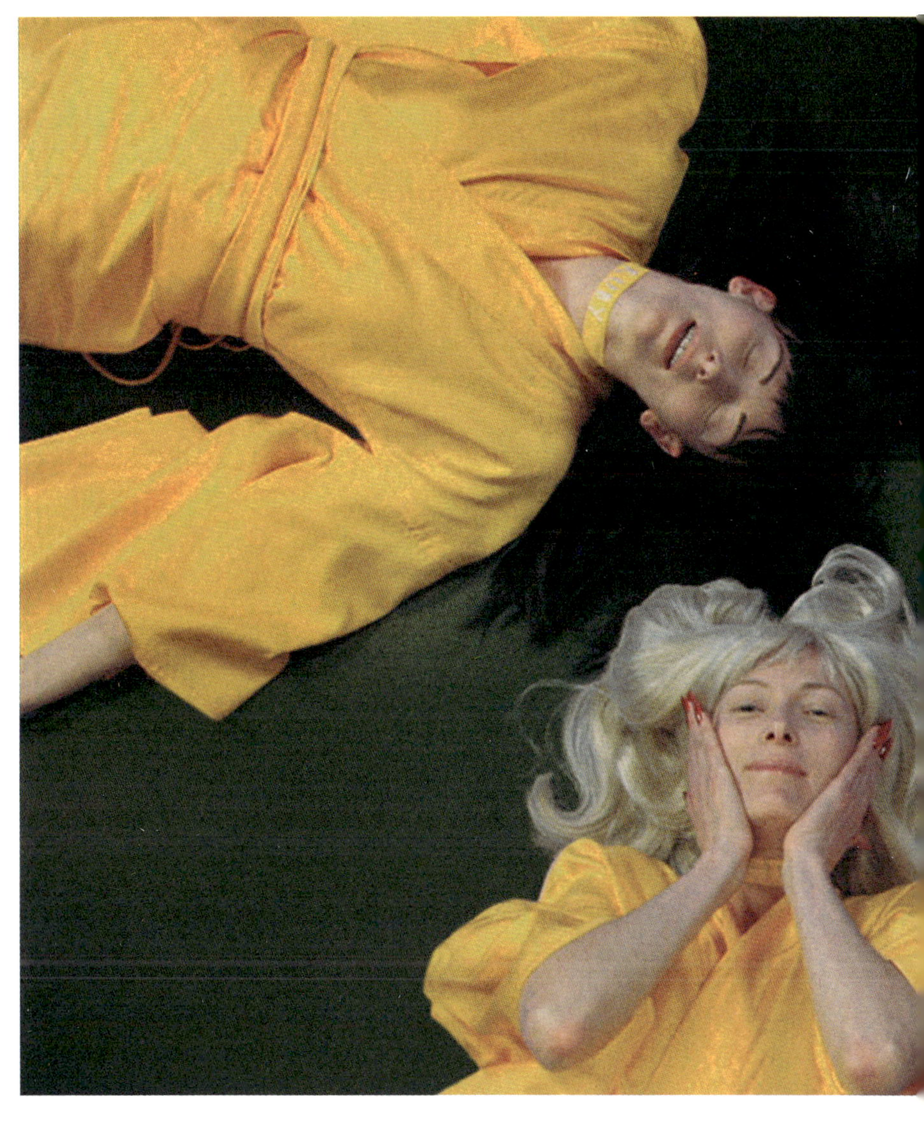

STILL FROM *TEKNOLUST*, 2002

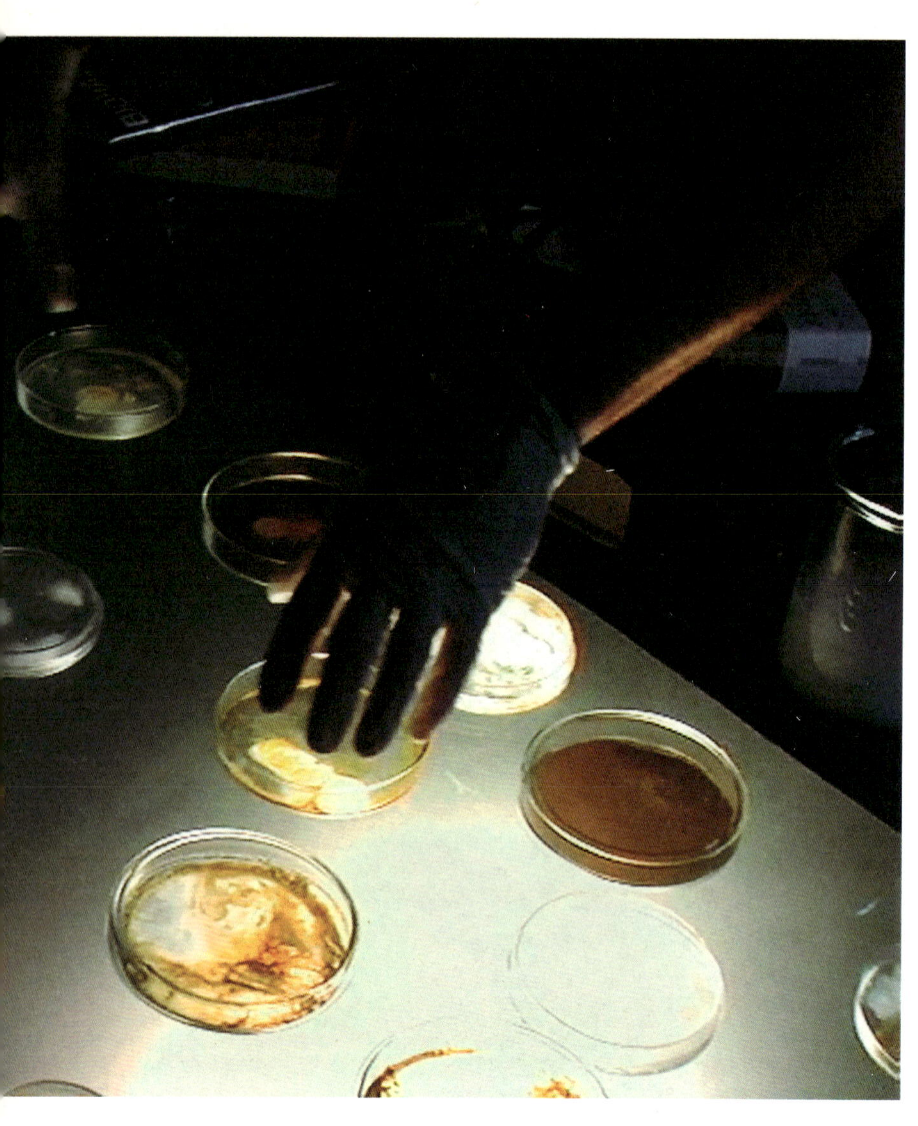

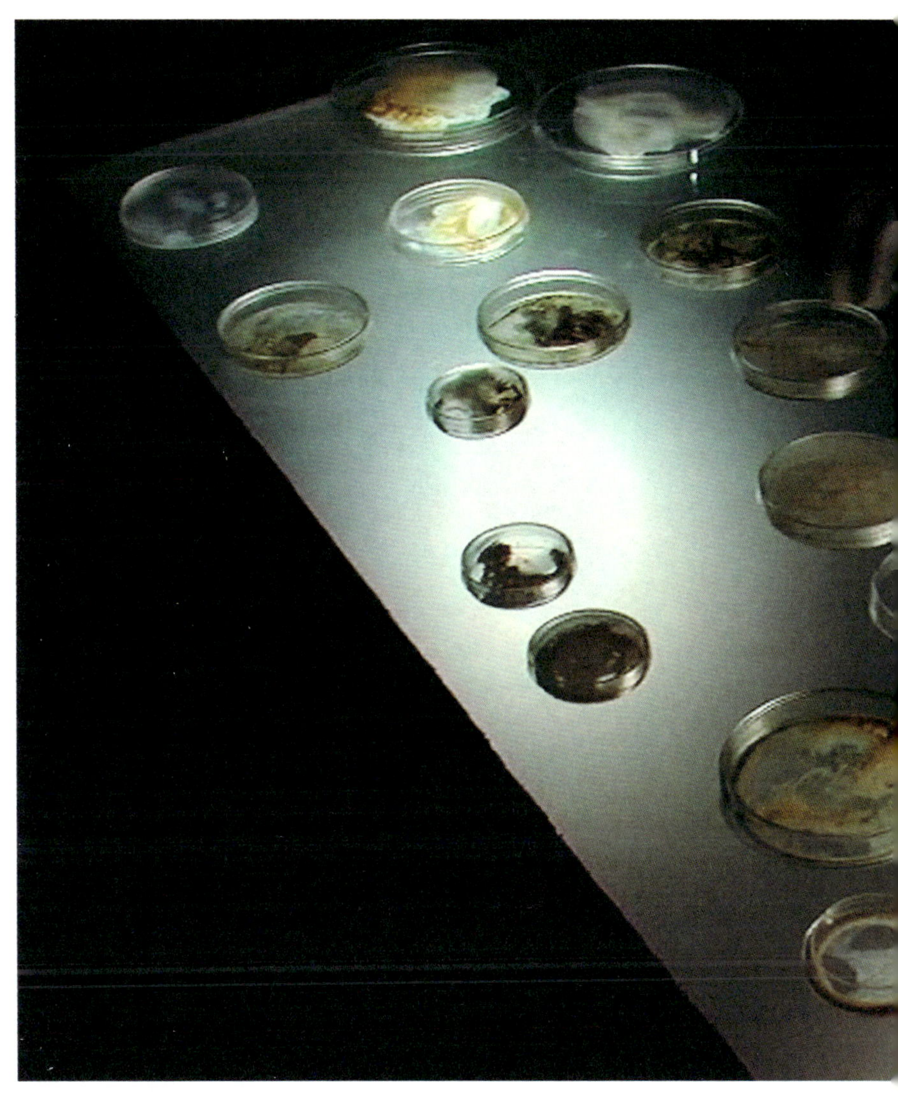

STILL FROM *STRANGE CULTURE*, 2007

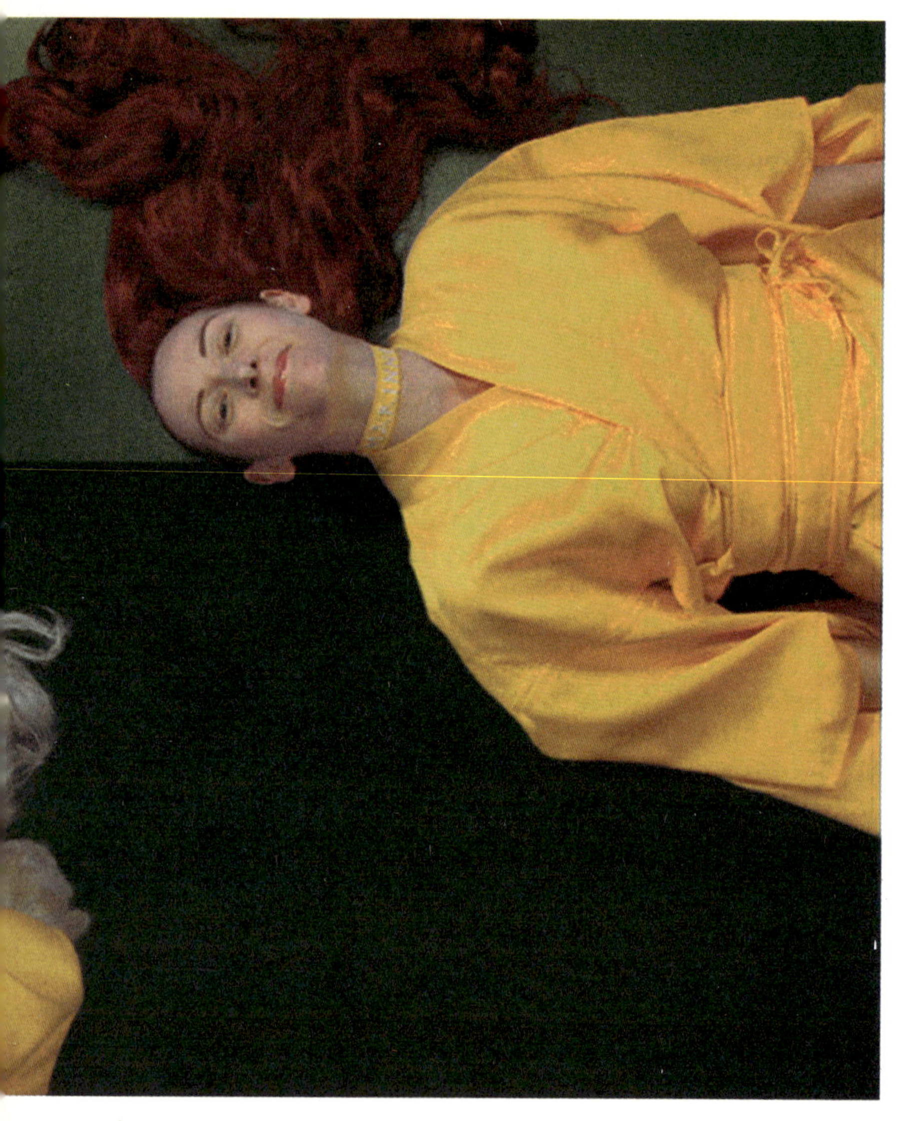

# 26
# DOING TIME

There was history and there was women's history. There was art making and there was women's art making. To give it the kind of power we felt it could have, we needed to make our work and create an institution, like the Woman's Building, for it to be seen in public.
—Sheila de Bretteville, Los Angeles, 1984

If, in these pages, I describe my work more than my life, it is because I had no other life. I was so obsessed with making these works, having them fabricated and finishing them, that it was, quite literally, all I did besides commuting, teaching, and sleeping. It is a miracle I am still married and remain close to my daughter and grandchildren.

When I was pregnant, doctors predicted that I was on the threshold of imminent heart failure. Although I was only twenty-three years old, at each visit they reiterated that I did not have long to live. This provoked a desperation and urgency to complete as much work as I could.

In defiance of my early traumas, I came to believe that making work only I could do was what gave my life meaning. This was how I overcame my depression and suicidal impulses, and why I battled to survive my cardiomyopathy.

I no longer had close friends in San Francisco. Ellie had moved with Francis to Napa. Dawn left for college and would later go on to medical school (her "rebellion" against the life she led with a mother who was an artist). I was married to George, who accepted me as I am, an artmaking-obsessed person with no social life. In writing these pages, I realize that my determination to complete work denied me that other world in which there were friends, family, hobbies, and a social life. I had no idea how my life could encompass both.

Becoming a tenured professor at U.C. Davis was grueling. After thirteen exhausting years of long-distance commuting, endless meetings, and classes, I retired with benefits in 2004 and intended to dedicate myself solely to my artwork. My last week at U.C. Davis, someone relayed a story about an artist named Steve Kurtz, who had been arrested and charged with bioterrorism because of the artwork he created. I found the situation alarming and very of the moment in terms of government repression of artistic freedom.

Steve was a member of the Critical Art Ensemble, an art collective. He and his wife, Hope, were preparing an exhibition about genetically modified food, scheduled to be shown at the Massachusetts Museum of Contemporary Art. One morning, he discovered that Hope had died unexpectedly in her sleep and called emergency medical services. When paramedics arrived, they noticed Petri dishes and scientific paraphernalia in the living room, which Steve and Hope were using for his show. The paramedics alerted the FBI. Within hours, Steve found himself in custody on suspicion of bioterrorism. His home was quarantined, raided by federal agents in biohazard suits, and his wife's body underwent an autopsy which showed she had died of natural causes. A week later, Steve was released back to his home, to await a trial on federal criminal charges.

In July 2004, a grand jury refused to bring any bioterrorism charges, but did indict Kurtz on federal criminal mail fraud and wire fraud charges along with Robert Ferrell, professor of Genetics at the University of Pittsburgh and a scientific consultant to the Critical Art Ensemble. They were accused of ordering and mailing $256 of harmless bacteria. On April 21, 2008, the indictment for mail and wire fraud was ruled "insufficient on its face." This means that, even if the actions alleged in the indictment were true, they would not constitute a crime.

Having lived through the 1960s and the Vietnam War protests, I was suspicious of the government's intrusion in the lives of Americans. Over the years, I had met counter-culture figures such as Timothy Leary, Abbie Hoffman, and Jerry Rubin, and watched the government persecute each of them. Steve's story urgently needed to be communicated to a broad audience.

When I phoned Steve, he confirmed the story and gave me permission to make a film about his situation, even though his attorney would not allow him to appear on screen. I cast Thomas Jay Ryan, an actor who had been in *Teknolust*, as Steve. Tilda, in town for a day, made herself available for about forty minutes to portray Hope. *Strange Culture* used news footage, dramatic re-creation of events with actors, animation, and testimonials and was made with no budget, on equipment borrowed from U.C. Davis and with only four days of actual shooting. I made a rough cut myself and then spent two days in an actual edit bay. It took around six months to make the film. The total cost was under $20,000.

*Strange Culture* explored how the government suppresses freedom of speech and freedom of artistic expression, and how the media blurs fact and fiction. It made a case for Steve having been targeted by the FBI because his work challenged government policies. I was thrilled when *Strange Culture* opened a section of the 2007 Berlin Film Festival and was also screened at the Toronto and Sundance festivals.

Jeannette Catsoulis described *Strange Culture* in *The New York Times*: "Somewhere between documentary and dramatization, fact, and impression, 'Strange Culture' molds one man's tragedy into an engrossing narrative experiment that defies categorization." She concludes by saying: "Alternately teasing and terrifying, 'Strange Culture' is a near-perfect alignment of subject and form. In its creative assessment of our current judicial climate, the need for artistic freedom has seldom seemed so urgent."

The film generated such outrage at Steve's mistreatment, and potential twenty-three-year jail sentence, that there were multiple protests and a flood of letters in his defense. Steve still considers that the charges against him were a response to his political activism. He has said on many occasions that *Strange Culture* was critical to

the government abandoning its charges.

After leaving U.C. Davis, I started organizing the hundreds of file boxes in my archive, stored in a variety of places, like in closets and under beds around my home, and in storage units in San Francisco. I was not sure what to do with them. I suffered several rejections before Stanford's Special Collections Library, to my great surprise and joy, decided to acquire the archive. Stanford had the added

attraction of being close, and made the archive accessible
online. I continue to send all my files and papers to Stanford.

In January 2007, Okwui Enwezor, a Nigeria-born art critic
and curator who had been artistic director of Documenta 1,
offered me the position of chair of the Film Department at
the San Francisco Art Institute (SFAI). Unlike my previous
commute, SFAI was only a few blocks from my apartment.

SFAI, established in 1871, was one of the oldest private art schools in the United States (it closed perma-
nently in 2022). My colleagues included not just Okwui, but
also Hou Hanru, who has curated exhibitions all over the
world and who was SFAI's director of exhibitions and
public programs, and the film department fixtures George
and Mike Kuchar, twin brothers who made underground 8
mm films. I imagined I would be part of a vibrant community of shared ideas and public critiques.

George Kuchar always made me laugh. He was
eccentric, a completely free thinker, and possessed
immense verve and enthusiasm. George was an icon
adored by students for his zany but witty low-budget
movies made with lunch money. His films ran anywhere
from five minutes to ninety. I do not think any of his films
cost more than a hundred dollars.

Unfortunately, we did not spend much time together.
A few years after I arrived at SFAI, George was diagnosed
with terminal prostate cancer. He died on September 6,
2011, on what would have been his sixty-ninth birthday.
The night George died I watched the moon as it moved
across the San Francisco skyline. From my window, I saw
what appeared to be a million souls rising and floating in
the sky. They all looked like George. At that moment I realized that nothing is lost forever.

Beyond his classes, George taught all of us to search
for our soul in a better world, to not be afraid, to live in the
raw, to be honest, naked, and funny, and to express the
irony of our frailty as we all approach extinction. George
celebrated the things that make us human and the
humanness in eccentricity.

Although I had hoped to find a community at SFAI,
that never happened. Soon Okwui left to become chief
curator at the Haus der Kunst in Munich, and Hanru
became artistic director at the Maxxi Museum in Rome. I
left as well, to dedicate myself once again to my work and,
most especially, to finish my film *!Women Art Revolution.*

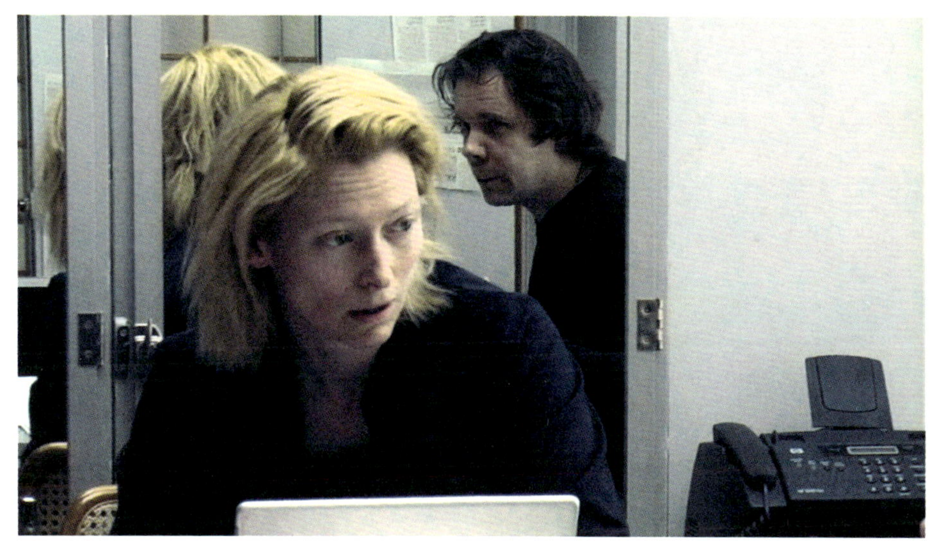

# STILL FROM *STRANGE CULTURE*, 2007

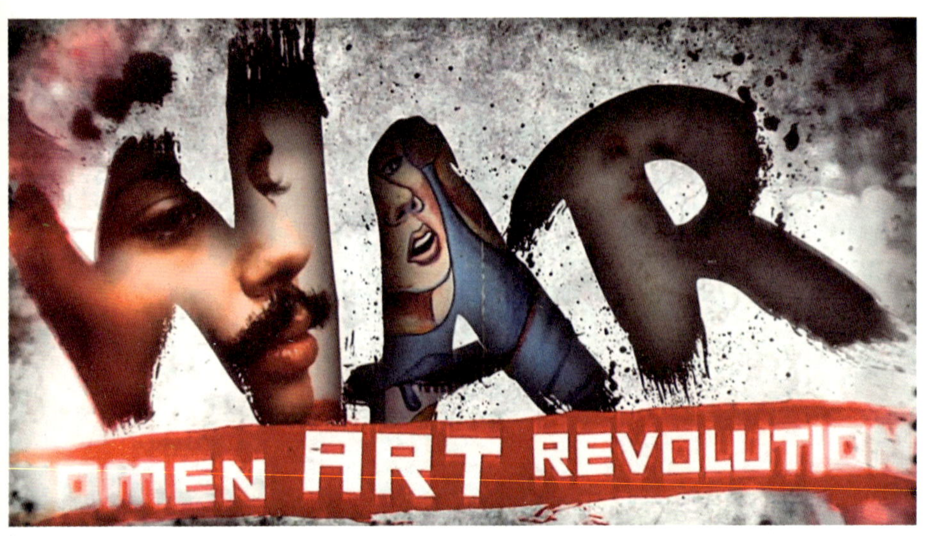

STILL FROM *!WOMEN ART REVOLUTION*, 2010

# 27
# !WOMEN ART REVOLUTION (!WAR), 1968–2010

For me, being a feminist meant that all other civil rights issues were part of my struggle. I have often said, I want to change the power structures that create inequities in the first place.
—Marcia Tucker, Santa Barbara, 2009

Beginning in 1968 when I recorded the first interviews until 2010, when I began editing *!Women Art Revolution*, I had amassed well over 1,500 hours of footage. There were never-seen conversations that detailed intimate stories and the struggles of sixty-five important art-world figures including Judy Baca, Connie Butler, Judy Chicago, the Guerrilla Girls, Alana Heiss, Suzanne Lacy, Sheila Levant de Bretteville, Lucy Lippard, Yvonne Rainer, B. Ruby Rich, Rachel Rosenthal, Faith Ringgold, Moira Roth, and Carolee Schneeman, among others. Though these artists were all part of an important cultural movement in America, none were included in any history of contemporary art.

These were women who invented methods to insert themselves directly into the culture. Their artworks addressed crucial issues of social justice, violence towards women, rape, as well as covert methods of media manipulation and censorship. By 2010, several of the women I interviewed had either passed away or were dying. When I mentioned their names to my students, they did not know who they were. Their stories needed to be told immediately.

Often, my interviews were the only video record of such highly influential feminists as Marcia Tucker, who founded the New Museum. I did not know many of these women before contacting them, and almost all were immediately taken with the idea of creating this historical record and allowed me to tape them. These artists pioneered radical performances and installations in non-traditional spaces. Their groundbreaking innovations were rarely acknowledged at the time. The intention of my film was to change that.

In 2010, forty-two years after I first began filming, I embarked on four grueling years of editing the footage, ten hours a day, six days a week—leaving no time for making any other artworks. It was important to spend time sitting in the company of these interviews. Their tenacity and hope caused my own thinking to evolve and mature, and taught me more about courage and vision.

Despite hiring several professional editors, none had managed to create a cohesive structure and make sense of this disconnected history. Because I had lived it, I took on the process. There were no shortcuts to making this film. Some days, progress meant locating a usable ten-second sequence. At times I wondered if it would ever be completed.

However, the story of the feminist art movement and its impact on society deserved to be told clearly, with honesty and humor. I incorporated archival footage of some artists I never met, such as Ana Mendieta. Editing the film and watching these women narrate their personal injustices often brought me to tears.

I begin the film by asking visitors to the Whitney Museum of American Art to name three women artists. Most could not. None of the women in my film, even Carolee Schneemann, Rachel Rosenthal, or Faith Ringgold, had gallery representation. Some had stopped making art. Listening to these interviews over and over, I realized I was not alone. We all suffered for decades, with little recognition or validation.

My goal was to make a film that was entertaining, inspiring, and informed the next generation of women artists. In addition to the already mentioned artists, the film's interviewees include artists and critics such as Susan Grode, Judith Brodsky, Harmony Hammond, Howardena Pindell, Martha Rosler, Nancy Spero, Miriam Schapiro, Sylvia Sleigh, Camille Utterback, Cecilia Vicuña, and Martha Wilson. Carrie Brownstein composed and performed the soundtrack. Working with art historians, we created a catalogue of exhibitions by these artists.

I reunited with Spain, who was sympathetic to the project because his mother was an artist who never had the opportunity to show her work. Spain, a feminist and champion of the underdog, designed the poster for the film as well as a graphic novel, printed on newsprint in the style of *Zap Comix*, with the cover a homage to Eugène Delacroix's 1830 painting *Liberty Leading the People*.

Over all these years, I financed the shooting of these interviews with income from my various teaching salaries. As I began editing, Creative Capital, the nonprofit arts organization, provided some grant money to complete the film, along with advice and support.

Once *!Women Art Revolution* was finished, the next challenge was getting it seen. Initially programmers at major film festivals thought there would be little interest in this subject. However, when they saw the completed film, they changed their minds. *!Women Art Revolution* was accepted by the trifecta of Sundance, Toronto, and Berlin film festivals, and received standing ovations at them all. When the feminist icon Gloria Steinem introduced the film at MoMA, she said, "Every frame of this film could be a novel." She recalled demonstrating outside the museum with the rallying cry: "MoMA is a female impersonator." Steinem observed, "This is such precious footage, because it's about the work as it is going on. It brings the other half of the human race into the art world."

Young women artists tell me they saw the film as part of their undergraduate art history courses. *!Women Art Revolution* is today in the permanent collection of many museums and educational institutions. The film, 83 minutes long, is merely a trailer for the full collection of interviews. There are seventeen hours of Judy Chicago interviews, twenty hours of Carolee Schneeman, eight hours of Faith Ringgold, as well as extensive examples of the work of the sixty-five women we interviewed. Stanford University acquired the interviews as a digital archive and, thanks to a grant from Preserving Creative America, put the entire video interviews online. They are all housed at the Stanford Special Collections Library, along with transcriptions, cross-linked for search purposes, making it all available globally 24/7/365. Zeitgeist Films, its distributor, reports that the film remains in great demand. It is the only video documentation on this history that exists, told by the women lived it.

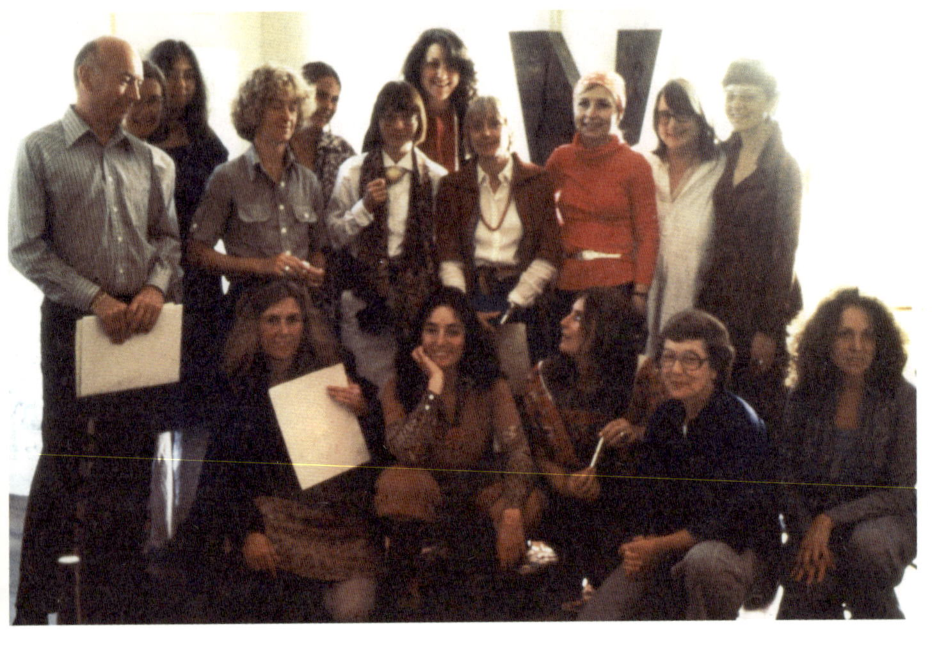

GATHERING OF WOMEN
ARTISTS WITH CRITICS.
INCLUDING: LYNN, SUZANNE
LACY, PAT TAVENER, NATASHA
NICHOLSON, JUDITH BARRY,
BONNIE SHERK, MOIRA ROTH,
HELÈNE AYLON, LAWRENCE
ALLOWAY, NATASHA
NICHOLSON, PAT TAVENER,
MARY STOFFLET. CIRCA 1988.

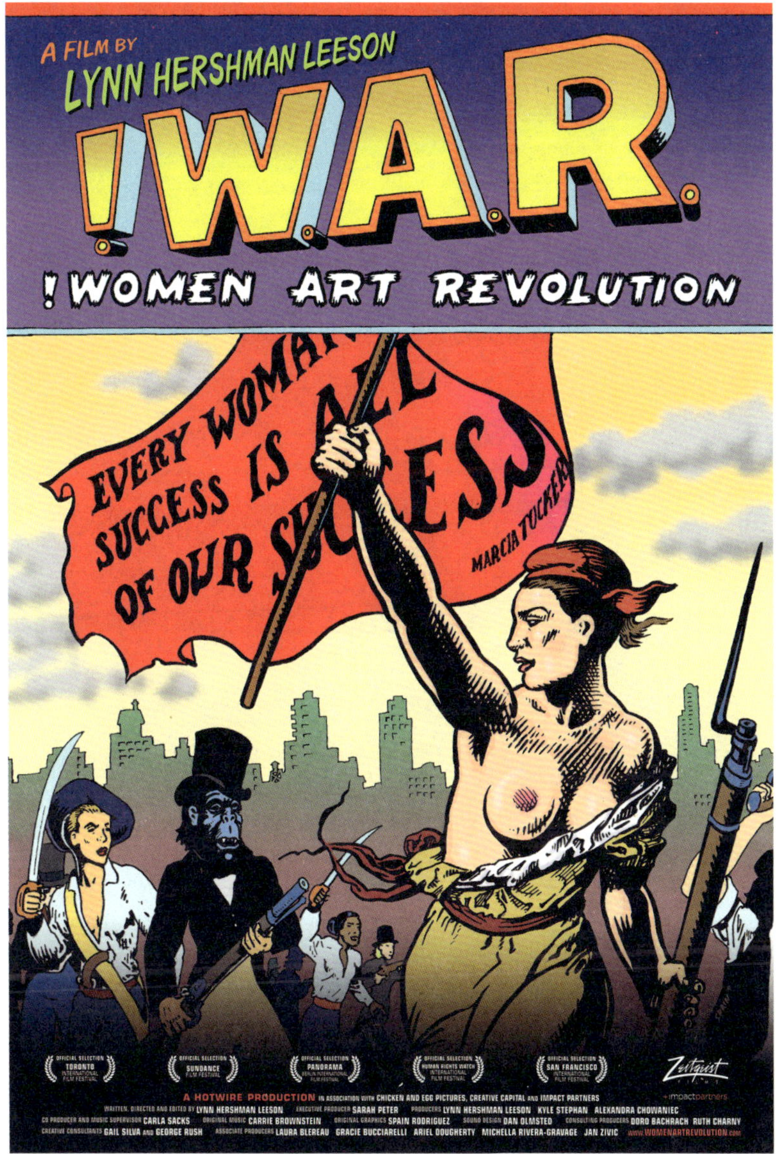



# COVER OF THE !W.A.R. COMIC BOOK WITH ARTWORK BY SPAIN RODRIGUEZ, 2010

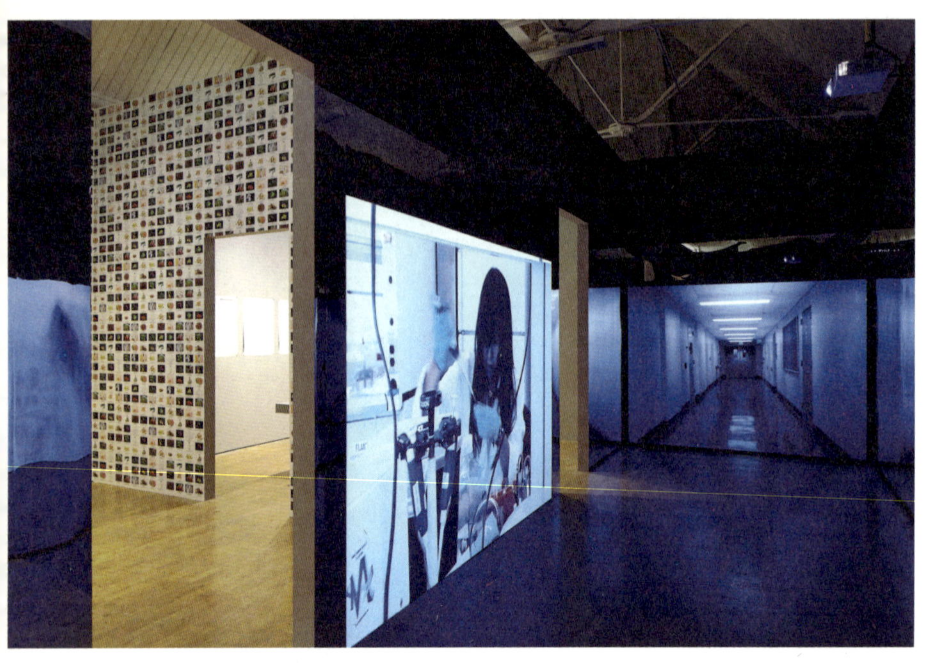

INSTALLATION VIEW OF THE *INFINITY* ENGINE, 2014, IN *ORIGIN OF THE SPECIES (PART II)* AT MODERN ART OXFORD, 2015. PHOTOGRAPH BY ANDY STAGG

# 28
# HOME AGAIN

> It was only when I realized who I was that I could really make art that interested me enough to really do a good job at it.
> —Martha Rosler, 1993

Perhaps it was karma. For over three decades I enabled other artists to complete their works. The list is long and includes Christo, Jeanne-Claude, Michael Asher, the more than one hundred artists who collaborated with the Floating Museum, and Steve Kurtz. I had given voice to the women artists featured in *!Women Art Revolution*. I accomplished all this while my own work was rarely acknowledged or exhibited, and often ignored, or worse, reviled.

As the Guerrilla Girls declared in one of their manifestos, as a women artist you do not have to worry about early success, and you can look forward to being discovered in your eighties. That is exactly what happened. The quote absolutely proved true for me.

The 1990s brought me sporadic moments of recognition. For instance, in 1994 I became the first woman to receive a tribute and retrospective at the San Francisco International Film Festival. In 1998, I was a Sundance Screenwriter Fellow and honored with the Flintridge Foundation Award for Lifetime Achievement in the Visual Arts. *Conceiving Ada* received the award of Outstanding Achievement in Drama from the Festival of Electronic Cinema. *Teknolust*, which had been so disparaged and booed when it first played at Sundance, received the

2003 Alfred P. Sloan Award for writing and directing. *Deep Contact* won an important prize at Ars Electronica.

Living in the Bay Area, I was privy to technologies as they were being developed. This would not have been possible anywhere else. In true cyborgian fashion, it was as if these technologies were members of my family. Even when they became obsolete, I kept them safe.

I still have my first iPhone. It drops words and does not ring but I have deep memories of our time together. I feel a kindred spirit with these devices and my history is planted within their outdated functions. I keep them close to me; they are like friends I do not want to lose.

Though I did not set out to dissect personal traumas in my artwork, they nevertheless often embed themselves. For instance, in the video sculpture *Look at Me*, a gray dollhouse projects a video in the kitchen window allowing viewers to witness a horrific scene of domestic violence. It is as if these works insist on making themselves. Often, I do not know what they are meant to say until they are completed. Many of these revelations are accidental, born of faith in the process.

In 2011, I received a life-changing phone call from Peter Weibel. Although three decades had passed, our memories, friendship, and trust remained intact. We giggled, remembering our meeting with August Coppola in front of his cappuccino machine, making predictions about the future of art (most of which turned out to be right). Peter had become the director of the ZKM Center for Art and Media, located within an enormous converted former arms factory in Karlsruhe, southwestern Germany. Founded in 1989, it is a pioneering institution whose mission is to exhibit the kind of work that I had been told in my whole career was "Not Art."

Peter was calling to invite me to participate in an upcoming exhibition at ZKM, *Moments: A History of Performance in 10 Acts*, in which he wanted to include the Roberta project. Among the other artists to be included were Marina Abramović, Graciela Carnevale, Simone Forti, Anna Halprin, Reinhild Hoffmann, Channa Horwitz, Sanja Iveković, Adrian Piper, and Yvonne Rainer.

The night I arrived in Karlsruhe, curators held a dinner for the exhibition's artists. Peter appeared in time for dessert. In the decades that had passed, we had both aged, adding time and weight to our appearance, yet I still saw him as he was then—young, thin, and handsome.

A casual remark about how much of my work had never been exhibited led Peter to propose organizing a very small retrospective with a small ZKM catalogue. This was a big deal! ZKM's catalogues are among the best in the world. I was seventy-three years old, and this would be the first catalogue of my entire career. When Peter and his associate Andreas Beitin realized how much of my work had never been exhibited or collected, and was still in my possession, they dedicated the central exhibition space of ZKM, its entire first floor, to *Civic Radar*, a full career retrospective. Almost two thirds of the 450 works to be exhibited had once been dismissed as "Not Art."

With this major museum retrospective looming, I approached galleries in New York yet again, hoping for representation. I was prepared for rejection, but among those who did respond, some were outright insulting. One prominent gallery director asked if I made my art on a card table in my bedroom. (What did that even mean?) It was shocking that gallery directors remained so officious, disrespectful, and out of touch about conceptual work by women artists. From my conversations with other women artists, I knew I was not alone.

Ruby Lerner, then director of Creative Capital, the non-profit that had helped fund *!WAR,* introduced me to Bridget Donahue. At our first meeting Bridget spent three hours going through my work, asking many questions. No gallerist had ever done that. A few weeks later, she revealed that she was planning to open her own art gallery and hoped to show my work as her first exhibition.

On June 14, 2014, *Civic Radar* opened. The title was a nod to mirroring as both words read the same backwards. For the first time, critics published research and consequential critiques of my work. The sound sculptures made in the early 1960s were acknowledged as the first multimedia artworks. *Lorna*, *Deep Contact*, the Telerobotic Dolls, *Dina, Synthia*, and *Agent Ruby* were recognized as anticipating technology's cultural impact.

ZKM commissioned *The Infinity Engine,* an installation investigating the consequences of genetic modification. Projects included genetically modified fish, a fish tank, images of genetically modified animals and foods, screens, projections, and a 3D-printed nose. To inform the intellectual underpinnings of *The Infinity Engine*, I worked with several pioneering scientists including Dr. George Church of Harvard University, Dr. Anthony Atala of Wake Forest Institute for Regenerative Medicine, Dr. Drew Endy of Stanford University, and Dr. Elizabeth Blackburn of the University of California.

I was very much looking forward to the ZKM catalogue but that, too, met with challenges. ZKM's regular partner, MIT Press, declined to publish the catalogue because its editor said he had never heard of me. Peter was furious. Instead, a collaboration with Hatje Cantz, an exceptional German publisher of art books, produced a 487-page catalogue, which included significant essays by respected scholars, and included an essay by Peter and a touching and moving letter from Tilda Swinton.

"I would say that your work is beyond modern," Tilda wrote. "It is beyond futuristic. It occupies a tunnel high above our heads and a time outside of any construct. There is no 'What if?' in your universe, only 'Why not?'"

One year later, in 2016, Holland Cotter in *The New York Times* selected the *Civic Radar* catalogue as one of the "Indispensable Books" of the year, listed as part of the "Best Art of 2016." Peter and Andreas sent fifty proposals to other museums in hopes of having the exhibition travel. Not a single U.S. museum responded.

Throughout my career, I was not looking for celebrity status or fortune. I wanted to be acknowledged as an artist, to be respected for the original ideas in my work, and for it to be exhibited, collected, and preserved. I had arrived at an age, and a point in life, where I had no reason to expect any of this to happen. And yet it did.

Teaching had provided me and my family with an income, health care, access to professional equipment and other resources for my work. Donald Hess lifted me out of debt. And George had shown me that I could have a loving marriage and that together we could be parents to my daughter, who is a remarkable individual. Dawn very much represents what first-stage feminists fought for: She enjoys a meaningful professional career doing important work where she is well paid, on parity with men in the same position, with a family, and children who see no barriers to what they can achieve. I am so proud of her, and gratified and amazed to see this occur in one generation's time.

Despite an early prognosis of infirmity and a short life, I am thankfully able to maintain good health and continue to work, always incorporating the latest technologies into my art.

Although I have sought out the most advanced technologies for my work, sometimes decades before they were popularly adopted, I retain a wariness about the dangers posed by modern technology, particularly when deployed by the government against its citizens. At the same time, my work also implicates viewers in technology's potential to be misused, to create digital dependencies, to surveil us. Yet what has kept me making art in the face of rejection is that I continue to believe art takes place in a space independent of life's travails and is an affirmation of a belief in the future.

Feline plus Jellyfish Gene
Use: Research for HIV and AIDS virus  Born: 2011  Mayo Clinic. USA

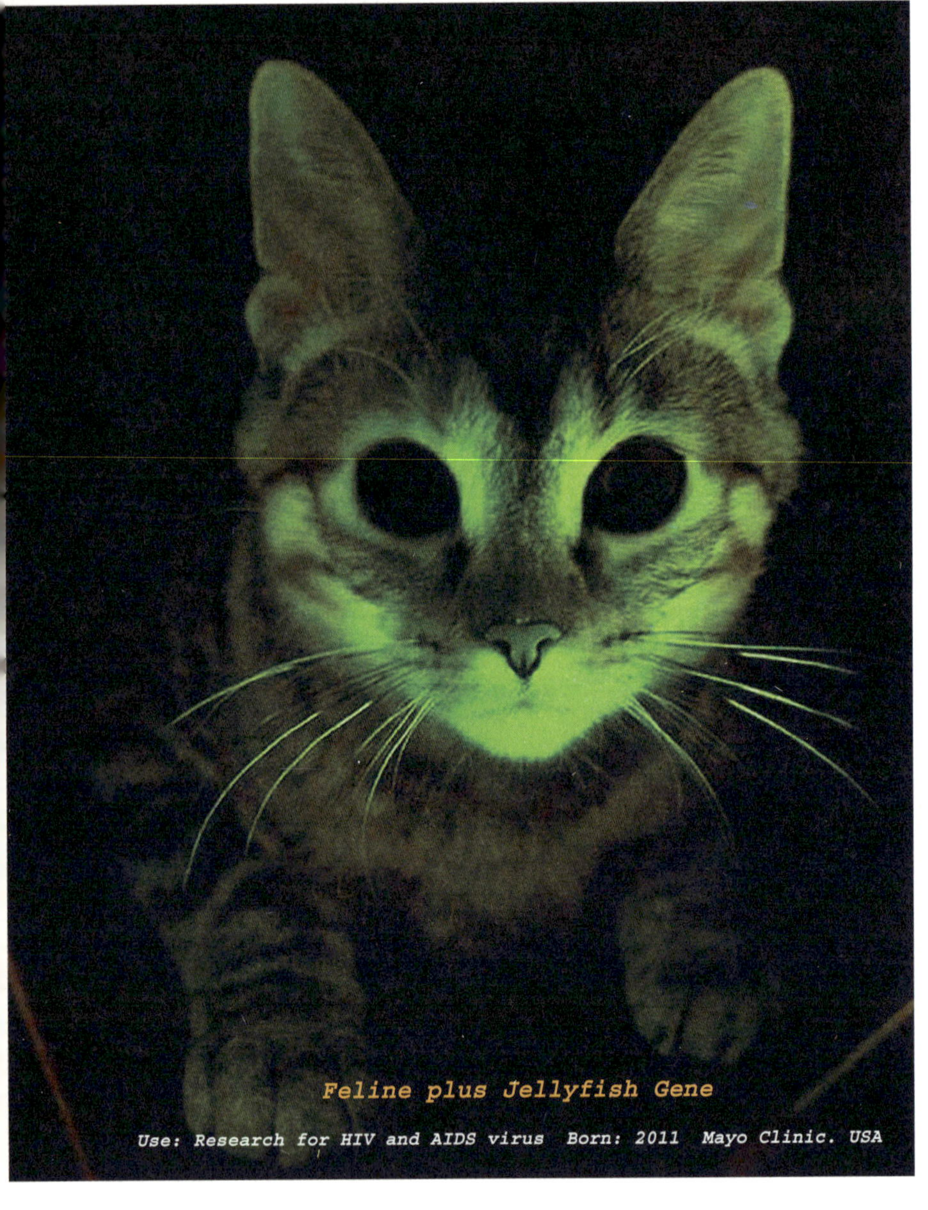

GLO CAT, 2013

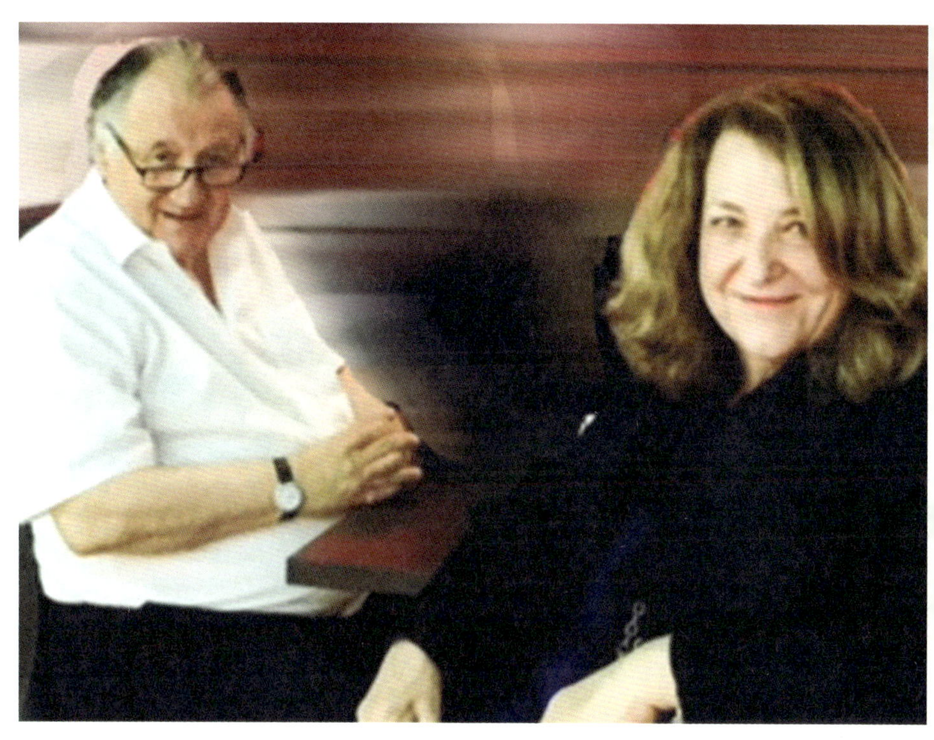

# LYNN WITH PETER WEIBEL, 2014

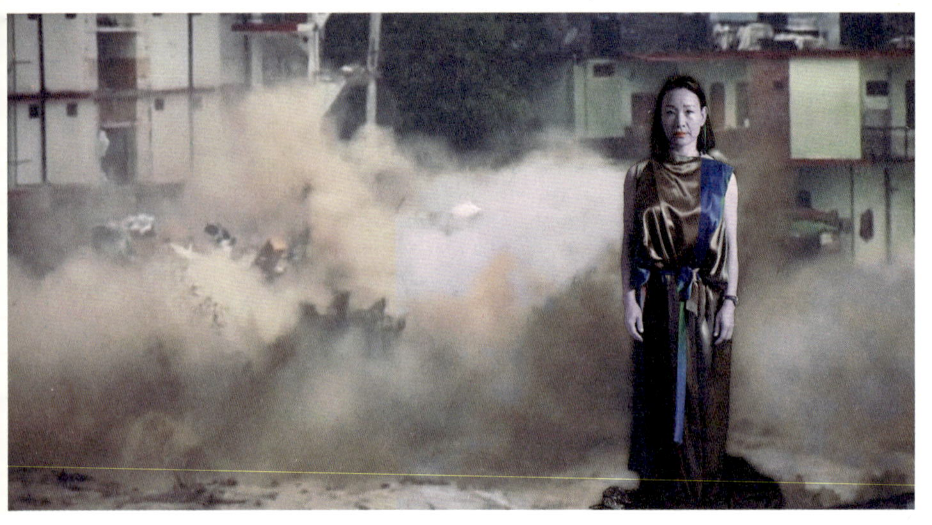

STILL FROM *LOGIC PARALYZES THE HEART*, 2022

# 29
# TIME SHOWS US WHAT WE CANNOT SEE AT THE TIME

The machine does not isolate man from the great problems of nature but plunges him more deeply into them.
—Antoine de Saint-Exupéry

In 2003, the human genome was sequenced. This critically important achievement was the result of a newly devised editing system for DNA, CRISPR, which allows researchers to edit genomic code and correct disease-associated mutations, thereby possibly overcoming our genetic limitations.

Advances in technology and science have often provided me with the tools and subjects of my work. In 2018, Sabine Himmelsbach, director of the House of Electronic Art in Basel, invited me to create an exhibition for which I converted the entire museum into a genetics laboratory. Dr. Thomas Huber, an administrator at Novartis, a leading biotech firm based in Basel, on the museum's board of directors, generously helped navigate the logistics.

For this exhibition, we created two original antibodies. An antibody identifies the toxins in culture(s) and finds a way to neutralize them. Our first antibody was derived from a code for the letters of my name, LYNNHERSHMAN, and the second antibody referred to the letters in ROBERTA. As there were no code possibilities for ROB, we used the last four letters, ERTA. Four months later, Thomas unveiled our formulations in a Novartis lab.

The LYNNHERSHMAN antibody would bind with anything. However, the (Rob)ERTA antibody possessed the property of not being able to bind. This was a "big deal." Novartis had for years tried without success to produce an antibody that would not bind with anything. Novartis executives proclaimed that we had "hit the jackpot." What a glorious surprise. The ERTA antibody could be used to identify, expose, and combat toxins existing in human circulation, thereby becoming an early detector of disease.

After the unexpected success of ERTA, a year later Thomas and I approached the Harvard Weiss Institute scientist George Church, known as the father of synthetic biology. George had converted his thesis and a short film into DNA. Meeting George inspired me to convert my research into DNA. At George's suggestion, I contacted Twist Biology, which performed a four- month process of molecular breakdowns and reconversions, producing two vials. One contained the (Rob)ERTA antibody and the other vial held my research that had been converted into synthesized DNA. Both vials were exhibited at the House of Electronic Art. *The Infinity Engine* was the culmination of a decade of investigations into questions of manipulated identity, as well as the fundamental issues of life and death in the face of scientific and technological advances.

In 2022, Thomas and I embarked on a second project, *Twisted Gravity*, which sought to find a solution to contaminated water. An estimated 502,000 people die each year from drinking water that contains plastic, bacteria, parasites, and other contaminants. Thomas and our team hoped to generate a "twist" of both art and science to make water that had been tainted by climate change, human carelessness, and pollution, safe.

The Weiss Institute at Harvard, led by Dr. Richard Novak, had developed the AquaPulse System, which inserts electrical pulses into water at a rate that dissolves plastics and contaminants, at one liter per minute. We also discovered that nature, on its own, has created a new species of wax worm that ingests and then dissolves plastic from water. This became the basis of our artwork.

The exhibition consists of six pedestals with three etched panels each. Images are etched into three layers of plastic lit with LED lights. The first is devoted to AquaPulse; the second to the Evolution Pedestal, which contained a system to propagate microorganisms that have the ability to degrade plastic; and a third one illustrates efficiency by changes in the brightness of the connected panels.

*Twisted Gravity* has been on view throughout the world, commissioned by Gwangju Biennale, Korea, and exhibited at VAC Museum Moscow, Poncher Foundation LA, and the New Museum.

"Working with Lynn," Dr. Novak wrote, "opened our eyes to the counterpoint of our water purification system W This collaboration did not just create an art installation, but new science as well."

In 2021, on my eightieth birthday, my first U.S. solo retrospective museum exhibition, *Twisted*, curated by Margot Norton, opened at the New Museum in New York City, described as follows: "Hershman Leeson has consistently worked with the latest technologies, from Artificial Intelligence to DNA programming, often anticipating the impact of technological developments on society. As the artist posited in 1998, 'Imagine a world in which there is a blurring between the soul and the chip, a world in which artificially implanted DNA is genetically bred to create a self-replicating intelligent machine, which uses a human body as a vehicle for mobility.'"

Although the exhibition featured works from throughout my career, there was no little irony in the fact that Covid prevented me from displaying any of my works that required direct touch or viewer interaction.

An invitation to participate in the Venice Biennale enabled me to complete a new video installation, *Logic Paralyzes the Heart*, in which the actor Joan Chen portrays the very first cyborg. It was awarded a special citation at the Biennale "for indexing the cybernetic concerns that run through the exhibitions in an illuminating and powerful way that also includes visionary moments of her early practice that foresaw the influence of technology in our everyday lives."

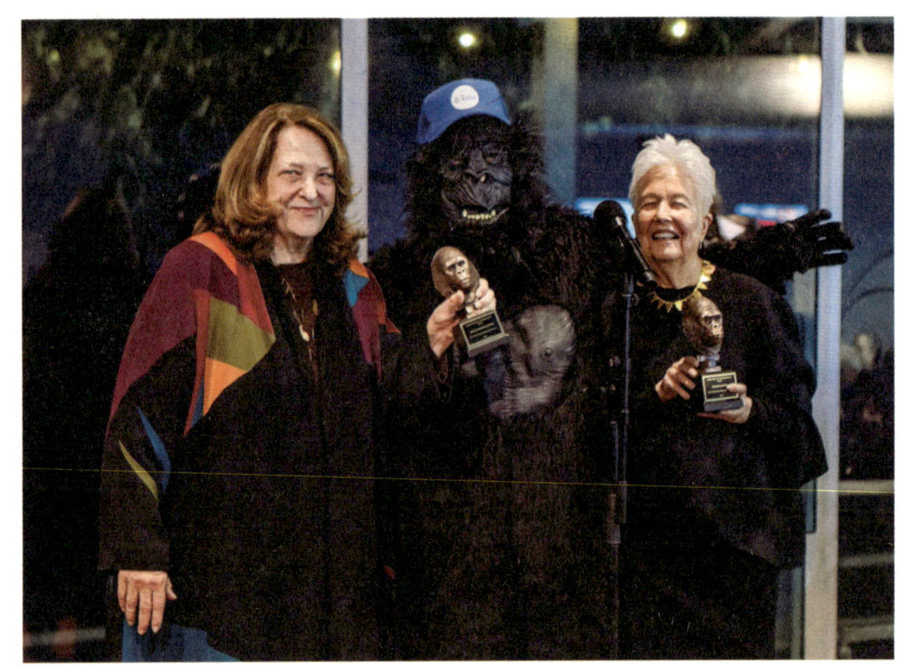

LYNN AND ELEANOR COPPOLA
RECEIVING AWARDS AT THE
DI ROSA CENTER FOR
CONTEMPORARY ART'S 25TH
ANNIVERSARY CELEBRATION
GALA, 2022

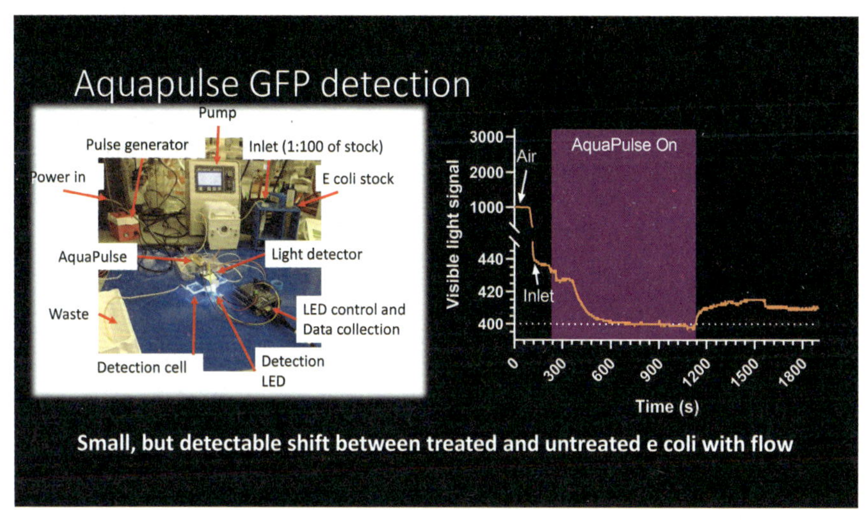



# *AQUAPULSE GFP DETECTION, 2022*

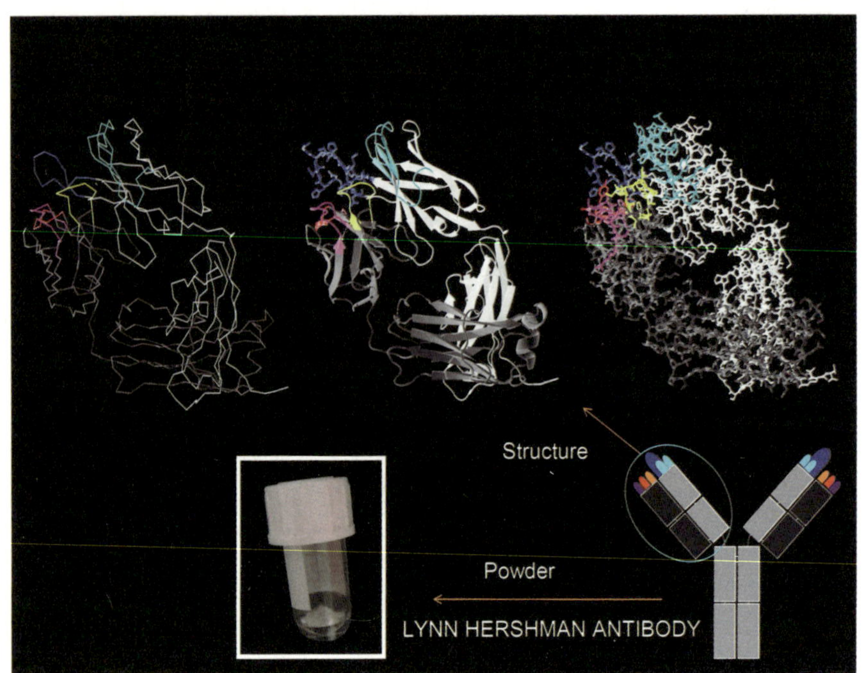


# LYNN HERSHMAN ANTIBODY PROCESS, 2018

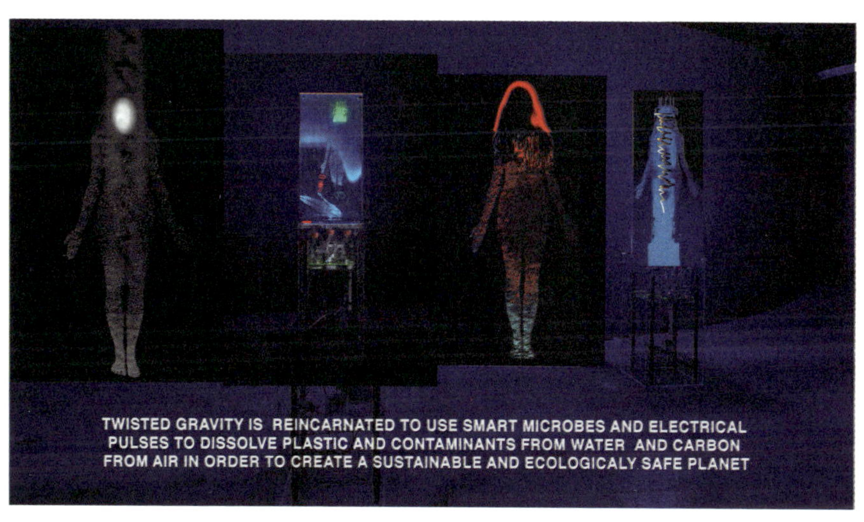


# OUTLINE OF PLANS FOR VENICE BIENALLE INSTALLATION (UNREALIZED), 2019

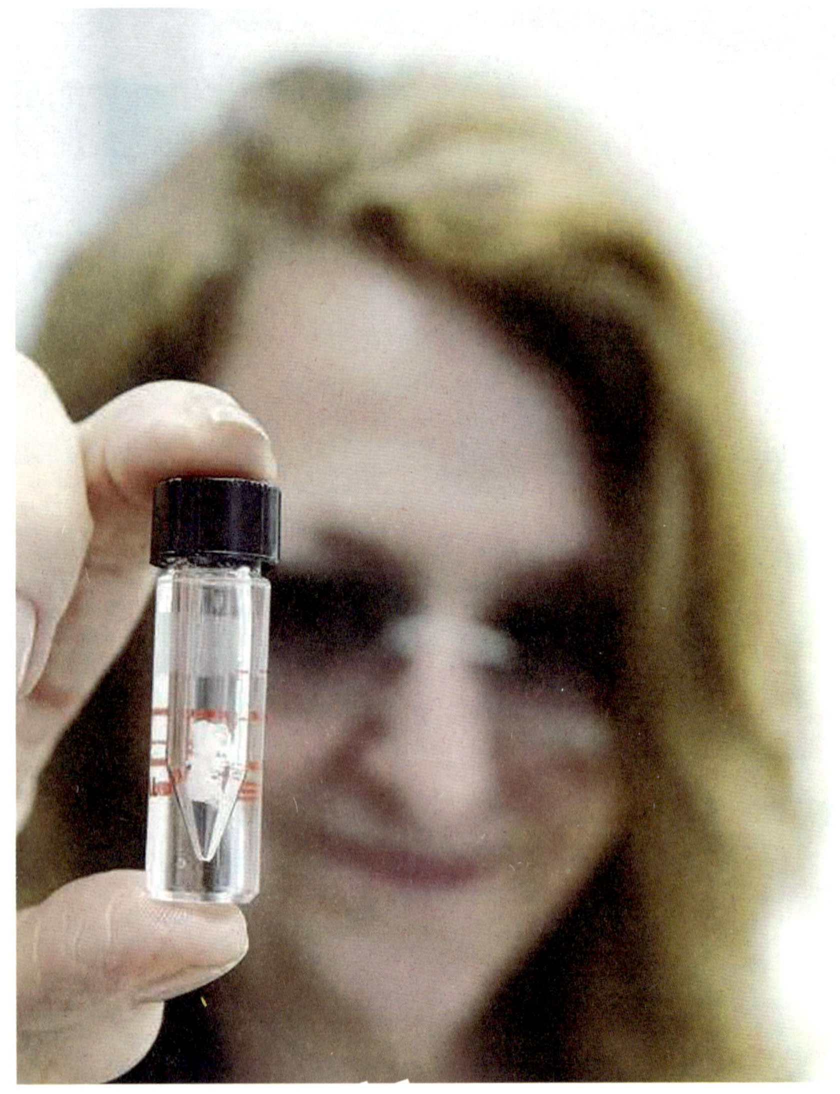

LYNN WITH THE
LYNNHERSHMAN ANTIBODY,
2018. PHOTOGRAPH BY
NOVARTIS/LAURIDS JENSEN.

# 30
# TIMING

> Life is like knitting an argyle sweater blindfolded.
> You can't see the patterns you've created till it's
> nearly over.
> —Lynn Hershman Leeson, San Francisco, 1986

Eleanor Coppola and I first met in the car pool for our two-year-olds' nursery school. It was transformative to meet another female artist who defied that era's embedded cultural prejudices by persisting in her art practice. We plotted projects together in stolen moments as we met at the Caffe Trieste, or after screenings at her home. Together we designed installations in hotel rooms, performances in coffee shops, or long-distance collaborative drawings. Very few people saw these works but creating them affirmed us as artists. Several of the projects are described throughout this book, which Ellie encouraged me to write. Although Ellie passed away recently, she was an extraordinary person whose friendship meant more than I can ever fully acknowledge.

Life is composed of choices made in the moment. But a memoir looks backwards at time and its long-term effects.

I recently saw Germano Celent at the New York Armory exhibition. He waved and we agreed to meet for coffee and catch up later that week. Regrettably, we never had that coffee. I remember driving Germano through Northern California to show him *Running Fence*. Covid had just begun its contagion and Germano was one of its first victims.

This is just one of the many memories exhumed in the writing of this book. Some of the joys and losses, opportunities, and friendships that this memoir uprooted ignited unexpected revelations not only of thrilling moments but also opportunities missed. For instance, speaking to my grandfather on the phone was, absolutely, more important than a Xerox project. Visiting Carolee would have meant an exquisite moment together. Instead, time passed, and this, like so much else, vanished.

Life cannot be lived without regret. I do not regret the life I lived, only some of the choices I made.

People are more important than art.

I have been relentless in the pursuit of my art. That, I have realized, is the MacGuffin in my life.

Persistence of vision has been attributed to the retina's imperfection. It is a way of seeing what we believe to be there. It is the afterimage of an optimist. It is an illusion that relies on time to wink into the future and coax it into reality. I have been nothing, if not persistent.

As Antoine de Saint-Exupéry wrote, "It is only the heart that can see clearly; what is essential is invisible to the eye." And I would add, it is often invisible to the "I."

Until very recently, my work was scattered among several locations. Uncollected and not archived, it would be lost. I have now rented a studio where more than 4,400 artworks from 1955 to the present are gathered in one space where archiving is under way.

Thomas Huber remains one of my collaborators. With his help an "Anti-Aging Serum" was recently created as well as a video titled *Cyborgian Rhapsody* in which a GPT-3 chatbot wrote and then performs a script about evolution and immortality.

As I write this, I am approaching eighty-four years old. How did that happen?

We share a brief time together. Evolution began with sharing, not just with other living creatures, but with the planet itself. We do not exist alone. Rather, we are in a partnership with all living things.

The challenge is in the moment. The time is always now.

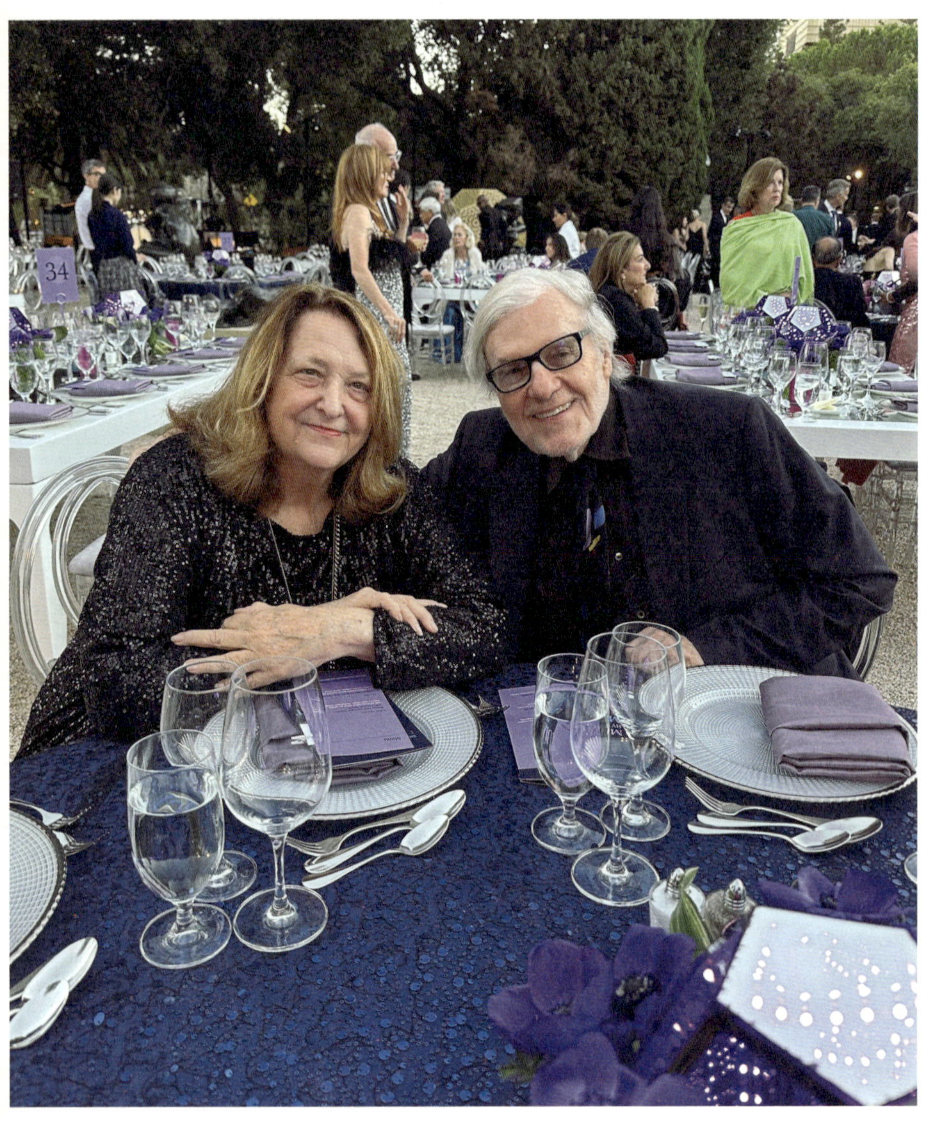

# HONOREE LYNN WITH HUSBAND GEORGE AT THE MUSEUMS BY MOONLIGHT GALA AT CANTOR ARTS CENTER, 2024

Acknowledgments

First and foremost, I would like to thank Tom Teicholz for his invaluable research, counsel, and editing of this memoir. This is the first book I have written, and I could not have done it without him.

I would also like to thank my assistant Noelle Barna, who so sensitively helped organize the images in this book, and Jiminie Ha and Milo Bonacci for the design of *Private I*, and John McGhee, proofreader extraordinaire.

I am especially grateful to the vigorous and sustained encouragement over the years of Hilton Als, Claudia Altman Siegel, Natasha Boas, Eleanor Coppola, Bridget Donahue, Rudolf Frieling, Eli Hankin, Noa Hankin, Richard Hankin, Dawn Hershman, Becky Koblick, George Leeson, Arthur Lester, Christiane Paul, Kyle Stephan, Tilda Swinton, Peter Weibel, and Michael Zilkha.

"I would make my work and wait for the world to catch up."

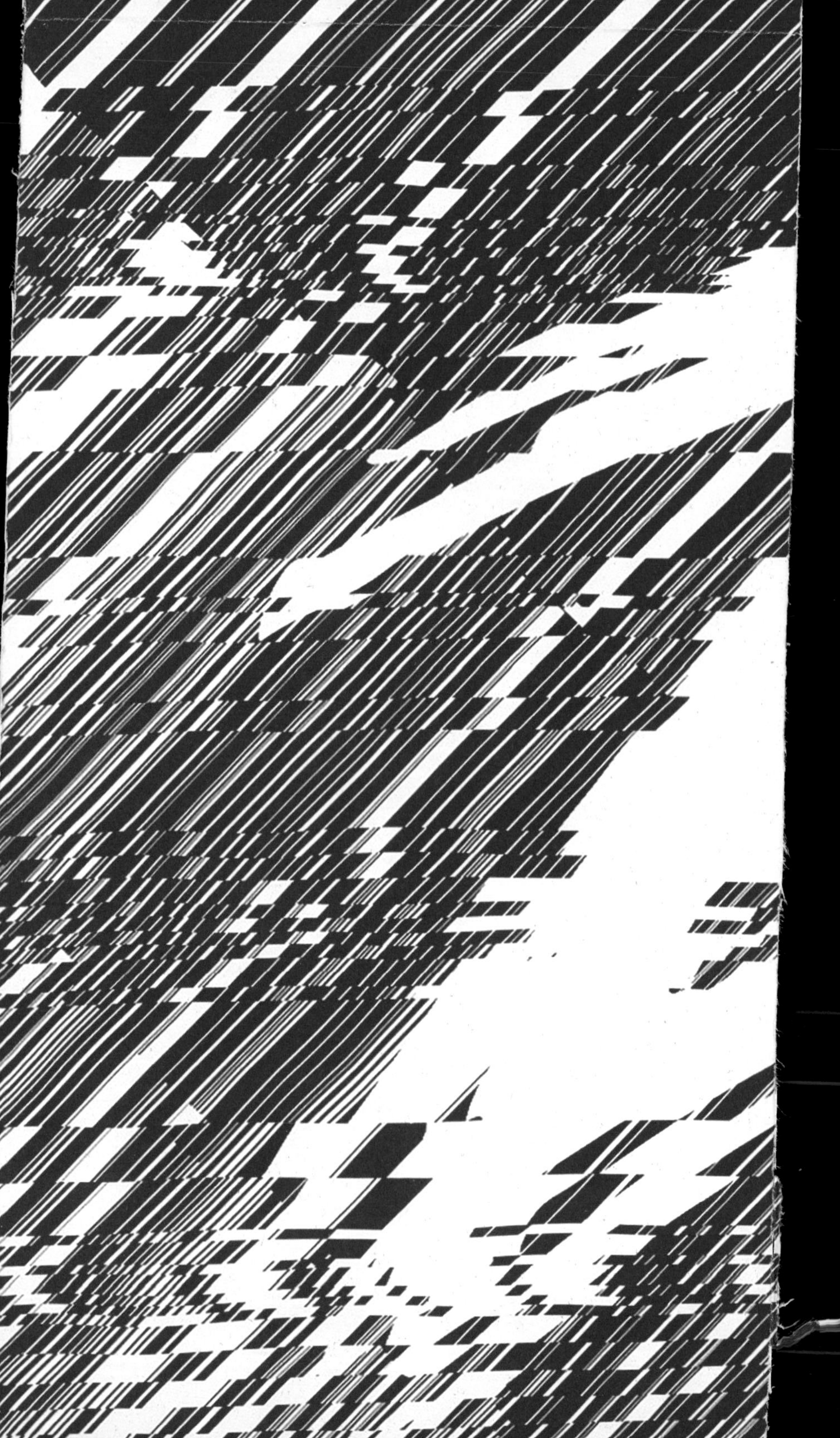